ANTITRUST ECONOMICS
AND LEGAL ANALYSIS

GRID SERIES IN LAW

Consulting Editor
THOMAS W. DUNFEE, The Wharton School, University of Pennsylvania

OTHER BOOKS IN THE GRID SERIES IN LAW

ANTITRUST ECONOMICS AND LEGAL ANALYSIS

Eugene M. Singer
Economic Consultant

Grid Publishing, Inc., Columbus, Ohio

© COPYRIGHT 1981, GRID PUBLISHING, INC.
4666 Indianola Avenue
Columbus OH 43214

Printed in the United States

1 2 3 4 ⊠ 4 3 2 1

Library of Congress Cataloging in Publication Data

Singer, Eugene M.
    Antitrust economics and legal analysis.
    (Grid series in law)
    Includes index.
    1. Antitrust law — United States — Cases.
    2. Antitrust law — Economic aspects — United States.
I. Title.
KF1652.S54   343.73'072   80-19847
ISBN 0-88244-227-9 (pbk.)

FOR DEBRA AND LISA

Contents

PREFACE

More than a decade has passed since the publication of my first book, *Antitrust Economics: Selected Legal Cases and Economic Models* (1968). In the interim, I have been an economic consultant to law firms on antitrust cases. My life has been spent visiting plants, meeting executives of companies, discussing the pricing, manufacturing and distribution of products, and theorizing with lawyers on the economic defense materials which could be presented in litigation in a courtroom or in a memorandum to the staff of the Department of Justice, Antitrust Division or the staff of the Federal Trade Commission.

I have tried to write a book in which the reader can feel some of the enjoyment I have had in the practice of antitrust economics. This book represents the reflections of the author, and is not intended as a survey of antitrust legal or economic literature.

I have urged as a theme in this book that antitrust policy cannot be determined solely or even in large part from economic models. Economic theory with its strong assumptions concerning "other things being equal," resource availability, knowledge, and foresight can reach a single solution. But I do not believe antitrust policy has, or should have, singular answers. There should be a rule of reason and a flexibility in antitrust policy which depends on a wide spectrum of legal and economic factors.

There does not have to be a single goal which all must be directed to in order for our nation to have an effective antitrust policy. Antitrust policy is not directed simply to further "competition," "efficiency," the "welfare of the consumer," or to perpetuate "an organization of small units which can effectively compete with each other." It is all of these things and more. Antitrust policy need not be blind to the conservation of resources, the employment of workers, the defense of the nation or the economic needs of a community.

A question in antitrust economics is seldom resolved by the data. Data can be presented, honestly and fairly, in a wide variety of formats. Numbers can be as effective as rhetoric provided the integrity of the argument is maintained. The major economic findings in a large number of antitrust cases can be repositioned, with the result that an opposite conclusion to the case can be justified. Therefore, analysis of antitrust economics should not be expected to yield unique answers from data; rather, the analysis of data should contribute, along with political ideology and social consciousness, to the formation of flexible answers for a changing world which keeps asking many of the same questions.

EUGENE M. SINGER
HARRISON, NEW YORK
January 1981

I. SELECTED TOPICS IN ANTITRUST ECONOMICS:
Economic Models, Concentration and Profits

INTRODUCTION

Economists can contribute with lawyers to the analysis of market facts in an antitrust case. Both come to the same problem with different training and discipline; both are highly educated individuals; and both should have the requisite ability to think and analyze a set of facts with logic and a spirit of humanism. A model, an equation, a market share, or a rule is too mechanical and simplistic for the professional.

The structural approach to antitrust is questioned in the first three chapters. Those urging a structural type antitrust policy have generally sought to establish rules and guidelines which would restrict the growth of larger companies and limit their levels of profits. Advocates of the structural approach to antitrust have sought to establish three critical propositions which would justify their using an indicator of structure, such as a market share or profit rate, as a sufficient basis for finding a violation of the antitrust laws.

The first proposition states that the model of pure competition, composed of small competing business units, is a suitable goal for achieving an optimum economic position for consumers. Chapter 1, Antitrust Policy and Economic Models, casts doubt on this proposition as a single policy in an economy which is simultaneously dedicated to other broad objectives, such as conservation of resources, product improvement, and full employment.

The second fundamental proposition which those advocating the structural philosophy have tried to establish is that industrial concentration is rising in the United States. "Big business" is alleged to be growing more rapidly and thus becoming more concentrated than the medium- or smaller-sized firms. If it can be established that there is a "rising tide of economic concentration" and economic concentration is bad for the country, a foundation is laid for breaking up big business or for stopping any further increases in industrial concentration through a strict merger policy.

The second chapter, Industrial Concentration, explains why the question whether industrial concentration is rising in the United States cannot be readily answered. There are problems in measuring industrial concentration and in defining products and industries.

As products change in our country, the compilation of sales data by the government is refitted into new product categories. Some industries which are becoming more important are split into new sub-groups, and other product categories of declining importance are combined. Therefore, studies of industrial concentration can only include data from a limited number of older industries with products which have not significantly changed. The dynamic and more interesting industries with rapidly changing products and technology have the greatest impact on the ultimate well-being of consumers, yet they are precisely the industries which have to be excluded from the tabulations of industrial concentration since no data exist for the earlier years being studied.

The third proposition which those advocating the structural philosophy in antitrust have sought to establish is that economic concentration results in non-competitive behavior reflected in higher prices and, consequently, high profits. Chapter 3, entitled Profits, explains some of the problems in calculating comparable profit rates for companies in different industries, or companies in the same industry with different types of capital equipment and various levels of vertical integration. Apart from all the numerical difficulties with profit data, there is a basic objection to criticizing earnings of the more profitable companies on the grounds that their high earnings *might* reflect monopoly power rather than superior skills. In terms of public policy, a standard which finds average profits or average size desirable will ultimately settle for average performance as a goal. There is also an interrelated concern in the study of industrial concentration: the larger or the more profitable firms may be stronger with the result that the weaker firms may be unsuccessful in the competitive struggle. If the smaller firms are unsuccessful, we must ask ourselves the profoundly difficult question, what is the price of economic growth and the cost of economic freedom?

ANTITRUST POLICY AND ECONOMIC MODELS

Since the Sherman Act was passed in 1890, there has been a similarity in the types of antitrust images that have been created. Many of the images were founded in the laissez faire political economy of the nineteenth century and were surrounded with the fears of "big business" and "big government." One of the most articulate expressions of an image of competition was stated by Judge Learned Hand in the Alcoa case in 1945:

> Throughout the history of these (antitrust) statutes it has been constantly assumed that one of their purposes was to perpetuate and preserve, for its own sake and in spite of possible cost, an organization of industry in small units which can effectively compete with each other.[1]

This is a powerful image. It pictures the United States economy as an organization of industry in small units and urges us, under the banner of antitrust, to perpetuate and preserve in spite of possible cost an economy of only small firms. It may be wise to question allegiance to this standard, especially if economic objectives such as conservation of resources, full employment, and product diversity are deemed more important to society. If these economic objectives are sufficiently important to us, we will have to reject as outmoded the imagery associated with the model of pure competition.

Although many of the classic images in antitrust have remained constant, the economic environment associated with these images has changed. Prior to the turn of the century the economic effects of the railroads interconnecting formerly protected markets accounted for a substantial amount of the sentiment of groups seeking to curb the distribution and market power of larger companies. Concepts such as "competition" or "industry concentration" were viewed in terms of an economic region, not on a national basis. Some economic corrections were undoubtedly considered to be in order, but the central theme of the proponents of the Clayton Act in 1914 was to protect the existing economy from lessening of competition, not to change the industrial structure of the economy. Since a free enterprise system was defined in terms not too different from the existing economy, the cost for obtaining such a system was not particularly great. Antitrust questions concerning economic concentration were being asked in an environment marked by a Federal Government of minor size, a trade union movement just under way, and unimportant foreign trade.

Today many of the same antitrust questions are being asked. But the environment has changed with the advent of intercontinental information and transportation systems; an economy in which federal, state and local government purchase over 20 percent of the annual goods and services; and regulated industries which account for over 30 percent of the annual new plant and equipment expenditures in the economy. Finally, in recent years we have seen, at least on a temporary basis, wage and price controls or guidelines affecting most of the private sectors of the economy.

CLASSICAL ECONOMIC MODELS IN ANTITRUST

The traditional starting point in antitrust economics has been the model of ''pure competition.'' Before discussing the assumptions and implications of this particular model, it may be helpful to comment in general terms on what an economic model is, and what it purports to do. Basically, an economic model is used to analyze the cause and effect between two or more variables. It is assumed that except for the variables under consideration, everything else in the world is held constant. Examination of an economic model will not yield a ready answer with regard to a specific course of action for antitrust policy. Furthermore, an economic model can suggest almost any alternative with regard to price or output depending upon which terms are treated as variables or constants. The phrase ''economic theory suggests'' can therefore be used by either side of any argument in industrial organization. Like a helicopter, an economic model can go in any direction depending upon which levers are moved and which are held constant.

The assumptions of the pure competition model reflect the basic structure of an undeveloped agrarian economy: standardized products, numerous firms in markets, each firm with a small share and unable by its action alone to exert significant influence over price, no barriers to entry, and output carried to the point where each seller's marginal cost equals the going market price.

The classical economists took considerable care to state their assumption that there would be not only perfect mobility of resources within the industry under consideration, but for all input and output industries in the economy. Thus, the firm in the model of pure competition could not encounter any raw material shortages; labor unions, regulated industries, national defense, social security systems, or any other constraint. Finally, the purely competitive firm had the advantage of perfect foresight of the types of products which consumers would demand. Most importantly, the term ''optimal'' for the classical economists implied merely that the supply-and-demand equation for the economic model could be solved within their theoretical framework. It did not purport to indicate that consumers would be happy or satisfied with their level of income, standard of living, or the quality of goods and services distributed in their economy.[2]

THE INADEQUACIES OF THE MODEL OF PURE COMPETITION FOR ANTITRUST POLICY

Antitrust statutes have not been directed to the narrow task of eliminating all monopolistic elements in our economy. Variations in products, advertising, and brand names give product diversity to our economy in contrast to the standardized products found in countries not operating within a free enterprise system. These monopolistic elements would not exist in a world of pure competition where a large number of firms manufacture a homogeneous product, and no one firm can materially affect the market price. To eliminate these monopolistic elements would destroy the distinctive traits and individuality of firms with respect to their services, products, and price policies. The basic point is that a belief in the value of competition does not require each and every move in antitrust policy to be made in the direction of a pure competition model. The pure competition model is neither a description of reality nor a normative standard toward which antitrust policy makers should strive.

Professor Edward Chamberlin, in describing his term "monopolistic competition," reaches basically the same conclusion:

> Now if pure competition is the ideal, the direction in which we should move is very clear. For it is easy enough to show that the actual economy is shot full of monopoly elements, and hence that any move to get rid of them or to diminish their importance is in the right direction. The main point I want to make is that the welfare ideal itself (as well as the description of reality) involves a blend of monopoly and competition and is therefore correctly described as one of monopolistic competition. If this is true, it is no longer self-evident which way we should move, for it is no longer self-evident on which side of the ideal lies the actuality for which a policy is sought. It is possible that the economy should be made 'more competitive' but it is also quite possible that it should be made 'more monopolistic' instead.[3]

An encouragement of some monopolistic elements does not require an advocacy of monopolies.[4] It is rather a recognition that the term competition encompasses a vitality of interacting market forces that are not always provided by moving in the direction of pure competition. The term "competitiveness" should not be shackled with the connotation that unless the market conditions simulate those of a theoretical model containing a large number of firms no one of which has any influence on price, and all of which produce a standardized product, the market structure lacks the vital rivalry and stimulus associated with a free enterprise system.

In a world of pure competition an optimum allocation of resources is determined only after the consumer preferences or the demand conditions of a community are known. The assortment of goods which maximizes the total utility of a community has presented economists with insuperable difficulties because of the incomparability of the utilities of different individuals. There is no economic or objective solution for finding a "bliss point" which maximizes the satisfaction of consumers.[5] Resort must be made to value judgments as to the favorability of income distribution and individual and social preferences. Thus, models dealing with optimum allocation of resources have not met the problem of determining the ideal product mix of the economy.

The unique features of products and services are emphasized by advertising. To the extent that consumers accept these differences as important, a differential in value is created between related products. Individualism becomes the keynote. Individualism in product encourages each company to manufacture, not an identical product, but a better product than its competitor. Individualism in service encourages each company to try harder to please customers. Individualism in price means that a company has some limited degree of price flexibility. These features are not present in a model of pure competition. However, each of these forms of individualism has been recognized as fundamentally important to the free enterprise system of the United States.

There are several reasons for rejecting the proposition that an image of competition such as that suggested by the economic model of pure competition is a suitable guide for a public policy directed toward the entire United States economy. The assumptions of the model of pure competition reflected the basic economic structure of an undeveloped agrarian economy with country stores selling plain soap, butter, flour and other undifferentiated products. Competition meant that if each farmer or producer maximized his output, the economy would achieve the best allocation of resources. Today this philosophy is being challenged.

First, conservation of natural resources. It is not clear that the economy is always better off if the output of any scarce natural resource industry is expanded. Nor is it clear that the members of an industry composed of many small units will be able to comprehend the responsibility, and exercise the necessary discipline, required to conserve the resources of our basic industries. Indeed, many companies lack the capital, financial resources, and research and development facilities required to redesign products with the objective of long-term conservation of resources. Misallocation of resources can occur not only with respect to other industries, but with respect to the future use of scarce resources. By deconcentrating one particular industry, the relative bargaining power of the deconcentrated firms will be weakened with regard to their suppliers and customers. Their marginal costs for raw materials may increase or the prices received for their output may be lowered. Resources will be reallocated to relatively stronger industries. A similar problem exists in allocating scarce resources between the present and future economy.

If the United States continues to maintain price controls, guidelines or regulations, the critical economic variable will become output. The energy crisis of the 1970's depicts the massive complexities inherent in the government's attempting to regulate both price and the allocation of petroleum output among industries with various levels of priorities. It has also dramatized the interdependence of the network of industries in the United States economy for basic natural resources. The nation realized after the Arab oil embargo that the curtailment of any basic input industry, such as petroleum, paper, lumber, aluminum or plastic, could slow down virtually every manufacturing and distribution facility. As a result of the interrelations of our industries, the regulation of any single natural resource industry increases the potential for not only further direct regulation of closely related industries, but indirect regulation of almost all industries which depend on this resource.

The reconciliation of our antitrust statutes with conservation needs may require joint industry cooperation which may have direct or indirect effects on price and output. A major objective of our antitrust statutes, and especially Section 1 of the Sherman Act, is to encourage and insure independence of competitive action. The public policy problem is that total independence of action will prevent some solutions from ever being reached where the outcome would benefit both industry, the consumer and free enterprise. For example, a joint warehouse distribution system open to any member of an industry could contribute to minimizing fuel, overhead and transportation costs. Such a system may not be able to be developed unilaterally. But the implications for competition are significant if there is a likelihood that smaller sized companies, which might not otherwise survive, would become more competitive by utilizing joint facilities. Similarly, joint research efforts of companies on resource conservation, or the building of joint recycling facilities may encourage the survival of companies by minimizing the threat of resource shortages.

Second, full employment. The problem of a nation attempting to maintain full employment would not be relevant to classical economic model builders. Social security, unemployment insurance, trade union collective bargaining, wage and price controls were not permitted in the calculation of the simple ratios of marginal costs and prices. External social and economic factors such as these were assumed away with the Latin rubric *ceteris paribus*, namely, "other things being equal." Unlike the classical economists, we cannot call forth the *ceteris paribus* rubric. Alteration of any industry structure to render firms unable to raise prices, without simultaneously modifying existing collective bargaining relationships and government controls, may misallocate resources. Furthermore, it is not clear that advocates of deconcentration would like the classical adjustment of output rather than price. Since no firm in a purely competitive market could affect price, the only variable which a firm could adjust was output. But the classical adjustment of a firm's output implies changes in employment levels, which may not be a desirable public policy.

The late Senator Philip Hart proposed an "Industrial Reorganization Act" (S.3832), which sought to "restructure industries dominated by oligopoly or monopoly power," by making them come closer to a model of pure competition.[6] Senator Hart believed that under his bill "competition would make prices and profits the variables — not production and employment." But there will always be changes in output as consumer demands change, and resources are reallocated. Any bill to restructure industry therefore will be self-defeating if it tries to bring industries closer to a model of pure competition and make price, not output, the variable. To predicate a restructuring of the American economy on a premise of eliminating changes in output is to follow a course of action which assumes that the American consumer will exhibit no change in consumption patterns, and industry will offer no product innovation.

Third, product diversity. Product diversity and brand differentiation were not present in classical models of pure competition. The output was always a standardized product. Again, there can be seen a corollary between the model of pure competition and an agrarian economy producing fungible commodities such as wheat and corn. A hallmark of the present United States economy is product diversity. Variations in products, advertising, and brand names give an individual identity to firms and products in our economy. This individuality of product can be contrasted to the standardized product found in countries not operating within a free enterprise system.

If a number of different varieties of a product are preferred by our society over a single standardized product, it is possible that our economy may have to maintain a greater number of plants, some of which may operate at higher cost levels than would result if society consumed standardized products. But this state of the economy is not one of misallocation of resources — if consumers prefer a wide diversity of sizes, shapes, and types of products. For example, there probably would be lower plant costs per unit of output if all garments were made of a standard black cloth and everyone drove a black Model T Ford. New car model changes or alterations in fashions which outmode last year's garments are not misallocations of resources if society prefers continually changing products and style.

The Federal Trade Commission has taken a different view of product differentiation. In a major structural case brought against the four major manufacturers of ready-to-eat breakfast cereals, the FTC charged that "brand proliferation" and "artificial product differentiation" were illegal methods of competition which serve to create "barriers to entry" for alleged oligopolists.[7] The remedy sought by the FTC was to break up the three major breakfast cereal manufacturers into smaller independent units with the expectation that this would result in less advertising, fewer brands and products, and lower prices. It is the contention of the FTC that the preferences of consumers for a wide variety of taste, colors, shapes, and forms of a given product type are irrational since many of the product differences, in the opinion of the staff of the FTC, are insignificant.

It is not clear how a company producing wide variations of a type of product with different brand names can create "barriers to entry." If consumers are accustomed to seeing a wide variety of brand names on a shelf, the marketing appeal of any single brand is weak. In short, proliferation of brands lowers barriers to entry by reducing consumer brand loyalty to any given trade name. Of course, if one company introduces many new products and another company introduces only a few products, the likelihood of continued product success might appear to be greater for the first company. In actuality, the strategies resemble those of roulette players that use chips all over the board versus others that play a few selected numbers. Unlike the model of pure competition, which assumes perfect knowledge and certainty, firms in our economy do not know which numbers to play on the roulette table, and which products will meet the taste-buds and fancy of the American public. A firm that correctly gambles on where the demand is going to be for a specific type of product with a particular style, fashion, or taste, will show low unit costs and high profits, even if it has no advantage over other firms in its industry in producing an identical product at an identical output level.

Fourth, profits. The classical economists had no reason to be particularly concerned with profits. None of the small firms in their model of pure competition had any advantages in physical location; nor were firms confronted with any scarcities of resources or constraints on capital. In the absence of barriers to entry associated with patents, know-how, capital, and management, new small firms could easily enter and erode the short-term profits of the older firms in an industry up to the limit of demand. In short, in classical economics all firms in an industry were created equal and were endowed with the same knowledge, management and availability of resources.

The environment of the classical model builders was clearly not one of high technology, or extensive research. In the last few years we have seen examples of staggering losses for individual companies in not entering, but withdrawing from research-oriented fields such as computers and aerospace. With the hindsight of today, consider the "attractive" level of profits anticipated by these firms a decade ago. At what point of time should we calculate the profits of one of these firms: (1) when the firm is succeeding in an entirely different product line and building a profit base for future expansion into possibly unrelated fields; (2) during the next stage, when the firm may be incurring losses in a new division while attempting to build a prototype or develop its own technology; (3) during the next five or ten years, when the firm may be earning attractive profits depending on the success of the product; or (4) during the subsequent years when their earlier technological advantage is copied by others, as product cycles change and as past technologies become outmoded? Alternatively, do we want the firm which has consistently succeeded for ten, twenty, or thirty years to bow out of the race and attempt to retire as the champion merely because he has been too good a player for too long?

The selection of an arbitrary profit level applicable to all industries as a presumptive measure of monopoly power is highly questionable. How can we meaningfully compare the rate of profit for an industry which has low capital requirement and primarily markets a product, possibly door to door, with a major chemical or metal industry requiring substantial capital outlays for production facilities? The company or industry which is primarily in distribution is labor intensive and will reflect a low net worth; the capital intensive industry will show larger net worth as a result of its capital needs and equity financing. The same dollars divided by different amounts of net worth will show different rates of return. Consider other companies which may sustain large current deductions as a result of sporadic advertising programs or research and development expenditures associated with the introduction of new products. Since accountants have no assurance that these types of expenditures will ultimately yield a profitable product, the common practice is to write these expenses off in the current year rather than capitalize them over-many years. This accounting practice causes widely different levels of profits as a percent of net worth. If the product succeeds, the firm no longer has the earlier costs to offset the current profits. In other words, we cannot meaningfully interpret current accounting profits as economic profits without examining the years of incurred costs during the development of a product.

There is a basic problem in using accounting values for depreciated assets rather than replacement values in computing economic profits. If the production process has not changed greatly for manufacturing or processing a commodity or a basic product, a plant which was built twenty years ago may have approximately the same output as a plant built this year even though a new plant may cost five or ten times more than the older plant. Furthermore, the new plant would have high depreciation charges offsetting its current profits. With high plant equipment and capital costs, the rate of profit for the new plant would be low. The industry therefore would not be particularly attractive for a potential new entrant. In contrast, the rate of profit for the older, more fully depreciated plant would be higher. It is erroneous to argue that the old plant has monopoly profits and the new plant has competitive profits. If the older plant were valued at replacement cost rather than the accounting book value, both plants would have the same low profit rate. The conclusion therefore is that if management has enough foresight to enter an industry which will not encounter major capital or technological changes for a period over 20 years, and if inflation persists, and if demand for the product continues, the company may be rewarded with higher profits than received by more recent entrants with higher capital costs.

CONCLUSION

Antitrust policy should be appraised in an economic environment in which regulated industries occupy a substantial segment, full employment goals are requisite, and product diversity is responsive to consumer tastes and preferences. To sacrifice these standards for the purpose of obtaining an organization of small units is to pay an immeasurably high price. There is a place in our economy for both larger and smaller sized firms, both of which can successfully develop new products and services.

Antitrust policy should not be oversimplified by fading images such as the economic model of pure competition. Reconciliation of the competition between and within concentrated and unconcentrated industries, between the smaller and larger sized firms, and between regulated and unregulated industries has historically raised difficult antitrust questions. These questions probably will become even more difficult to answer in the years ahead. Easy answers will not remove these difficult questions. Free enterprise will always be marked by disparities — in the size of firms, in profits, and in products. These are not differences to fear. These disparities are the basis of competition and the economic strength of this nation; and they are the basis on which we can build a meaningful antitrust policy.

ENDNOTES

1. *United States* v. *Aluminum Company of America* , 148 F. 2nd 416 (2nd Cir., 1945).
2. See J. M. Henderson and R. E. Quandt, *Microeconomic Theory* (New York: McGraw-Hill Book Company, 1958), pp. 202-8; T. Scitovsky, *Welfare and Competition: The Economics of a Fully Employed Economy* (Homewood, Ill.: Richard D. Irwin, Inc., 1951); R. H. Leftwich, *The Price System and Resource Allocation* (New York: Holt, Rinehart & Winston, Inc., 1956); A. Lerner, *The Economics of Control: Principles of Welfare Economics* (New York: The Macmillan Company, 1944).
3. E. H. Chamberlin, *Towards A More General Theory of Value* (New York: Oxford University Press, 1957), p. 93.
4. Monopolists, in their attempt to maximize profits, restrict output. Therefore, in an economy mixed with monopolies and competitive industries resources will tend to be over-allocated to competitively produced commodities and under-allocated to monopolistically produced commodities. However, in a world of monopolies, where no industries are competitive, a misallocation of resources does not necessarily result. Professor William Baumol makes this point with an interesting metaphor: "Given the level of employment of resources, a misallocation can arise only if the demand for inputs of one set of industries (the monopolists) is low in comparison with that of the remaining industries. If each of a number of runners slows down, none of them need come in ahead of the others, and if each industry is weak in its bidding for resources, no lopsided allocation of these resources need result. We see, then, that some competition may conceivably be worse than none!" *Economic Theory and Operations Analysis*, (Englewood Cliffs, N.J.: Prentice-Hall, Inc., 1961) p. 257 Cf. J. S. Bain, *Price Theory* (New York: John Wiley & Sons, Inc., 1966) p. 240-47; and Lipsey and Lancaster, "The General Theory of Second Best," p. 12.
5. Professor Paul Samuelson states, ". . . the new welfare economics is a body of doctrines which attempts to go as far as possible in preparing the way for the final a-scientific step involving value judgments . . ." See his "Evaluation of Real National Income," *Oxford Economic Papers*, New Series, Vol. II (1950), pp. 1-29. Also see T. C. Koopsman's "Allocation of Resources and the Price System," the first of *Three Essays on the State of Economic Science* (New York: McGraw-Hill Book Company, 1957), pp. 41-66; M. W. Reder, *Studies in the Theory of Welfare Economics* (New York: Columbia University Press, 1947); I. M. D. Little, *A Critique of Welfare Economics*, 2nd ed.

(London: Oxford University Press, 1957); A. Bergson, "A Reformulation of Certain Aspects of Welfare Economics," *Quarterly Journal of Economics,* Vol. LII (February, 1938), 310-34; W. J. Baumol, *Welfare Economics and the Theory of the State* (London: Longmans, Green & Company, Ltd., 1952); and J. de V. Graaff, *Theoretical Welfare Economics.*
6. *Congressional Record* (July 24, 1972).
7. *In the Matter of Kellogg Co., General Mills Inc., General Foods Corp. and The Quaker Oats Co.,* FTC Dockett 8883. Complaint issued April 26, 1972.

THOUGHT QUESTIONS

1. Should antitrust policy be determined primarily by an economic model concerned with allocation of resources?
   a) Are the criteria or assumptions of an economic model more important than social or political objectives?
   b) Does Congress legislate with a goal of maximizing consumer welfare, or with a mixture of objectives, such as by compromising conflicting special interests?
   c) Should antitrust policy reflect a compromising of alternative goals or seek to maximize a singular objective?
2. Should we encourage a proliferation of products to satisfy a wide diversity of consumer tastes even though higher production costs may be involved?
   a) Should we have a single type of breakfast cereal, such as corn flakes, or many types of cereals which may require higher per unit costs?
   b) Should cereal companies be allowed to advertise an old established cereal or only new brands?
   c) Do you believe that the government should regulate any of the following: (1) the size of raisins in a cereal, (2) the quality of raisins, (3) the amount of vitamins added to these products, (4) the label on the package of the ingredients, (5) a requirement to publish on a package the percent of minimum daily nutritional needs contained in a typical portion of cereal both with and without milk, and (6) the addition of milk, orange juice and toast in all television advertisements of cereal, as well as a statement as to what constitutes a good nutritional breakfast?
3. Would you characterize a new plant as "non-optimum" this year if it was designed for peak production levels in five years?
   a) Should we wait five years before building this plant?
   b) At what point of time would the output of this plant first be characterized as "efficient?"
   c) If demand for the company's product continued to grow for the next seven years, would the plant still be characterized as "efficient?"
   d) If economic "efficiency" is related to foresight in guessing correctly the size and type of future demand, which is always in flux, how can the general equilibrium equations for allocating resources ever reach a theoretical finite solution?

2

INDUSTRIAL CONCENTRATION

The government embarked on a program in 1975 entitled Line of Business Reporting, which requires approximately 500 of the major companies in the United States to file for each plant detailed shipment and asset data for various product categories. A substantial amount of the political pressure for this reporting system came from the Federal Trade Commission which sought to establish a data base which could be used eventually for a structural *per se* attack against major companies.[1] Industries with high concentration for the leading firms and high levels of profits were to be selected as candidates for closer scrutiny.

If it can be established that concentration is increasing and concentration is bad for the nation, a basis is established for stopping further increases in concentration through a strict anti-merger policy or by forcing larger companies to be broken up. This chapter will show how difficult it is to measure industrial concentration. First, there are problems of product classification. Should we divide the cars by price range so that sub-compacts and limousines are in different categories? Should four-wheel drives, diesels, two-door coupes, convertibles, dune buggies, electric cars, U.S. Army jeeps, electric golf carts, and foreign cars be included or excluded in the product categories being studied? There are also problems in double counting shipments from one plant, such as tires, which are included again in a finished assembled product, such as an automobile. Finally, there is the problem of technological change. The Model T Ford is replaced by a Pinto. Jet planes replace propeller planes, electronic word processing equipment replace typewriters, and small chips replace circuit boards in computers. New industries are born and others are replaced with the result that a considerable portion of the data becomes non-comparable over time. The comparison of concentration ratios or trends of concentration in these fundamentally different industries is not meaningful even though the industries may be directed to performing the same function for the consumer or end-user.

THE STANDARD INDUSTRIAL CLASSIFICATION CODE (SIC)

Comprehensive tabulations on concentration generally follow the definitions of products and industries set forth in the Standard Industrial Classification Code, abbreviated SIC.[2] The definitions in the classification system become progressively narrow or more particular with successive additions of numerical digits. Starting with the broadest definitions, there are twenty 2-digit major manufacturing industry groups, which are shown below in Table 2-1.

TABLE 2-1
SIC 2-Digit Manufacturing Industry Groups

SIC Code	
20	Food and kindred products
21	Tobacco manufactures
22	Textile mill products
23	Apparel and other fabricated textile products
24	Lumber and wood products
25	Furniture and fixtures
26	Pulp, paper and products
27	Printing and publishing
28	Chemicals and allied products
29	Petroleum and coal products
30	Rubber products
31	Leather and leather products
32	Stone, clay, and glass products
33	Primary metal products
34	Fabricated metal products
35	Machinery except electrical
36	Electrical machinery
37	Transportaton equipment
38	Instruments and related products
39	Miscellaneous manufacturers

United States Bureau of the Budget, *Standard Industrial Classification Manual 1972*, (Washington D.C.: Government Printing Office, 1945); and United States, Bureau of the Census, *1972 Census of Manufactures*, Industry Statistics, (Washington D.C.: Government Printing Office, 1976).

These major industry groups in 1972 were subdivided into 143 3-digit industry groups; which were further divided into 451 4-digit industry and product groups; 1,293 5-digit classes and, finally, 10,500 7-digit individual products. The SIC system of product and industry subdivision can be observed in the illustration from the food industry in Table 2-2.

TABLE 2-2

SIC Code	Number of Digits	Designation	Name
20	2	Major industry group	Food and kindred products
203	3	Industry group	Canning, preserving
2033	4	Product group or industry	Canned fruits and vegetables
20332	5	Product class	Canned seasonal vegetables
2033211	7	Product	Canned asparagus

The standard industrial classification of products and industries seldom coincides with market definitions utilized in the analysis of competition. For example, the 4-digit industry, Cookies and Crackers (SIC 2052) includes two 5-digit product classes: Crackers and Pretzels (SIC 20521) and Cookies and Ice Cream Cones (SIC 20522). The product class of Crackers and Pretzels includes both Matzoths and Communion wafers, which we shall conclude are not in competition. The product class also includes a number of other non-competitive consumer products: graham crackers, pretzels, saltines, cracker crumbs and melba toast.

In some cases a physically identical product can be assigned to more than one industry. For example, process cheese from an integrated firm is assigned to Industry 2022, Natural Cheese; when produced by a non-integrated firm, which purchases the cheese before processing it, the product is assigned to Industry 2025, Special Dairy Products. Similarly, frankfurters are classified in two different industries depending upon whether they are manufactured in meat packing plants which do their own slaughtering (SIC 2011), or in plants which purchase their meat from the outside (SIC 2013). In both these cases, the controlling factor was the extent of vertical integration by the reporting plants.

Many of the apparent incongruities in the classification of products result from the practicalities of reporting data. A plant which is vertically integrated into several stages would be double counting if it added its products from each of its stages of production. More important, a fundamental change in compilation would occur if production data were assembled for each vertical stage of production rather than for shipments out the door of a plant. The result is that physically identical products are not grouped together to the extent that different production processes or vertical production stages are involved.

Some of the problems associated with classifying products can be observed in the "Not Elsewhere Classified" industries, which are not really industries but groupings of miscellaneous products. For SIC 2099, Food Preparations, Not Elsewhere Classified, the products include chocolate syrup made from purchased materials; peanut butter; instant tea; potato, corn and other chips; and vinegar and cider. The chocolate syrup was not a candy, and therefore could not be classified in SIC 2065, Candy and other Confectionary Products. Nor could the chocolate syrup be classified under SIC 2066, Chocolate and Cocoa Products since it was made from purchased chocolate, and industry 2066 is confined to plants which make their own chocolate by shelling, roasting and grinding cacao beans. The peanut butter also had trouble finding a classification. If it was in liquid oil form, it could have been classified in SIC 2079, Shortening and Cooking Oils. The tea was unable to fit into the Beverage industry since it was neither bottled nor canned. A similar problem was presented by potato chips. If the chips had been dehydrated and dried, rather than cooked in oil, they could have been included in SIC 2034, Dried and Dehydrated Fruits, Vegetables and Soup Mixes, which includes potato flakes, granules and other dehydrated potato products and dried fruits such as dates. The potato *chips* could then have joined the potato *flakes* along with the dried dates, provided that the dried dates were not chocolate covered, in which case they would be reclassified to SIC 2065, Candy and Other Confectionary Products. The point of these examples is simply that economic data based on product categories are as ambiguous as the definitions of the products which underlie the data.

CONCENTRATION RATIOS IN MANUFACTURING
Excerpt from United States, Dept. of Commerce,
Bureau of the Census, *1972 Census of Manufactures*

TABLE 6. Share of Value of Shipments of Each Class of Product Accounted for by the 4, 8, 20, and 50 Largest Companies; 1972 and Earlier Years — Continued

1972 Code	Class of product and year	Value of shipments				
		Total	Percent accounted for by			
		(million dollars)	4 largest companies	8 largest companies	20 largest companies	50 largest companies

Major Group 20. - Food and Kindred Products-Cont.

1972 Code	Class of product and year	Total (million dollars)	4 largest companies	8 largest companies	20 largest companies	50 largest companies
2087-	Flavoring extracts and sirups, n.e.c.–Continued					
20872	Liquid beverage bases not for use by soft drink bottlers	1972.. 97.9	65	79	93	99
		1967.. 129.9	74	87	96	99
		1963.. 76.1	73	85	93	99
		1958.. 59.2	63	78	91	99
		1954.. 38.3	83	89	95	(NA)
20873	Flavoring sirups for use by soft drink bottlers	1972.. 637.1	89	94	98	99+
		1967.. 353.0	(D)	97	99	99+
		1963.. 298.7	(D)	91	95	98
		1958.. 217.4	89	93	96	98
		1954.. 194.2	89	95	97	(NA)
20874	Other flavoring agents (except chocolate sirups)	1972.. 529.9	68	74	82	92
		1967.. 410.6	(D)	72	81	92
		1963.. 299.1	51	61	73	87
		1958.. 162.8	(NA)	(NA)	(NA)	(NA)
		1954.. 159.5	38	47	62	(NA)
20870	Flavoring extracts and sirups, n.s.k.	1972.. 71.8	(X)	(X)	(X)	(X)
		1967.. 49.4	(X)	(X)	(X)	(X)
		1963.. 17.1	(X)	(X)	(X)	(X)
		1958.. 12.0	(X)	(X)	(X)	(X)
20910	Canned and cured seafood, including soup (except frozen) (1967 product class 20310)	1972.. [9]585.0	38	56	71	85
		1967.. [9]421.1	34	52	68	82
		1963.. [9]384.5	33	47	62	78
		1958.. [9]367.0	([11])	([11])	([11])	([11])
2092-	Fresh or frozen packaged fish (1967 product group 2036-)	1972.. [9]1,000.2	21	32	52	72
		1967.. [9]529.7	24	35	53	71
		1963.. [9]362.8	23	34	49	65
		1958.. [9]274.1	18	28	45	66
		1954.. [9]158.0	23	36	53	(NA)
20922	Fresh packaged fish and other seafood (1967 product class 20362)	1972.. [9]135.2	28	39	59	80
		1967.. [9]66.2	23	35	58	83
		1963.. [9]76.6	14	21	37	58
		1958.. [9]58.4	16	26	42	63
		1954.. [9]53.6	20	31	50	(NA)

(X) Not applicable
(NA) Not available
[9] Value of production
([11]) Establishments in Alaska and Hawaii are important producers of these products. Recomputed figures cannot be shown for the 4, 8, 20 and 50 largest companies prior to 1963 without disclosing the operation of individual companies in Alaska and Hawaii.

RECLASSIFICATION OF PRODUCT CATEGORIES OVER TIME

The decision to split a four digit product group into additional product classes or to divide one product class into several product classes is in part a function of the changing importance of various consumer products. For example, as frozen foods became more important consumer goods, plants emerged which specialized in segments of the frozen food industry, and finer distinctions in product classification became appropriate. The 1967 5-digit *product class*, Frozen Specialties (20373) was divided in 1972 into a 4-digit *product group*, Frozen Specialties (2038), which was in turn broken into four 5-digit *product classes*: Frozen pies and other frozen baked goods (20381); Frozen dinners (20382), and two other miscellaneous categories. Shipments of another closely related product group, Frozen Fruits and Vegetables (2037), were added to the new product group of Frozen Specialties (2038), since the more elaborate and fancy frozen fruit and vegetable mixtures approached the specialty status.

The split of 1967 product class, Frozen Specialties into additional classes in 1972 such as, Frozen Pies (20381) and Frozen dinners (20382) showed dramatically different levels of concentration. The product group, Frozen Specialties had a top four company concentration ratio of 36 in 1972. But the new classes had a top four company concentration ratio of 51 for Frozen Pies and 58 for Frozen dinners. The continual changes in product classifications, which are made by the Bureau of the Census in an attempt to keep pace with the changing product mix in the economy, alter the measured levels of concentration.

Part of the answer to the question whether concentration is increasing in the United States depends on how products are reclassified into changing product sets. The greater the sub-division of product groups into the component product classes, the greater is the likelihood that at least one of the product classes will have a higher concentration ratio than that of the product group. Table 2-3 shows the high and low top four concentration ratios for the product classes within the 4-digit product groups in the Meat Industry. The four digit product group, Meat Packing Plants (2011) with a top four concentration ratio of 26 had eleven component product classes with top four concentration ratios ranging from a high of 68 to a low of 26. Similarly, the product group, Poultry Dressing (2013) with five component product classes had a top four company ratio of 16 and component product classes with concentration ratios ranging from 69 to 17. The important point of Table 2-3 is to appreciate the wide range of concentration ratios which underlie a single product group concentration ratio.

Concentration ratios have been used in a wide number of economic studies which attempt to link concentration with profits, advertising or other variables. Seldom is there a prefatory note on the frailty of a concentration ratio and how vulnerable the absolute level of the concentration ratio is to the alternative product definitions and classifications. Each of the component product classes could easily be branched into further classes. It would be difficult to conclude that a top four company concentration ratio is above or below some "critical range" of concentration in a study which attempts to link concentration with monopoly or non-competitive behavior. Instead, a concentration ratio should be viewed as one of numerous possible alternative product groupings, each one of which may offer some degree of insight into the interrelations of plants which have either similar production processes, similar types of end-products or similar sources of supply.

TABLE 2-3
Top 4 Company Concentration Ratios
for Meat Product Classes, 1972

SIC Code	Title	Number of Component 5-Digit Product Classes	4-Digit Product Group Top 4 CR	5-Digit Product Class Top 4 CR
2011	**Meat Packing Plants 4)**	11	26	
20111	Beef a)			30
20112	Veal a)			27
20113	Lamb & mutton a)			55
20114	Pork, fresh & frozen			37
20115	Lard			37
20116	Pork, processed a), b) & 4)			34
20117	Sausage & similar Products b), c) & 4)			26
20118	Canned meats b), 4) & 5)			68
20119	Hides, skins & pelts			30
2011X	Other meatpacking plant products			(S)
20110	Miscellaneous by-products			(X)
2013	**Sausages & Other Prepared Meats 4)**	5	16	
20136	Pork, processed or cured a), d) & 4)			24
20137	Sausage & similar products c), d) & 4)			23
20138	Canned meats d), 4) & 5)			34
20139	Natural sausage casings			40
20130	Sausages & other prep. meats, n.s.k.			(X)
2016	**Poultry Dressing Plants**	5	16	
20161	Young chickens			17
20162	Hens and/or fowl			39
20163	Turkeys			40
20164	Other poultry and small game			69
20160	Poultry dressing plants, n.s.k.			(X)
2017	**Poultry & Egg Processing**	3	23	
20171	Processed poultry, except soups			34
20172	Liquid, dried & frozen eggs			36
20170	Poultry & egg processing, n.s.k.			(X)

a)   not canned or made into sausage
b)   made in meatpacking plants
c)   not canned
d)   not made in meatpacking plants
(S)   withhheld because data did not meet publication standards
(X)   not applicable
n.s.k. not specified by kind
4)   Appreciable amounts of this product can be found in other product categories. For example, shipments of sausages come from both SIC 20117, sausages, made in meatpacking plants and SIC 20137, sausages not made in meatpacking plants.
5)   Comparability of this industry has changed slightly as a result of the 1972 SIC revision. The change is estimated to be less than 3 percent of the total value of shipments.

The use of concentration ratios in this context is limited to similar types of industries. The extension of concentration ratios to cross-sectional studies of a multitude of industries which have some common structural attributes is open to question. The concentration index is not being used in its deductive capacity of showing permutations and combinations of a substantially similar set of products. Rather it is being used as an absolute measure, such as temperature on a thermometer, without sufficient consideration being given to the fact that the scale of the thermometer can be as easily changed as Chinese frozen vegetables can be broken out of Frozen vegetables (SIC 20372) with a 35% concentration ratio and put into Frozen Dinners and Nationality Foods (SIC 20382) with a 58% concentration ratio.

SELECTION OF A SAMPLE OF INDUSTRIES

Any study of industrial organization must omit a considerable number of industries or product groups, due to various data problems. In the *1972 Census of Manufacturers* there were 451 product groups of which 72 were listed as "not elsewhere classified" or "miscellaneous." The products in these remainder categories are so diverse that they are beyond economically meaningful product groupings. Consequently, they are omitted in most studies of industrial concentration. Other product categories have their data withheld by the Census to avoid disclosing figures for individual companies. For example, the product class, Chocolate Candy made in the same establishment (20662) had (D) in place of its concentration ratio to indicate a disclosure problem, namely, the data would disclose information largely related to the Hershey Company.

Another problem concerns duplication or double-counting of shipments in an industry by shipments between plants in the same industry. A computer manufacturer may manufacture a transistor in one plant and ship it to another plant where it is affixed to a circuit board, which is in turn shipped to another plant where it is assembled into a memory module which may in turn be shipped to a final plant where the module is assembled into the central processor of the computer. The same transistor would be counted at least four times in the value of shipment figures. The plants could all be in the same industry, Electronic Computing Equipment (3573). The Census uses a concentration ratio based on value added rather than value of shipments for this industry and a number of other industries: Meat packing (2011), Sausages (2013), Wines and brandy (2084), Woven Carpets (2271), Blast Furnaces (3312), Primary Copper (3331), Primary lead (3332), Refrigeration and Heating Equipment (3585), and Telephone apparatus (3661). The use of value added to measure concentration in industries with a high degree of vertical integration minimizes the duplication problem, but makes these concentration ratios non-comparable to industries which have their concentration ratios based on value of shipment data.

The more extensive is vertical integration, the greater will be the duplication in shipments within the same industry. The presence of duplication in an industry imparts an upward bias in the level of a concentration ratio. For example, if the value of shipments of the top four companies was $1 million and the industry had shipments of $2 million, the concentration ratio would be equal to $\frac{1}{2} = .50$. If duplication occurred and $1 million is added to the numerator and denominator, the ratio would be equal to $(1 + 1)/(2 + 1) = \frac{2}{3} = .66$ Any study of industrial concentration should segregate industries in which the products shipped are used as materials, parts or components, in the manufacture of other products in the same category. For example, the concentration ratio (84%) of Chewing gum (2067), which has almost no vertical integration since it purchases from different industries its two basic material inputs, sugar and flexible wrapping materials, is not readily comparable to the concentration ratio of the more complex, vertically integrated industries such as Guided Missiles and Space Vehicles (3761) or Motor Vehicles (3711).

CONCENTRATION TRENDS

Antitrust legislation has generally been related to a need to slow or reverse an assumed rapidly increasing or high level of concentration. In its first case under the 1950 Celler-Kefauver Anti-Merger Act, amending Section 7 of the Clayton Act, the Supreme Court stated in the *Brown Shoe* decision: "The dominant theme pervading congressional consideration of the 1950 amendment was a fear of what was considered to be a rising tide of economic concentration in the American economy."[3] Similarly, in June 1969, the Attorney General of the United States observed: "The danger that this superconcentration poses to our economic, political and social structure cannot be over-estimated."[4]

Proponents of legislation which would break up large companies through the divestiture of many of their plants seek to find sets of industries or product classes which will confirm a supposed "rising tide of concentration" and thereby justify their proposed legislation. An example of this type of legislation is the Industrial Reorganization Act (S.1167) which proposed that there be a rebuttable presumption that monopoly power is possessed if a top four company concentration ratio in any line of commerce exceeded 50 percent.

(1) Aggregate Concentration

The Census does not publish concentration ratios for product groups and product classes which show the percentage of total shipments accounted for by the *identical* leading companies. An unchanged top four company concentration ratio of 50 for ten years may not necessarily reflect stability in the sizes of the leading companies. The four leading companies today may be entirely different companies than they were a decade earlier. The Census publishes aggregate concentration data for the top *identical* 50 manufacturing companies in terms of value added (equal to the differences between total shipments and cost of materials).[5]

TABLE 2-4
Share of Total Value Added by Manufacture
Accounted for by the 50 Largest Manufacturing
Companies, 1963, 1967, and 1972

		1963	1967	1972
1.	Share of Value Added Accounted for by the Identical Largest 50 Companies	22%	23%	25%
2.	Share of Value Added Accounted for by the Largest 50 Companies (Not the Identical Companies)	25%	25%	25%
3.	Number of Companies Surviving in the Top 50	50	43	40

These data are shown in Table 2-4 for the decade 1963 to 1972. The share of value added for the top 50 identical manufacturing companies rose from 22 percent to 25%. If the top 50 companies are selected, regardless of whether they were the identical companies in the time period covered, the share of value added remains constant at 25% from 1963 through 1972. Of the top 50 manufacturing companies in 1972, only 40 were in the top 50 manufacturing company group in 1963. If a longer span of time is selected, such as from 1947 to 1972, only 25 of the top 50 companies in 1972 were in the top 50 in 1947. Fifteen of the top 50 manufacturing companies in 1972 were not even in the top 100 manufacturing companies in 1947.

(2) Average Concentration

A study of trends in *average* economic concentration in the United States economy, with a flavor of politics, can be seen in the report published by the Cabinet Committee on Price Stability established by President Johnson in 1969. The report concluded that "average market concentration of manufacturing industries has shown no marked tendency to increase or decrease between 1947 and 1963, according to an analysis of 213 essentially comparable industries."[6] These industries were then further divided into 81 consumer industries and 132 producer goods industries although the Bureau of the Census provides no such distinction. The study found: "The average decline in concentration in producer goods industries was offset by a substantial upward movement in consumer goods industries." This upward movement was found by dividing all consumer goods into three categories: undifferentiated, moderately differentiated, and highly differentiated. In the nineteen-year period under consideration, the undifferentiated consumer goods showed an increase in average concentration of less than 1 percentage point, the moderately differentiated goods showed an increase of 4.5 percentage points, and the highly differentiated goods had an increase of 12 percentage points. Thus, the crux of the Price Stability Committee's conclusion of a "sharply upward movement" in consumer goods industry concentration is based on 17 highly differentiated product categories.

Table 2-5 shows the list of seventeen highly differentiated consumer goods industries used by the Committee.[7] Throughout their study the Committee used unweighted averages of concentration ratios. Thus, the concentration ratio of the top four companies producing Chewing Gum is given identical weight in being averaged with the ratio of the leading producers of Motor Vehicles and Parts. By definition, each of these industry concentration ratios is a percent with a different base. The unweighted averaging of the percentages is therefore statistically erroneous.[8] In Table 2-5 the Cabinet Committee's list of highly differentiated consumer goods industries is, contrary to their procedure, weighted by value of shipments. Two of the industries, Wines and Brandy and Motor Vehicles and Parts have concentration ratios based on value added rather than value of shipments, due to the presence of extensive duplication. These industries have been placed in Part II of Table 2-5 along with Greeting Cards, which is misclassified as highly differentiated. If these three industries are eliminated from the group of seventeen industries, there is an unchanged weighted average concentration ratio of 48 in 1947 and in 1963. Only by including in the weighting a questionable value of shipment figure for Motor Vehicles and Parts (which has horrendous problems in duplication of shipments) can one produce an upward movement. Almost all of the increase in concentration in this industry occurred by 1954 when the top four

TABLE 2-5
List of Highly Differentiated Consumer Industries
Used by President Johnson's Cabinet Committee
on Price Stability

SIC Code	Industry	Top Four Company Shipments Concentration Ratio		Industry Value of Shipments - in Thousands of Dollars	
		1947 (1)	1963 (2)	1947 (3)	1963 (4)
	PART I:				
2043	Cereal Preparations	79	86	284,320	625,058
2072	Chocolate and Cocoa Products	68	75	349,907	479,085
2073	Chewing Gum	70	90	148,286	224,844
2082	Malt Liquor*	21	34	1,316,005	2,315,068
2085	Distilled Liquor*	75	58	870,235	1,090,462
2086	Bottled and Canned Soft Drinks	10	12	748,196	2,210,920
2087	Flavorings	50	62	313,573	729,704
2111	Cigarettes*	90	80	1,131,891	2,655,346
2121	Cigars*	41	59	311,401	358,463
2834	Pharmaceutical Preparations	28	22	941,290	3,314,323
2844	Toilet Preparations	24	38	381,376	1,792,662
3421	Cutlery (Includes Razor Blades)	41	66	142,571	283,352
3633	Household Laundry Equipment	40	78	422,297	760,161
3861	Photographic Equipment	61	63	457,497	1,851,213
	Sub Total	698	823	7,838,845	18,690,661
	PART II:				
2084	Wines and Brandy +	26	44	167,418	368,281
3717	Motor Vehicles and Parts +	56	79	11,564,913	36,181,007
2771	Greeting Cards	39	57	123,856	345,961
	Sub Total	121	180	11,856,187	36,895,249
	Total	819	1,003	19,695,032	55,585,910
	Part I Weighted Concentration Ratio	48	48		
	Parts I and II Weighted Average Concentration Ratio	52	68		
	Parts I and II Unweighted Average Concentration Ratio (Price Stability Committee)	48	59		

* Value of production data.
+ The presence of substantial duplication in the shipment figures for SIC 2084 and 3717 resulted in the Census Bureau computing the concentration ratios of these industries in terms of value added. The shipment figures for these industries are shown, with the duplication, in columns (3) and (4). If value added is used as a weight instead of value of shipments, the weighted average in 1963 of Part I is 47, and of Parts I and II, 64. Census concentration ratios in terms of value added are not available for 1947.

Source: U.S. Dept. of Commerce, *1947 Census of Manufactures*, Vol. I (Washington, 1949)

companies accounted for 75 percent of the industry value added. Since 1954 there has been a substantial increase in the share of imported cars; however, imports were excluded in the computations of concentration ratios in Table 2-5.

The important point is that public policy conclusions cannot be drawn meaningfully with respect to all highly differentiated consumer goods from a list of so few industries that the inclusion or exclusion of one industry from a weighted average causes widely differing results. Even more questionable is the procedure of averaging data from industries as diverse as Chewing Gum, Greeting Cards and Motor Vehicles and Parts. If apples and oranges are not additive, why should it be perfectly acceptable to add or average the concentration ratios of the apple industry with the orange industry?

Before one starts to calculate concentration trends, the initial question should be whether there exists a sufficient number of similar economic characteristics to make an average or trend of substantive value. The dollar magnitude of different product classes being compared cannot be so disparate in size that averaging renders a meaningless conclusion.[9] With this *caveat* in mind it is difficult to see how a single 5-digit product class in 1972, such as Lampshades (SIC 39995), with $37 million of shipments, can be meaningfully compared or averaged with an enormous 5-digit product class such as Passenger Cars (SIC 37111) with $29.2 billion shipments in 1972. The same point also raises the specter whether any multiple industry averaging of not just concentration data, but of any industry variable, such as sales or profit data, should be put together as a pot-pourri in a kettle and averaged. Respect for the basic principles of arithmetic would direct studies in industrial organization away from the multiple industry approach and toward single industries or similar types of industries.

SELECTION OF A CONCENTRATION INDEX

The concentration ratios published by the Bureau of the Census show the percent of domestic plant shipments for various groups of products which were made by the top four, eight, twenty and fifty largest companies. A top four company concentration ratio of, say 80 percent, does not show whether the component firms were all the same size with 20% of the industry or whether the top firm had 74 percent and the next three firms each had 2 percent. The problem relates to arithmetic: different distributions of numbers can give the same average value.

In an antitrust case the procedure followed by the federal agencies and the courts is to request, by subpoena if necessary, the shipments and imports of all of the leading companies in the industry being examined. But the analysis does not stop there. It only begins a long, in depth examination of many alternative product groupings which offer different concentration ratios. Consideration is also given to future expected changes in market shares resulting from the probability of new entrants. A top four company concentration ratio in the context of antitrust litigation therefore presents only a limited amount of information and, as a short-hand expression, is analogous to a person's nickname in contrast to his biography.

The product categories utilized by the Bureau of the Census are seldom used in an antitrust case. This should not be surprising when the flexibility of product classification is appreciated. Each alternative classification or regrouping of products generally shows different market shares and allows an alternative insight into a competitive framework as the effects of imports, substitute products and various geographic considerations are taken into account. The objection that a top four company concentration ratio does not impart sufficient information is often related to a search for a unique number from some formula, ratio or index that can be characterized without qualification as "the" concentration ratio for an industry. This is the quest for a world of absolutes and seldom stops at just measuring industrial concentration. The target often is the more ambitious desire to achieve a single number which can describe competition as being satisfactory or unsatisfactory. Antitrust law by its fundamental jurisprudential nature examines the world of relatives, the matrix of alternative explanations which consider the shadow of doubts, the plausible and the implausible, and in this twilight, the law seeks an ultimate balance of evidence.

In an antitrust case concerned with monopoly or the effect on competition from a merger of firms, the interest is confined to the top eight or ten companies. The trends in market shares of each leading company and its changes in ranking are studied. This examination of the top part of the distribution of firms in an industry can generally be performed with simple market shares or a concentration ratio which aggregates the market shares for the top four or top eight companies. In this context, a concentration ratio has no more profundity than an elementary average of four numbers. Since the market share of each of these leading firms is being analyzed on an individual basis, the concentration ratio is to a large extent superfluous.

Other indexes of concentration, referred to as "summary measures," are employed to examine the full distribution of firms in an industry. The most frequently used summary measure of industrial concentration is the Herfindahl Index.

The Herfindahl Index is defined as the sum of the squares of the market shares of firms in an industry. If there were only four firms in an industry, each equal in size with 25% of industry sales, the Herfindahl Index would be equal to .25.

Four Firms Equal Size
Herfindahl Index $= (.25)^2 + (.25)^2 + (.25)^2 + (.25)^2 = .25$
Five Firms Equal Size
Herfindahl Index $= (.20)^2 + (.20)^2 + (.20)^2 + (.20)^2 + (.20)^2 = .20$
Five Firms Unequal Size
Herfindahl Index $= (.90)^2 + (.02)^2 + (.02)^2 + (.02)^2 + (.02)^2 = .97$
One Firm
Herfindahl Index $= (1.00)^2 = 1$

If all the firms in an industry are equal in size, the Herfindahl Index is equal to $1/n$ where n is the number of firms. Thus, an industry with four equal sized firms has an index value of $1/4$ or .25, and an industry with five equal sized firms has an index value of $1/5$ or .20. The value of index decreases toward zero as the number of firms of equal size increases in an industry. In the extreme case of a single firm monopoly, the index has a value of one. In practice it is difficult to use the Herfindahl Index since the Bureau of the Census will not disclose individual company data for all the firms in an industry.

(1) The FTC-Litton Typewriter Matter

Most of the points mentioned in this section can be observed in the economic analysis of a well written Federal Trade Commission, Initial Decision involving the merger of *Litton Industries*, which owned Royal typewriter, with Triumph-Adler typewriter.[10] The Bureau of the Census published a top four company concentration ratio for Typewriters (3572) of 81 percent for 1967. See Table 2-6. The 4-digit product group (3572) was identical to the single 5-digit product class (35720) and included standard electric and non-electric typewriters, portable typewriters, as well as highly specialized typewriters used by the media for composing. The Census listed dollar shipments, but not a concentration ratio, for 7-digit products: Standard Electric Typewriters (35720-01), Standard Non-electric Typewriters (35720-03), Standard Portable, Electric and Non-electric (37520-05) and Specialized Typewriters (35720-12). The data for the last two categories were combined to avoid a disclosing individual company data. In addition, typewriter parts were divided into different categories depending upon whether the parts were shipped from a vertically integrated plant which manufactured complete typewriters.

TABLE 2-6
Bureau of the Census Product Classification
for Typewriters in 1967

SIC Code	Title
3572	Typewriters, including specialized units for composing
35720	Typewriters, including specialized units for composing
35720-01	Standard Electric Typewriters
35720-03	Standard Non-electric Typewriters
35720-05	Standard Portable (electric and non-electric)
35720-12	Specialized Typewriters
35720-40	Typewriter Parts sold separately Produced by Complete Machine Manufacturers
35720-51	Other Typewriter Parts sold separately

The Federal Trade Commission's Hearing Examiner, disregarded these data and categories. Data for imported typewriters by foreign competitors such as Olivetti, Facit, Olympia, Brother, Nippo and the acquired company, Triumph-Adler, were not included in the Census figures which covered only shipments from domestic plants. The Census product classifications were also found to be inappropriate by the FTC Examiner. The Examiner considered three basic product groupings. The largest group was the "U.S. Office Typewriter Market," which excluded specialized typewriters. The "Heavy Duty Office Typewriter Market," was studied which included standard office electric typewriters, both new and factory-reconditioned, and automatic typewriters. "Portable Typewriters" were found to be another relevant product market with the portable electric sub-market as the most important segment.

Market shares of each typewriter company were examined for the period 1963 to 1969. A concentration ratio for the top four companies in the "U.S. Typewriter Market" category, shown in Table 2-7 shows only a slight change of 2 percentage points from 89 to 91 percent in the six year period. However, the Herfindahl Index for the whole distribution of firms showed a jump of 20 percentage points or 66 percent from .30 to .50. In the space of six years, IBM's market share rose from 47.2 percent to 68.9 percent. But the next three companies lost their former market positions. Litton (Royal) declined from 20.6 percent to 11.6 percent; Sperry Rand

TABLE 2–7
Comparison of Top Four Concentration Ratios with Herfindahl Index and Market Shares of Companies Selling Typewriters in the U.S. 1963 and 1969

Manufacturer	U.S. Office Typewriter Market (%)		U.S. Heavy-Duty Office Typewriter Market (%)		U.S. Portable Typewriter Market (%)		U.S. Electric Portable Typewriter Market (%)	
	1963	1969	1963	1969	1963	1969	1963	1969
IBM	47.2	68.9	71.8	85.7	–	–	–	–
Litton (Royal)	20.6	11.6	5.7	3.1	24.5	16.3	–	16.3
SCM	7.3	2.5	7.8	.6	44.7	57.0	100.0	77.9
Sperry Rand	6.7	4.3	5.6	2.4	8.8	5.5	–	1.5
Olivetti	13.9	5.9	7.7	4.3	8.7	5.8	–	–
R.C. Allen	.6	.3	–	–	–	–	–	–
Olympia	2.7	3.1	.6	1.7	7.0	3.5	–	–
Adler	.5	1.9	.5	1.8	.5	1.3	–	.9
Facit	.3	.3	.2	.2	.5	.7	–	–
Paillard	.3	.3	.1	.1	2.9	1.6	–	–
Brother	–	1.0	–	–	2.5	7.1	–	3.4
Messa (Sears)	–	–	–	–	–	.6	–	–
Nippo	–	–	–	–	–	.6	–	–
TOTAL	100.0	100.0	100.0	100.0	100.0	100.0	100.0	100.0
Top 4 Company Concentration Ratio	.89	.90	.93	.96	.87	.85	1.00	.99
Herfindahl Index	.30	.50	.53	.74	.28	.37	1.00	.63

fell from 6.7 percent to 4.3 percent; and Olivetti fell from 13.9 percent to 5.9 percent. The Examiner found that the grouping of all typewriters together was not economically meaningful in the determination of probable competitive effects:

> Such a grouping lumps together many different kinds of typewriters with completely different physical characteristics and uses with no reasonable interchangeability of use. For example, portable typewriters, designed for home and student use, are not functionally interchangeable with heavy duty office electric machines, which are designed to withstand heavy duty typing tasks in commercial, government and school offices. Moreover, such a grouping brings together typewriters with vastly different prices. For example, the IBM Model D standard office electric typewriter retails for $510, while portable typewriters sell for as low as $29.95.

Diversity of leadership in the leading companies in component product categories is dramatic in the complete absence of IBM from the portable typewriter market. SCM with only 2.5 percent of the U.S. typewriter market had 77.9 percent of the U.S. electric portable sub-market. There was testimony presented showing Royal which was number two in the U.S. office typewriter market, had annual losses over $9 million a year for the past three years. The Examiner also recognized that the typewriter industry was about to undergo a substantial technological upheaval with new entrants marketing electronic typewriters and word processing equipment. The Federal Trade Commission first found a violation and ordered Litton to divest itself of Triumph-Adler. Two months after its decision, the Commission reopened the proceeding to reexamine the question of relief. The FTC judge concluded,

"It is to be anticipated that, in the exercise of good business judgment, Litton would withdraw from the office typewriter market and terminate its efforts to enter the automatic submarket thereof if it were required to divest itself of Triumph-Adler. . . . Competition in the office typewriter market narrows itself down to an effort by others to compete with IBM, . . . it is recommended that the Commission modify its order of March 13, 1973, by rescinding that portion which requires Litton to divest itself of Triumph-Adler."[11]

The Commission followed this recommendation and did not require Litton to divest itself of Triumph-Adler.

CONCLUSION

The basic question in the selection of either a percentage type concentration index, such as the top four company concentration ratio, or a summary measure, such as the Herfindahl Index, is not which one is the best measure of concentration, but which one describes the aspect of the distribution in which the investigator is concerned. The ultimate purpose of measures of industry concentration should be the comparative analysis of concentration of the same or a similar set of industries over time. Neither a single concentration index nor a combination of concentration indexes can be used as a direct measure of the degree of competition. Except in extreme cases where a few firms produce almost all of the output of an industry, the knowledge of the distribution of firms is insufficient, in and of itself, for the making of an even cursory judgment as to the nature of competition. A concentration index is only a partial description of an economic group. Measuring and comparing the concentration ratios of widely differing industries in an attempt to evaluate competition is probably as foolhardy a venture as taking a ruler into a zoo to measure the size of all animals. Additional information is required, such as whether the industry is expanding or contracting, the extent of mergers, the rates of entry and exit of firms, the capital and technology required for entry, the level of advertising, the level of research and development expenditures, the rate of technological change, the importance of substitute products, imports, exports, price flexibility, raw material shortages, and the physical age and replacement cost of plants and equipment.

ENDNOTES

1. See B. Bock, "Line of Business Reporting: A Quest for a Snark?" *The Conference Board Record* (November, 1975), pp. 10-19; G.J. Benston, "The Baffling New Numbers Game at the FTC," *Fortune* (October, 1975); and Motion by Aluminum Company of America, et al., to quash order to file Line-of-Business Report (August 20, 1974), reprinted in Daily Executive's Report, The Bureau of National Affairs, Inc. (August 20, 1974).
2. United States Bureau of the Budget, *Standard Industrial Classification Manual 1972,* (Washington, D.C.: Government Printing Office, 1945); and United States, Bureau of the Census, *1972 Census of Manufactures,* Industry Statistics, (Washington, D.C.: Government Printing Office, 1976).

3. *Brown Shoe Co.* v. *United States*, 370 U.S. 294 (1962) p. 315.
4. J. N. Mitchell, Address before the Georgia Bar Association in Savannah on June 6, 1969. Reprinted in Commerce Clearing House, *Trade Regulation Reporter* (Chicago, 1969) pp. 505-09.
5. U.S., 1972 *Census of Manufactures*, Concentration Ratios in Manufacturing, Tables 1-3.
6. United States, *Studies by the Staff of the Cabinet Committee on Price Stability* (Washington, 1969).
7. The method by which the seventeen industries were selected was footnoted at page 60 in the study as follows: "Generally speaking, industries classified as undifferentiated make advertising expenditures of less than 1 percent of sales, and those classified as highly differentiated make substantial expenditures for advertising, often in excess of 10 percent of sales and usually are heavy users of television advertising media. See Federal Trade Commission, Industry Classification and Concentration (1967). Inspection of the FTC document, which is the basis for the differentiation classifications, shows the identical footnote plus the following sentence: "Incomplete information makes classification into differentiation categories somewhat subjective." The result is that an industry can be considered highly differentiated in Table 2-5 even though its advertising expenditures are less than 1 percent of sales. The range of subjectiveness is apparent when an industry such as greeting cards is included in Table 2-5. It is difficult to perceive the distinguishing characteristics that would enable a consumer to differentiate between the cards of different manufacturers.
8. F. E. Croxton, D. J. Cowden, and S. Klein, *Applied General Statistics*, 3rd. ed. (Englewood Cliffs, N.J., 1967).
9. See *United States* v. *Crocker-Anglo National Bank*, 277 F. Supp. 133 (N.D. Calif., 1967) at p. 166. A witness in this bank merger case testified that any concentration ratio in California would be overwhelmingly dominated by the Bank of America: "It is like trying to combine a giant and a pigmy and say something about the size of a man by so doing. They are two separate classes of men and you cannot draw off a conclusion as to the average of a man by combining a 20 foot giant and a 4 foot pigmy."
10. U.S., Federal Trade Commission, *In the Matter of Litton Industries, Inc.*, Dkt. 8778, Initial Decision by Walter R. Johnson (February, 1972). Part of the explanation for excellence in economic analysis is attributable to the testimony and extensive exhibits offered on behalf of Litton by two leading antitrust economists: Dr. Betty Bock of the Conference Board and Dr. J. Fred Weston of the University of California, Los Angeles.
11. *Litton Industries, Inc.*, Dockett 8778, FTC Transfer Binder, 1973-1976, *Commerce Clearing House*, 1974, Para. 20,664 (July 12, 1974).

THOUGHT QUESTIONS

1. What is the difference between a "summary measure" of concentration and an "absolute measure?"
   a) Is one necessarily more useful than another?
   b) What is "aggregate concentration?"
2. Should we encourage the participation of smaller firms in larger capital projects in instances where it is known that the total cost of the project will be higher if it is done in piecemeal production?
3. Should there be an absolute level of concentration for an industry, or alternatively a market share for a company, which is presumably anticompetitive?
4. In 1973 the Federal Trade Commission dismissed a complaint against General Mills with regard to their purchase of Gorton, the leading frozen seafood company. The conglomerate acquisition raised a number of product definition and concentration questions:
   1) Was the appropriate market to judge the acquisition "frozen packaged fish" or "frozen prepared foods?"
   2) If the market was "frozen packaged fish" as the FTC staff contended, should "frozen shrimp" have been excluded by the FTC because its price per pound is

more expensive than frozen fillets and sticks, or because it was a shellfish, or for some other reason?

3) The FTC submitted concentration data based on domestic production only. Should imported fish have been excluded in computing market shares? Note: If several fishing boats docked at Cape Cod after fishing in Nova Scotia, the catch from those flying foreign flags are treated as imports and the catch from those flying the U.S. flag are treated as domestic production.

4) Should all fresh fish be grouped with frozen fish?

5) Assume some large fishing vessels have freezing facilities on board and others use freezing facilities on land. Should the fresh fish which is subsequently frozen on land be combined with the fish which is brought in already frozen?

6) Should frozen fillets (individual fish) be combined with frozen fish sticks (made from two or three segments of individual fillets)?

7) Should frozen fish dinners, including mashed potatoes and a vegetable, be included with frozen fillets and sticks?

8) Should breaded frozen fish fillets be included with non-breaded frozen fillets?

9) Should breaded frozen fish sticks made into triangles to imitate a single fish fillet be combined with actual frozen fish fillets?

10) Should expensive cod frozen fish sticks be combined with considerably less expensive haddock fish sticks?

11) Should the market shares be based on pounds of fish or dollar sales? Should we separate out, in dollars, the unprocessed frozen fish in ice blocks from the processed breaded fish fillet sold in retail packages?

12) Should the large ice blocks of frozen fish which are resold by Gorton to smaller companies which cut the blocks into small individual portions for making breaded sticks and fillets be counted twice: once when sold by Gorton and second when sold by the manufacturer?

13) What value should the ice-block take in terms of dollars: the Gorton raw material price or the more expensive finished product price?

14) Frozen fish sticks and fillets are sold in large institutional packages to schools, hospitals, prisons and restaurants. Should these products be combined with the smaller retail packages sold in supermarkets?

15) If the frozen retail and institutional markets were combined, and the market shares were calculated in terms of dollars, should there be an adjustment for the higher priced retail packages which are combined with the lower priced bulk institutional packages?

16) Should frozen "fish chowder" in cans be included with primarily non-frozen canned "soups" or with "frozen packaged fish?"

5. In the Gorton case, none of the competitors in the frozen fish industry expected General Mills to enter its industry directly. General Mills stated one of its principal interests was the fact that Gorton had frozen food warehouses throughout the United States which could handle all types of frozen prepared food products. Should the market have been "frozen food warehouses?"

6. The Federal Trade Commission concluded the appropriate market in the *Gorton* case was "prepared frozen food products," and not "frozen packaged fish, excluding shrimp." Illustrate the range of frozen food products which could be included under the category "prepared frozen foods." Can a category this broad be a "market" for analyzing competition under the antitrust laws?

3

PROFITS

QUESTIONING THE ALLEGED RELATIONSHIP BETWEEN PROFITS, CONCENTRATION AND MONOPOLY POWER

Few relationships in antitrust economics will ever be statistically established without some group dissenting in the conclusion. The passage of time alone will generate another set of data for new scholars to test old propositions. Wisdom and considerable restraint is often required in antitrust economics to know what one has not proved despite an apparent relationship between broad economic variables such as profits and concentration.

The study of competition requires an analysis of manufacturing and distribution techniques, pricing, innovation, and multiple-product relationships. In contrast, the term "concentration" requires only an arithmetic computation of a percentage. By substituting "concentration" for "competition" in the analysis of antitrust, one can conveniently solve the difficult problem of ascertaining a tendency for a substantial lessening of competition by simply finding a numerical increase in concentration. Market concentration is then used as a proxy for competition.

By showing a correlation between high concentration and profit rates, some economists have sought to establish that high concentration results in less competition and is reflected in high profits. The basic inference of these studies is that competition will be lessened as profit rates increase. To quote the final report of President Johnson's Council of Economic Advisors: "Numerous studies have shown a significant relationship between high concentration and high profit rates — an indication of weak competitive pressures."[1] A far more conservative position was taken by Professor Joe Bain in his pioneer work of this relationship: "The unadjusted accounting rate of profit, as computed by the usual methods from balance sheets and income statements, is *prima facie* an absolutely unreliable indicator of the presence or absence either of monopoly power or of excess profits. . ."[2]

If concentrated industries lower costs by improving manufacturing processes or expand sales by introducing new and improved products, their increased profits are not necessarily the result of monopoly power. Profits flowing from these forms of beneficial economic activity should be encouraged; instead, profits are generally stigmatized. Similarly, if the leading companies in concentrated industries were to invest more heavily in capital equipment than labor intensive smaller firms, their profits may be the result of economies of scale. A company which correctly predicts and designs the type of product which customers seek should also be expected to earn high profits. Professor John McGee states:

> A firm that correctly gambles where the big demand is, and tools to produce for it, will grow large, and show low costs and high profits, even if it has no advantage over others in producing an *identical* product at *identical* rates and volumes.[3]

In any given industry the earnings among competing firms can be expected to differ as a result of variations in the quality of management, the historical decisions made in designing the location of plants, and the technology of both equipment and production processes. If the best in efficiency, technological change, marketing and management is expected to rise as cream to the top, the leading firms should be expected to be the most successful and the most profitable.

INADEQUACIES OF AVERAGE PROFITS AS A PERFORMANCE STANDARD

To compare a single relatively high profit rate of a given company or industry to the average of all manufacturing industries or to all other companies in an industry, and to attribute the difference from this average as "monopoly profits" is to accept the "average" as the standard of performance. All companies that have profit rates above some average should *not* be presumed to be tainted with illegal monopoly profits; nor should those companies with profit rates at or below some average be presumed to be performing in a satisfactory manner or within a competitive environment.

A few recent examples illustrate the use of the "average profit standard" in antitrust. President Jimmy Carter appointed a commission in 1978 to recommend certain reforms of our antitrust laws. The report of the commission concluded that the regulation of trucks had created "monopoly profits" as evidenced by the high rate of return on investment.[4] The commission noted, without any economic analysis, that the 100 largest regulated trucking companies realized a 19.7 percent ratio of profits to equity as against 14 percent for all manufacturing.[5]

The same reasoning for an average profit level can be seen in the recent ReaLemon decision of the Federal Trade Commission where Borden was charged with monopolizing the processed lemon juice market with their ReaLemon brand.[6] The Commission found that ReaLemon's return was higher than that of all Food and Kindred Product companies and for All Manufacturing companies. The Commission stated, "This persistent high profitability is further evidence of Borden's monopoly power." An economist examining this same evidence of a deviation of profits from an average level could just as intelligently conclude that the high profitability is evidence of Borden's persistently high management ability, marketing skill and product quality standards — all of which helped bring Borden from a single horse-drawn, milk delivery wagon up to a multi-billion dollar food and chemical corporation.

To castigate all those above an average profit level and approve or condone those at or below an average level is akin to criticizing the smartest students in a class for possibly cheating on their examinations. The average profit standard reflects the lethargy found in the absence of competition where each company plays it "safe," and does *not* attempt to charge lower prices, create better products, or provide more efficient production and service. Superior performance with concomitant high profits is the basis of success and should be grounds for celebration, not criticism, in a free enterprise system.

THE STATISTICAL SIGNIFICANCE OF THE ALLEGED RELATIONSHIP BETWEEN PROFITS AND CONCENTRATION

The statistical relationship between profits and concentration has been one of the most widely studied areas in antitrust.[7] Almost all of the studies show a positive relationship with the more concentrated industries earning higher profits. In some time periods the positive correlations between profits and concentration are attributed to variations in the sizes of firms: more concentrated industries have firms with larger physical facilities and economies of scale in manufacturing and distribution. The profit data in the vast majority of studies includes domestic and foreign earnings as well as the profits from all the diverse and sometimes conglomerate enterprises of a company. The capital structures of various industries included in the sample differ markedly. A huge industry such as petroleum refining, which is heavily dependent upon fixed capital, will be included along with small labor intensive industries, such as fountain pens, which can be assembled in a leased floor of a building.

Companies and industries with older, but efficient plants, have their assets undervalued in an inflationary economy. Newer industries with high growth rates may have higher asset costs for their recent plants, but these costs may be more than offset by higher prices resulting as the demand for their new products outstrips their expanding capacity. Thus, the level of profits of a company or an industry is a reflection of demand conditions, cost and supply constraints, and a dimension of time.

The existence of a positive relationship between profits and concentration does not necessarily prove that competition is less in concentrated industries. The higher profits earned by the leading firms in concentrated industries may reflect better run companies with greater perception of market demand, improved production methods and superior product performance. All the factors that push the leader to the top, both competitive and non-competitive, are combined in a company's total profit. There is no more reason to describe these earnings as "monopoly profits" than as "competitive success." There is therefore no standard answer to the dual questions: Did the leader in a field earn high profits merely because it was the leader? Or were the high profits a reflection of the leader being the best in its industry?

In 1951 Professor Joe Bain published a paper entitled: "Relation of Profit Rate to Industry Concentration: American Manufacturing, 1936-1940."[8] Despite the breadth of the title, the paper covered only 42 manufacturing industries and was based on the comparison of the average profit rates of two groups of industries: those with top eight firm concentration ratios above 70 percent, and those below. Bain then employed a statistical significance test, and concluded that there was less than a 1 percent chance that the difference between these two means could be due to random factors. Similarly, on the basis of 21 industries in a concentrated group and only 9 industries in an unconcentrated group, Professor Michael Mann concluded that "the difference between average rates of return is statistically significant at the .01 level."[9] Professor Leonard Weiss noted a significant relationship between profits and concentration in over 80 studies by various economists.[10] An unsophisticated student might conclude that all these studies which found a significant relationship between profits and concentration were 99% irrefutable. Such a conclusion would be erroneous, and a result of not understanding the limited use of the term "significance" in statistics.

Most elementary statistics courses begin with an analysis of how to portray a distribution of data, and how to measure its center and its dispersion. Various tables are furnished as appendices to elementary text books on statistics showing values of various idealized symmetric curves (such as the bell-shaped Normal Curve or the "t" Distribution) which extend indefinitely in both directions as tails. The logic relating to these basic symmetric curves is critical to the overall concept of proving "significance" between and among variables being analyze© in industrial organization.

At the heart of classical statistics is a repetitive experiment being performed an enormous number of times from a huge population which has continuous and symmetric properties. These types of experiments are more likely to be found in the physical sciences than the social sciences. For example, a swimming pool owner has to find the pH value of the water each day in order to determine whether more chlorine should be added. After taking a few samples in a vial, a conclusion is reached about the pH value of the whole pool. If one could quickly test, say 100,000 small vials from the pool and find the average pH value, it would be almost identical to the average obtained from the billions of samples required to test every drop of water in the entire pool. The *Central Limit Theorem,* which is at the core of classical statistical methods, states that the distribution of the values of these 100,000 samples can be approximated by a symmetric bell-shaped curve referred to as the Normal Curve. We therefore are able to extend our knowledge from the mean of our samples to a conclusion as to the mean and dispersion or shape of the population consisting of the pH value of all the water in the pool.

Every five years the United States Department of Commerce publishes the *Census of Manufactures* which provides concentration ratios and other information on the share of industrial activity accounted for by the largest companies in approximately 450 manufacturing industries. Any broad based study of industrial concentration must utilize to some extent the data compiled by the *Census of Manufactures.* Many of the 450 industries have data problems with the result that only a limited number of industries can be selected in studies of concentration. But the industries chosen are not "samples" randomly selected as vials of water in the swimming pool example. Nor is there any basic homogeneity or continuity of that which is being sampled. The basis of the sampling is simply whether the data can be used. Thus, the studies of the relationship between profit and concentration do not really draw a random sample as required for a statistical significance test, nor is the population of 450 industries a symmetric type distribution such as the bell-shaped Normal Curve derived from the theoretically expected data base of infinite homogenous units. The "sample" selected in these studies of industrial organization is basically their limited population of a few hundred or less industries for which data are available. In this context, it is arguable whether statistical significance tests are appropriate.

CONCLUSION

A positive relationship between concentration and profits does not imply that competition is lessened as profits increase. If the leaders of an industry offer the best in service, quality and efficiency, they should be expected to earn high profits. If these profits reflect success in performance, they should not be stigmatized as "monopoly profits." A simple correlation between one *structure* element such as a concentration ratio, and a *performance* variable, such as a profit rate, will not provide an easy formula for finding a "critical value" for determining the presence or absence of competition. An approach which examines in detail the nature of competition in specific industries gives a greater opportunity for appreciating interdependence among variables, and is more likely to bring us closer to an understanding of American enterprise.

ENDNOTES

1. United States, *Economic Report of the President,* Annual Report of the Council of Economic Advisors (Washington, 1969).
2. J. Bain, "The Profit Rate As A Measure of Monopoly Power," *The Quarterly Journal of Economics* (February, 1941).
3. J. S. McGee, *In Defense of Industrial Concentration* (Praeger, 1971), p. 40.
4. *New York Times* (December 16, 1978).
5. Since the trucking industry is not even part of the manufacturing sector but part of the transportation sector, it is questionable why the commission would compare it to the average rate of return of the manufacturing sector.
6. *In the Matter of Borden, Inc.,* FTC Docket No. 8978, (November 7, 1978).
7. The literature is summarized in papers by Harold Demsetz and Leonard Weiss in *Industrial Concentration: The New Learning*, ed. H. J. Goldschmid, H. M. Mann and J. F. Weston, (Little, Brown; 1974), pp. 162-245.
8. *Quarterly Journal of Economics*, (August, 1951), pp. 293-324.
9. H. M. Mann, "Seller Concentration, Barriers to Entry, and Rates of Return in Thirty Industries, 1950-1960," *Review of Econ. and Statistics* (August, 1966), pp. 296-307.
10. See footnote 7.

THOUGHT QUESTIONS

1.   Give some examples of food companies which manufacture non-food items, the profit of which are included in their published aggregate net profit figure.
     a)   How meaningful is a profit rate for all companies which are classified in the

2-digit Standard Industrial Classification Industry of "Food and Kindred Products?"

2. Should companies be forced to disclose more market information, such as sales and
    profits, than they are presently required to do?
    a) Give one example of how knowledge of a company's costs, or market share,
        could prove to be anti-competitive and another example of how it could be
        pro-competitive.
    b) Should a company be required to report the number of employees, sales or profits
        of a particular 7-digit product made with other products in the same plant?

3. Consider a hypothetical product that accounts for 5% of a plant's output and does not
    have sufficient volume to be made solely in one plant. What are the problems
    associated with "indivisibilities," for example, the use of a pro-rata cost or profit
    figure with the knowledge that 5% of a large steam boiler which is required to generate
    the temperature to make this product cannot be meaningfully isolated? Since most
    plants are multi-product operations, what does the above example suggest about the
    extent that allocations affect the cost and profit of most products?

4. Large antitrust cases, such as a number of government and private cases against IBM
    or AT&T, involve thousands of exhibits, hundreds of witnesses, and millions of
    documents.
    a) Compare the examination and cross-examination of the various witnesses on
        economic, engineering, and financial data with the simple correlation of concen-
        tration and profit rates followed by some earlier economic studies.
    b) Are the courts presently more sophisticated in analyzing the variables affecting
        the basic data than many earlier economic studies were?
    c) Do you believe that a simple concentration ratio or profit rate is sufficient for the
        government to start a case against a company or industry?

5. Discuss how the following factors could affect a company's profits: a creative
    advertising campaign, a new management team, the permanent closing of an older
    plant, a new style and product design, a shortage of critical input, the opening of a new
    production line, a strike, a reevaluation of inventory, the acquisition or sale of a
    division, a change in foreign exchange rates, the existence of a favorable long term raw
    material supply contract, and a business contraction or general inflation in the
    economy.
    a) Could "monopoly profits" be separated from these factors?

6. The oil industry has a relatively low top four company concentration ratio but earned
    historically *high* profits in 1979. The automobile industry has a relatively high top four
    company concentration ratio but earned historically *low* profits in 1979. Explain.

7. In 1980, U.S. Steel announced the closing of 15 steel plants.
    a) Should the economic profit rates of this company be adjusted in the past to take
        account of the huge write-offs?
    b) Should anticipated plant closing in future years be written-off presently in order to
        ascertain economic rates of return?
    c) Should the earnings of a company's remaining plants be viewed in isolation after
        other plants are closed, or should their earnings be offset by the cost of closing the
        former plants?

8. Compare and discuss the profits for three plants owned by different companies making
    an identical product: (1) a 1940 plant which is fully depreciated with very few fixed
    costs and a low rate of productivity, (2) a 1970 plant with high fixed costs and high
    depreciation charges and a relatively average rate of productivity, and (3) a 1980 plant
    with new technology, relatively high fixed costs and an extremely high rate of
    productivity.
    a) What would an average profit rate of this industry suggest?

9. The recent windfall oil tax is only 30% rather than 60% of the difference of the market
    price from a lower base price for independent oil producers who have an output of less
    than 1,000 barrels a day.

a)   What is the objective of this favored legislation?
b)   What is the expected effect on development and exploration drilling as well as imports?
c)   How does this legislation reconcile with the goals of a model of pure competition or the goals of an ''optimum'' allocation of resources?

II. SELECTED ANTITRUST LAW CASES:

Monopoly, Price Fixing, Vertical Integration, Tying Arrangements, Price Discrimination and Mergers

4

INTRODUCTION TO ANTITRUST CASES

Antitrust cases have been selected in Part II to cover six major legal subjects: Monopoly, Price Fixing, Vertical Integration, Tying Arrangements, Price Discrimination, and Mergers. The earlier monopoly cases, such as the *Standard Oil* case (1911) and the *Alcoa* case (1945), are classics in antitrust law. A number of newer cases selected, such as the District Court opinion in the *Berkey Photo-Kodak* (1978) case and the Federal Trade Commission *ReaLemon* opinion (1978) are not Supreme Court opinions nor, at this stage, landmark cases. But they are stimulating opinions in terms of their language and facts and the type of economic evidence which was introduced at trial.

MONOPOLY

The Supreme Court has shown a remarkable flexibility in examining economic evidence in antitrust cases. In the 1911 *Standard Oil* attempted monopoly case, the Supreme Court stated with respect to the Sherman Act that, ''in every case where it is claimed that an act or acts are in violation of the statute the *rule of reason*, in the light of the principles of law and the public policy which the act embodies, must be applied.'' The size of the company or its market share was not deemed relevant to a finding of monopoly unless there was also evidence of unreasonable, predatory practices. The Supreme Court rejected a structural approach for a behavioral approach based on the reasonableness of the business conduct of the defendant.

In 1920 the Supreme Court examined the activities of U.S. Steel which was charged with monopolizing the iron and steel industry. The Court rejected the structural approach and found that ''the corporation is undoubtably of impressive size, and it takes an effort of resolution not to be affected by it or to exaggerate its influence. But we must adhere to the law, and the law does not make mere size an offense, or the existence of unexerted power an offense.''

The *Alcoa* opinion (1945) was not a Supreme Court case, but the language of Judge Learned Hand is colorful. A number of diametrically opposite positions are stated in the opinion. For example, a *per se* structural approach to monopoly is suggested by the statement that, "The percentage we have already mentioned — over ninety . . . is enough to constitute a monopoly; it is doubtful whether sixty or sixty-four per cent would be enough; and certainly thirty-three per cent is not." But Judge Hand also stated that, "size does not determine guilt; that there must be some 'exclusion' of competitors. . . . A market may, for example, be so limited it is impossible to produce at all and meet the cost of production except by a plant large enough to supply the whole demand . . . A single producer may be the survivor out of a group of active competitors, merely by virtue of his superior skill, foresight and industry."

In 1956 the Supreme Court in the *Cellophane* case marked a high point in the use of theoretical economic concepts in its opinions by employing the term "cross-elasticity of demand." In finding that DuPont had not monopolized the cellophane market, the Supreme Court considered a wide array of market data showing the price, quality and end use of various competing flexible packaging materials.

In the *Kodak-Berkey Photo* case (1978) the Southern District Court in New York considered a private treble damage suit by Berkey Photo which alleged that Kodak had used monopoly power in the film market to monopolize and attempt to monopolize the still camera market. Berkey Photo alleged that when Kodak introduced its 110 camera, it should have given prior disclosure to its competitors in order for them to have an opportunity to develop a similar competitive product. The District Court held that Kodak had such a duty since Kodak was, ". . . a 'giant,' with a nearly unique agglomeration of enormous powers over adjoining markets in a huge industry." The Court of Appeals reversed, holding that, "If a firm that has engaged in the risks and expenses of research and development were required in all circumstances to share with its rivals the benefits of those endeavors, this incentive would very likely be vitiated." At issue in this case is whether the antitrust laws should require a large company with a large market share, such as Kodak, to soften the vigor of competition where a smaller rival might be injured by conduct which in other circumstances might be normal and acceptable.

The recent *ReaLemon* opinion shows the outer boundaries in the law of monopoly and the possibility of extreme remedies. The Federal Trade Commission held that Borden had monopolized the market for processed lemon juice with its ReaLemon brand. The Commission refused to follow the recommendation of the lower Administrative Law Judge that Borden be compelled to license to competitors the "ReaLemon" label for ten years. The FTC opinion suggested that Borden must refrain from vigorous price competition: "As a monopolist it is obliged to refrain from the sort of retaliatory price-cutting that would be allowed a sub-monopolist." Finally, the FTC opinion ordered Borden not to sell at "unreasonably low prices." This provision is diametrically opposed to the longstanding doctrine of the Supreme Court in the *Trenton Potteries* case (1927) which held that, "The reasonable price fixed today may through economic and business changes become the unreasonable price of tomorrow." Therefore, the Supreme Court in that case concluded that prices which were illegally fixed in violation of the Sherman Act were *per se* illegal "without the necessity of minute inquiry whether a particular price is reasonable . . . and without placing on the government in enforcing the Sherman Law the burden of ascertaining from day to day whether it has become unreasonable through the mere variation of economic conditions.'' The FTC opinion, in its concern for smaller companies, is advocating a rule making procedure with more government control and surveillance over the pricing and output decisions of larger companies which may injure smaller rivals through hard competition.

PRICE FIXING

Direct price fixing agreements among competitors to adhere to a particular price are considered *per se* illegal. The *per se* illegality refers to the level of the price. The fixed price is deemed unreasonable, and therefore illegal, regardless of whether it is a high or low price. However, considerable economic evidence is admissible in price fixing cases with regard to whether the parties had the *intent* to fix prices. Evidence showing that prices did not advance as fast as the published list prices or were substantially discounted from list prices is frequently introduced to show the lack of parallel conduct and, therefore, the absence of intent to fix the prices. Evidence of substantial cost increases resulting from higher raw material prices or higher labor rates is also generally allowed in evidence as an alternative explanation of simultaneous price advances in an industry by competitors.

In the *Sugar Institute* case (1936), the Supreme Court held illegal under the Sherman Act a trade association price-filing plan which required members to announce their prices publicly in advance of sales, and to adhere to these prices until they publicly announced changes. The Court found that the purpose of this system was to stop secret price discounting. The basis of illegality was the requirement that the various trade association members *adhere* to their publicly announced price lists. In 1969 the Supreme Court heard the *Container* case which involved the exchange of price information among eighteen leading corrugated box manufacturers. Unlike the *Sugar Institute* case, there was no agreement to adhere to a price schedule. The Supreme Court nevertheless found the practice to be illegal since the exchange of price information concerning specific customers had the effect of "keeping prices within a fairly narrow ambit." Three justices of the Supreme Court dissented on the grounds that "it is just as likely that price competition was furthered by the exchange as it is that it was depressed." The dissent noted that in all cases the information exchanged with regard to a particular customer informed the defendants of the price they would have to beat in order to obtain a particular sale. The result was not necessarily a stabilization of prices since sometimes the lower prices were matched.

In 1978 the Supreme Court was again confronted with the issue of price verification among competitors, as well as the criminal indictments of executives from several major gypsum board manufacturers. The defendants followed the practice of calling each other on the telephone to ascertain the price being charged to a specific customer. The defendants argued that they were trying to avoid being tricked by customers "lying" that they were being offered a lower price by a competing manufacturer. The defendants also argued that the intent in verifying the prices was not to stabilize or fix the prices, but to establish a "meeting competition" defense to a possible charge of price discrimination between competing customers. The Supreme Court held that, because this was a criminal case, an *intent* to fix prices had to be established before the defendants could be found guilty. The requirement for criminal *intent* reflects a more flexible attitude toward alternative explanations by defendants for alleged price fixing. Although the reasonableness of the prices is not opened to question, the circumstances surrounding the alleged fixing of prices was permissible evidence to establish that there was no intent to fix prices.

VERTICAL INTEGRATION

The vertically integrated firm, by virtue of its multiple operations in production and distribution, can further its interests at one level with its market strength at another level of competition. In the *Alcoa* case (1945), the sole domestic producer of virgin aluminum was charged with "squeezing" independent fabricators of aluminum sheet by selling them ingot at a high price, and then competing with them in the market with low fabricated sheet prices. Alcoa was alleged to be using its profits from ingot sales to subsidize its sheet fabricating operations until, presumably, its competitors went under. The offense of Alcoa was the continuation of this pricing policy *after* it had been put on notice that the survival of independent fabricators was in imminent danger.

In the *Standard Oil of Indiana* case, a price squeeze existed which was almost the reverse of that found in the *Alcoa* case. Instead of following the Alcoa pattern of selling a raw material at a high price to customers, and attempting to undersell them at the lower outlet level, Standard Oil sold gasoline at a high price to its own dealers at the outlet level and sold gasoline at a low price to wholesale jobbers. The Standard Oil dealers objected that they had to face competition from gasoline discounters who were buying inexpensive gasoline from wholesalers doing business with Standard Oil. Standard Oil successfully defended its pricing by proving that it sold the gasoline to the various wholesale jobbers at discriminatorily low prices in order to meet the competition of other oil companies offering an equally low price to them. The policy issue in the *Standard Oil* case was whether one level of competition should be encouraged, such as the wholesale jobber market, even though smaller companies at a lower level, such as retail gasoline dealers, might suffer in terms of harsh price competition.

The same policy issue was raised recently in the *GTE-Sylvania* case (1977) in which the Supreme Court was asked to review the practice of Sylvania in imposing territorial restrictions on its dealers which prevented them from selling television sets from locations other than their franchised stores. The Supreme Court held that territorial restrictions, without any constraints on prices, should be analyzed under the rule of reason. The Court overruled the earlier *per se* rule in the *Arnold, Schwinn* case (1967) which prohibited a manufacturer from restricting the sales territory of its products once title had passed to the dealer. The Supreme Court reviewed economic evidence showing that a weak manufacturer, such as Sylvania with only a 2% market share, needed to obtain stronger dealers in order to compete against the industry leader, RCA. However, Sylvania could only obtain stronger dealers by promising to insulate them from competition by neighboring stores selling the same product. Both from the point of view of the weak manufacturer or the vulnerable retailer, the theme of the Supreme Court in *GTE-Sylvania* was protectionism and, paradoxically, it was done in the name of competition.

PRICE DISCRIMINATION

In the *Corn Products* case (1945) the defendant operated a plant in Chicago which produced glucose used by candy manufacturers. The glucose was sold at a delivered price which was computed by adding to a base price at Chicago the published railroad rate to the point of delivery. Corn Products opened a second plant in Kansas City, but continued to maintain Chicago as its basing point for computing the railroad charge which was added to its final delivered price. The Supreme Court found that the Kansas City candy manufacturing customers had to pay "phantom freight" from Chicago even though they received the glucose from the near-by new Kansas City plant. The Supreme Court held that Corn Products illegally discriminated in price between its candy manufacturing customers purchasing from its Kansas City plant and those customers purchasing from its Chicago plant. From the point of view of the candy manufacturers in Kansas City, they were being charged the same price for glucose both before and after the Kansas City plant was constructed by Corn Products. The candy manufacturers located near Kansas City were not necessarily entitled to the cost savings resulting from Corn Products locating a new plant in Kansas City. Rather, it can be argued, the company constructing the new plant or warehouse should receive the resulting profit from lower transportation costs.

In a recent opinion, *A&P (Borden)* v. *Federal Trade Commission* (1979), the Supreme Court examined whether A & P was liable for knowingly inducing and receiving a discriminatory price when A&P failed to inform its milk supplier (Borden) that its bid was lower than necessary to meet a competitive price. The case is noteworthy in considering the amount of disclosure required of a buyer during contract negotiations involving competitive bidding. A&P urged Borden to submit a second bid because its first bid was above the bid of a competitor. A&P refused, however, to inform Borden of the precise amount it had to lower its price in order to meet the competitor's bid. The second bid submitted by Borden was lower than the competitor's bid. A&P remained silent and kept the difference. The FTC challenged the transaction on the grounds that A&P had illegally induced and received a discriminatory price. After seventeen years of litigation, the Supreme Court heard the case and held that Borden had a legal "meeting competition" defense, and therefore A&P did not illegally induce a discriminatory price. The Supreme Court concluded that A&P did not have a legal duty to tell Borden what the lowest price was which had to be met.

MERGERS

The same problems of product definition encountered in Chapter 2, Industrial Concentration, are present in merger cases. The level of concentration, measured by the share of industry shipments accounted for by the leading companies, is dependent upon the definition of the industry. In the *Continental Can (Hazel-Atlas)* case (1964) the Supreme Court held that the merger between the second largest manufacturer of metal containers (Continental Can) with the third largest manufacturer of glass containers (Hazel-Atlas) was illegal. The Supreme Court held that the inter-industry competition between metal and glass containers brought them under one combined product market for judging the merger. Any other definition by the Supreme Court would not allow it to reach a finding of illegality since Continental Can did not produce glass containers and Hazel-Atlas did not produce metal containers. The majority of the Supreme Court referred to their opinion decided the previous year in the *Philadelphia Bank* case (1963), which involved only bank deposits.

> By the acquisition of Hazel-Atlas stock Continental not only increased its own share . . . from 21.9% to 25%, but also reduced from five to four the most significant competitors who might threaten its dominant position. The resulting percentage of the combined firms approaches that held presumptively bad in *United States* v. *Philadelphia Bank*. . . .

The quotation shows a basically *per se* structural approach to mergers which was followed by the Supreme Court in the 1960's under Chief Justice Warren. In a strongly worded dissent to the case Justice Harlan wrote,

> The bizarre result of the Court's approach is that market percentages of a nonexistent market enable the Court to dispense with ''elaborate proof of market structure, market behavior and probable anticompetitive effects . . . the Court has 'dispensed with' proof which, given heed, shows how completely fanciful its market share analysis is.''

The structural approach of the 1960's was replaced by a more flexible analysis of economic factors by the Supreme Court in the 1970's under Chief Justice Burger. In the landmark opinion in the *General Dynamics* (1974) case, the Supreme Court noted that the effect of adopting the *Philadelphia Bank* approach which was advocated by the Government would be ''to allow the Government to rest its case on a showing of even small increases of market share or market concentration where concentration is already great or has recently been increasing.'' In allowing the merger of two coal mining companies into the fifth largest coal company in the United States, the Supreme Court held the appropriate standard for evaluating economic data is the future not the past:

> Evidence of past production does not, as a matter of logic, necessarily give a proper picture of a company's future ability to compete.

The Court concluded that the General Dynamics acquisition was legal and would not substantially lessen competition since the acquired company lacked sufficient coal reserves to be a significant competitive factor by itself in the future.

In 1979 the Circuit Court of Appeals for the Eighth Circuit in *Federal Trade Commission* v. *National Tea (Applebaums)* relied primarily on the *General Dynamics* decision in denying the FTC a preliminary injunction to stop the acquisition by National Tea of 26 grocery stores operated by Applebaums in the Minneapolis-St. Paul metropolitan area. At the time of the merger, National Tea operated 19 stores in the Minneapolis-St. Paul market and was incurring substantial losses in the majority of its generally small, outmoded stores. As a result of the merger, National Tea would become the number one firm in the Minneapolis-St. Paul area and the top four concentration ratio would increase from 44.5% to 49%.

Neither the lower District Court nor the Court of Appeals in the *National Tea (Applebaums)* case were content only to rely on market shares. The Court of

Appeals noted:

> . . . while market share is an important indicator of a firm's future competitive strength, other factors may discount its significance.

The Court recognized that National Tea's market share was obtained by extensive losses over a protracted period of time, and was therefore not an economically meaningful number in reflecting either market power or its future competitive strength.

There was considerable testimony in the *National Tea (Applebaums)* case concerning whether a relationship existed in food retailing between increased concentration and competition. The Court of Appeals held that,

> There was considerable conflict in the evidence as to whether increases in the top four firms' market concentrations in the interval from 40% to 50% of the total market, implied more than marginal increases in price, that is, decreases in competition.

In both *General Dynamics* and *National Tea (Applebaums)* the finding of economic concentration was not deemed by the courts to be a controlling factor. The courts looked beyond the present level of market shares and, with reason and flexibility, examined a wide spectrum of economic evidence in considering the future competitive environment of the merged firms.

5

MONOPOLY CASES

THE STANDARD OIL CASE (1911)

In 1862 John D. Rockefeller advanced $4,000 to Samuel Andrews to improve an oil refinery. The oil refinery prospered and in 1870 John D. Rockefeller, William Rockefeller, Henry M. Flagler, and several other individuals formed the Standard Oil Company of Ohio. By 1880 Standard had acquired a large number of refineries in New York, Pennsylvania, and Ohio.

The United States government brought legal proceedings in 1906 against Standard of New Jersey, John D. and William Rockefeller, Henry M. Flagler, and a number of other corporations and individuals. The government charged that a violation of Sections 1 and 2 of the Sherman Act occurred by reason of the defendants' conspiracy to monopolize and restrain trade in crude oil, refined oil, and other petroleum products. The conspiracy was alleged to have begun through the formation of Standard Oil of Ohio in 1870. The defendants were charged with having used Standard of Ohio as a means to obtain from the railroads large preferential rates and rebates over competing oil companies. The advantage of preferential railroad rates was alleged to have been used by Standard of Ohio to force smaller competitors to join their company, or alternatively, to drive these independents out of business. In addition to the power held by Standard over the railroads, Standard was also alleged to have exerted control over the pipelines from the eastern oil fields in Pennsylvania to the xid-western oil refineries.

THE RULE OF REASON

Standard Oil Company of New Jersey v. *United States*[1] became a landmark decision in antitrust law with the statement by Chief Justice White of the "rule of reason" for judging the legality of various business contracts and arrangements alleged to be in restraint of trade. The Government urged a *per se* application of Section 1 of the Sherman Act whereby *all* contracts or combinations in restraint of trade would be illegal. Chief Justice White, however, held that *every* contract or combination in restraint of trade was not illegal; only *unreasonable* restraints of trade were unlawful under the Sherman Act. The rule of reason has developed considerably beyond this early application to monopoly cases. The language of the Supreme Court in 1911 is still noteworthy:

> In substance, the propositions urged by the government are reducible to this: That the language of the statute embraces every contract, combination, etc., in restraint of trade, and hence its text leaves no room for the exercise of judgment, but simply imposes the plain duty of applying its prohibitions to every case within its literal language . . . the construction which we have deduced from the history of the act and the analysis of its text is simply that in every case where it is claimed that an act or acts are in violation of the statute the *rule of reason*, in the light of the principles of law and the public policy which the act embodies, must be applied.[2]

THE *PER SE* DOCTRINE

Justice Harlan dissented in part from the majority opinion in the *Standard Oil* case. Harlan maintained that the arguments in favor of a rule of reason interpretation of Sec. 1 of the Sherman Act had been expressly rejected by the Supreme Court fifteen years earlier in the *Trans-Missouri Freight Association* case, which held that an agreement among railroad companies for maintaining reasonable rates was *per se* illegal.[3]

Justice Peckham, speaking for the majority in the *Trans-Missouri* case, rejected the plea for the establishment of a rule of reason in the interpretation of the Sherman Act. The concept of *per se*, which is commonly treated as the antithesis of the rule of reason, emerges from the following passage in Justice Peckham's opinion:

> This agreement so made, the government alleges, is illegal as being in restraint of trade, and was entered into between the companies for the purpose of enhancing the freight rates. The companies, while denying the illegality of the agreement or its purpose to be other than to maintain reasonable rates, yet allege that without some such agreement the competition between them for traffic would be so severe as to cause great losses to each defendant and possibly ruin the companies represented in the agreement . . . Under these circumstances we are, therefore, asked to hold that the act of Congress excepts contracts which are not in unreasonable restraint of trade, and which only keep rates up to a reasonable price, notwithstanding the language of the act makes no such exception. In other words, we are asked to read into the act by way of judicial legislation an exception that is not placed there by the law-making branch of the government, and this is done upon the theory that the impolicy of such legislation is so clear that it cannot be supposed Congress intended the natural import of the language it used. This we cannot and ought not to do.[4]

The *Trans-Missouri* case was basically a price-fixing case and, consequently, might have been disposed of by the Court on the basis that conspiracies among competitors to fix prices are by their inherent nature unreasonable restraints of trade, *i.e.*, no reason exists which could justify the fixing of prices.[5] Justice Peckham believed that a decision as to the reasonableness of a *contract* necessitated a judgment as to the reasonableness of the *level of prices* resulting from the contract. This type of inquiry, Justice Peckham foresaw, would create considerable uncertainty as to the legality of business conduct. The passage also raises many of the same questions being currently debated concerning the competitive implications of high profits. In the words of Justice Peckham,

> If only that kind of contract which is in unreasonable restraint of trade be within the meaning of the statute, and declared therein to be illegal, it is at once apparent that the subject of what is a reasonable rate is attended with great uncertainty. What is a proper standard by which to judge the fact of reasonable rates? Must the rate be so high as enable the return for the whole business done to amount to a sum sufficient to afford the shareholder a fair and reasonable profit upon his investment? If so, what is a fair and reasonable profit? That sometimes depends upon the risks incurred, and the rate itself differs in different localities: which is the one to which reference is to be made as the standard? Or is the reasonableness of the profit to be limited to a fair return upon the capital that would have been sufficient to build and equip the road, if honestly expended? Or is still another standard to be created, and the reasonableness of the charges tried by the cost of carriage of the article and a reasonable profit allowed on that? And in such case would contribution to a sinking fund to make repairs upon the roadbed and renewal of cars, etc., be assumed as a proper item?[6]

THE DICHOTOMY OF THE RULE OF REASON AND THE *PER SE* DOCTRINE

Both the *per se* doctrine and the rule of reason are essential elements in the interpretation of our present antitrust laws. "Antitrust reflects," in the words of Professor S. Chesterfield Oppenheim, "the never-ending conflict between the desire for certainty and the desire for flexibility that is as old as the processes of the law itself."[7] The *per se* doctrine offers greater certainty to the antitrust laws, but sacrifices the vital elements of flexibility which are associated with the rule of reason. The methodologies of the two approaches have been distinguished by Professor Oppenheim as follows:

> Whereas a *per se* rule immediately brands the operative fact embraced by it as unreasonable, the Rule of Reason opens the way to reliance upon a broad range of discretion in weighing the evidence of defenses of justification compatible with the purposes of the antitrust statutes. The Rule of Reason operates through a process of inclusion and exclusion in a case-by-case consideration of all the facts. The per se illegality doctrine operates by converting predetermined single-fact categories into fixed rules of law."[8]

THE SPECIFIC INTENT TO MONOPOLIZE

The *Standard Oil* decision is also significant for its analysis of the prerequisite legal elements for monopolization. Chief Justice White, in contrasting the abusive market practices of Standard Oil with "advancing the development of business power by usual methods," implied that the Sherman Act condemned a specific intent and positive drive for monopolization rather than the resulting market structure of monopoly. In the following passage, Chief Justice White finds the defendants had the *specific intent* to monopolize the oil industry:

> . . . the acquisition here and there which ensued of every efficient means by which competition could have been asserted, the slow but resistless methods which followed

by which means of transportation were absorbed and brought under control, the system of marketing which was adopted by which the country was divided into districts and the trade in each district in oil was turned over to a designated corporation within the combination, and all others were excluded, all lead the mind to a conviction of a purpose and intent which we think is so certain as practically to cause the subject not to be within the domain of reasonable contention.[9]

LEGAL AND ECONOMIC CONCEPTS OF MONOPOLY

In the *Standard Oil* case the Supreme Court, in finding Standard Oil violated both Sections 1 and 2 of the Sherman Act, presented only a limited analysis of the structure of the oil industry and the market position held by Standard Oil. The Court mentioned that by the end of the first period, 1870-82, or approximately 30 years before the writing of the opinion in the case — and before the passage of the Sherman Act — Standard of Ohio had obtained "mastery over the oil industry, controlling 90 per cent of the business, and was thus able to fix the price of crude and refined petroleum."[10] Nevertheless, the Court conceded that Standard controlled only a "very small percentage of the crude oil produced."[11] Standard Oil's market power existed in the refined oil market; this power, maintained the Court, permitted the company to control the crude oil market despite the fact that Standard produced very little crude oil. In the words of Chief Justice White:

> The inference that no attempt to monopolize could have been intended, and that no monopolization resulted from the acts complained of, since it is established that a very small percentage of the crude oil produced was controlled by the combination, is unwarranted. As substantial power over the crude product was the inevitable result of the absolute control which existed over the refined product, the monopolization of the one carried with it the power to control the other; and if the inferences which this situation suggests were developed, which we deem unnecessary to do, they might well serve to add additional cogency to the presumption of intent to monopolize which we have found arises from the unquestioned proof on other subjects.[12]

The Court concluded that Standard Oil had monopolized the crude and refined oil markets. It is noteworthy that the Court did not follow an economic concept of monopoly in the sense of a company in control of all the output of an industry. Rather, the Court employed a legalistic concept of monopoly in which the market share of a company became important only when accompanied by predatory or abusive market practices.[13]

ENDNOTES

1. 221 U.S. 1 (1911).
2. *Ibid.*, pp. 63-66; italics added.
3. *United States* v. *Trans-Missouri Freight Assn.*, 166 U.S. 290 (1896).
4. *Ibid.*, p. 340.
5. Cf. *Chicago Board of Trade* v. *United States*, 246 U.S. 231 (1918).
6. 166 U.S. 290, 331 (1896).

7. S. C. Oppenheim, "Federal Antitrust Legislation: Guideposts to a Revised National Antitrust Policy," *Michigan Law Review*, Vol. L (June, 1952), 1149.
8. *Ibid.*, pp. 1151-52.
9. 221 U.S. 1, 75-77 (1911).
10. *Ibid.*, p. 33
11. *Ibid.*, p. 77
12. *Ibid.*
13. E. S. Mason, "Monopoly in Law and Economics," *Yale Law Journal*, Vol. XLVII (November, 1937), pp. 34-49; reprinted in his *Economic Concentration and the Monopoly Problem* (Cambridge, Mass.: Harvard University Press, 1957), p. 342.

THOUGHT QUESTIONS

1. Compare the "per se" and "rule of reason" approaches to antitrust.
2. Discuss the claim of the defendants in the *Trans-Missouri* case that "without some such agreement the competition between them for traffic would be so severe as to cause great losses to each defendant and possibly ruin the companies represented in the agreement . . . ?"
   a) Compare the agreement among railroad companies for reasonable rates in the *Trans-Missouri* case with the rate making procedure followed today by the Interstate Commerce Commission.
3. Do you agree with the Supreme Court that Standard Oil had 90% of the oil business even though it controlled only "a very small percentage of the crude oil produced?"
4. Would the Standard Oil case have been decided differently if Standard Oil tried to protect smaller crude oil producers from low profits or losses?
5. Compare the U.S. oil refiners in 1973, after the Arab oil embargo, with the Ohio crude oil producers in the 1890's.
   a) Did the market power at the refinery level in the U.S. carry with it control over the imported crude oil?
6. In the late 1970's, legislation was proposed in Congress to separate ownership of oil refineries from pipelines. Is there a need for this type of legislation?
7. Would the Alaskan pipeline have been built without the investment by major oil companies?
8. Would any major oil pipeline or refinery be built today without a captive source of supply to guarantee long term output?

THE UNITED STATES STEEL CASE (1920)

In *United States* v. *U.S. Steel Corp.*[1] the Government charged U.S. Steel with monopolizing the iron and steel industry by bringing under control in 1901 approximately 180 independent concerns accounting for about 50 percent of the national iron and steel output. It was argued on behalf of U.S. Steel that the corporation was not formed with the purpose to monopolize trade or restrict competition, but rather it was the natural response to the metallurgical methods of making and handling steel. Vertical integration, or the continuity in the processes of the industry from ore mines to the finished product, as well as plant specialization, whereby one plant makes a single product continuously rather than 20 or 50 products, offered mutual advantages to the member firms. A further purpose of the organization was the building up of export trade in iron and steel which previously involved sporadic dumping of products upon foreign markets. The Supreme Court found that U.S. Steel had not violated the monopolization provisions of the Sherman Act by its formation or subsequent conduct.

Justice McKenna of the Supreme Court noted that U.S. Steel employed none of the abusive trade practices which were alleged to exist in the earlier *Standard Oil* case. In his words,

> It resorted to none of the brutalities or tyrannies that the cases illustrate of other combinations. It did not secure freight rebates; it did not increase its profits by reducing the wages of its employees — whatever it did was not at the expense of labor; it did not increase its profits by lowering the quality of its products, nor create an artificial scarcity of them; it did not oppress or coerce its competitors — its competition, though vigorous, was fair; it did not undersell its competitors in some localities by reducing its prices there below those maintained elsewhere, or require its customers to enter into contracts limiting their purchases or restricting them in resale prices; it did not obtain customers by secret rebates or departures from its published prices; there was no evidence that it attempted to crush its competitors or drive them out of the market, nor did it take customers from its competitors by unfair means, and in its competition it seemed to make no difference between large and small competitors.[2]

THE ABUSE THEORY OF MONOPOLY

With substantial evidence showing the absence of abusive market practices, the foundation was laid for the Supreme Court to enunciate the so-called "abuse theory," namely, in the absence of abusive market practices the law does not make mere size an offense. In the words of Justice McKenna,

> Competition consists of business activities and ability — they make its life; but there may be fatalities in it. Are the activities to be encouraged when militant, and suppressed or regulated when triumphant, because of the dominance attained? To such paternalism the government's contention, which regards power, rather than its use, the determining consideration, seems to conduct. . . . We have pointed out that there are several of the government's contentions which are difficult to represent or measure, and the one we are now considering — that is, the power is "unlawful regardless of purpose" — is another of them. It seems to us that it has for its ultimate principle and justification that strength in any producer or seller is a menace to the public interest and illegal, because there is potency in it for mischief. . . . The Corporation is undoubtably of impressive size, and it takes an effort of resolution not to be affected by it or to exaggerate its influence. But we must adhere to the law, and the law does not make mere size an offense, or the existence of unexerted power an offense. It, we repeat, requires overt acts, and trusts to its prohibition of them and its power to repress or punish them.[3]

Despite the above pronouncements, the *U.S. Steel* case was not decided technically in terms of the "abuse theory." Rather, the decision in the case turned on the finding that U.S. Steel lacked the necessary market power for monopolization.[4] The Court noted that "whatever there was of wrong intent could not be executed" because U.S. Steel was unable *by itself* to control steel prices. Illegal conspiratorial conduct, such as pools, and industry gatherings called "Gary

Dinners," which were given by E. H. Gary while he was president of U.S. Steel, were offered as evidence by U.S. Steel for showing that it was not a monopoly and, consequently, had to persuade rather than coerce its competitors in order to control steel prices. In the words of the Court,

> Monopoly, therefore, was not achieved, and competitors had to be persuaded by pools, associations, trade meetings, and through the social form of dinners, all of them, it may be, violations of the law, but transient in their purpose and effect. They were scattered through the years from 1901 (the year of the formation of the corporation) until 1911, but after instances of success and failure were abandoned nine months before this suit was brought.[5]

The District Court opinion of Judge Bufferton in the *U.S. Steel* case offered considerable evidence showing the declining market position of U.S. Steel during the period 1901 to 1911.[6] The share of the nationwide steel business accounted for by U.S. Steel fell from 50.1 to 40.9 percent, and in the important steel ingot sector, its market share fell from 66 percent in 1901 to 54 percent in 1911.

INJURY TO COMPETITORS VERSUS INJURY TO COMPETITION

In the *U.S. Steel* case there was abundant evidence of injury to competition, such as price fixing, but the record was devoid of evidence showing that any competitors had been injured. Illegal collusive arrangements tended to protect the smaller steel producers by allocating territories to them and allowing them to charge higher prices. The sympathetic attitude of the Supreme Court toward U.S. Steel may have been more of a reflection of their concern with injury to competitors, of which there was none, rather than injury to competition, of which there was ample evidence. U.S. Steel did not attempt to drive out independent concerns from its industry. In fact, the business policy of U.S. Steel against directly injuring its competitors accounts in large part for the decline in market position of the various combinations absorbed by the parent company. For example, the American Tin Plate Company produced 95 percent of all the tin plate in the United States in 1899 before it was merged into the U.S. Steel Corporation. Its market control gradually decreased thereafter until in 1912 its proportion of the manufactured tin plate output was 53.7 percent. The Court noted, "After it was absorbed by the corporation, it ceased to rely upon its own power to fix and maintain prices, complete as was its power at first, and, like the other subsidiaries, was forced to cooperate with its competitors."[7] The gradual reduction in the market position of U.S. Steel in the decades following its formation provided the Supreme Court in 1920 with a rationale for dismissing the monopolization charge against U.S. Steel.

ENDNOTES

1. 251 U.S. 417 (1920).
2. 251 U.S. 417, pp. 440-41.
3. *Ibid.*, pp. 450-51.
4. A. D. Neale, *The Antitrust Laws of the U.S.A.*, p. 109.

5. 251 U.S. 417, pp. 444-45.
6. 223 F. 55 (1915).
7. *Ibid.*, p. 70. For an analysis of subsequent developments in the tin plate market, see J. W. McKie, *Tin Cans and Tin Plate* (Cambridge, Mass.: Harvard University Press, 1959).

THOUGHT QUESTIONS

1. What is the difference between "injury to competition" and "injury to competitors?"
2. Debate the following statement: the Supreme Court forgave U.S. Steel for "soft competition," but condemned Standard Oil for "hard competition."
3. Does the defense by U.S. Steel that it called price fixing meetings to "persuade rather than coerce its competitors in order to control steel prices" suggest that conspiratorial meetings are more likely to occur with weak market power?
4. Did the specialization of U.S. Steel in making a single standard product continuously in one plant give it a decisive competitive advantage in terms of economies of scale which precluded smaller companies from competing with it in given products? Should we encourage mergers which provide economies of scale even though concentration may increase?
5. Comment on the Court's finding that U.S. Steel's conspiratorial meetings, scattered for a 10 year period from 1901 to 1911, "were abandoned nine months before this suit was brought."

THE ALCOA CASE (1945)

In *United States* v. *Aluminum Company of America*,[1] the Government charged Alcoa with monopolizing the following markets: bauxite, water power, alumina, virgin aluminum (pig and ingot), castings, cooking utensils, pistons, extrusions and structural shapes, foil, miscellaneous fabricated articles, sheet and cable. Judge Caffey in the District Court found that Alcoa had not monopolized any of these markets. Judge Learned Hand, in the Court of Appeals, which was sitting as a court of last resort since the Supreme Court did not have a sufficient number of justices who were qualified to hear the case, reversed the District Court and held that Alcoa had monopolized the virgin aluminum ingot market.

Judge Hand rested his finding that Alcoa was a monopoly primarily on a market definition which showed Alcoa accounted for 90 percent of the output of virgin aluminum ingot in the United States. Judge Caffey, in the lower court, employed a market definition which showed Alcoa held only 33 percent of the market. The difference between market definitions was therefore critical to the finding of monopoly. Judge Caffey calculated Alcoa's share by adding together its virgin ingot production and its "secondary" or scrap ingot production. Judge Caffey did not include Alcoa's captive or "own use" production of ingot which it used internally to make fabricated aluminum products.

In contrast, Judge Hand included the captive or own use production of Alcoa in calculating its market share even though this production never reached the merchant or commercial ingot market. However, Judge Hand excluded the secondary or scrap ingot which competed with virgin ingot. Any other definition by Judge Hand would not have allowed him to reach the 90 percent figure upon which his finding of monopoly rested. In the words of Judge Hand,

> There are various ways of computing "Alcoa's" control of the aluminum market — as distinct from its production — depending upon what one regards as competing in that market. The judge figured its share — during the years 1929-1938, inclusive — as only about thirty-three percent; to do so he included "secondary," and excluded that part of "Alcoa's" own production which it fabricated and did not therefore sell as ingot. If, on the other hand, "Alcoa's" total production, fabricated and sold, be included, and balanced against the sum of imported "virgin" and "secondary," its share of the market was in the neighborhood of sixty-four percent for that period. The percentage we have already mentioned — over ninety — results only if we both include all "Alcoa's" production and exclude "secondary." That percentage is enough to constitute a monopoly; it is doubtful whether sixty or sixty-four percent would be enough; and certainly thirty-three percent is not. Hence it is necessary to settle what we shall treat as competing in the ingot market.[2]

The three methods of defining the aluminum market are as follows:

Computation of Alcoa's Market Share of Ingot

Sources of Aluminum Ignot

(1) Open market virgin ingot   (3) Secondary or scrap ingot
(2) Alcoa's own use virgin ingot   (4) Imported virgin and secondary ingot

Judge Caffey's formula:
(virgin + secondary)
$$\frac{(1) + (3)}{(1) + (3) + (4)} = 33\%$$

Judge Hand's formula:
(virgin + own use)
$$\frac{(1) + (2)}{(1) + (2) + (4)} = 90\%$$

A third formula:
$$\frac{(1) + (2)}{(1) + (2) + (3) + (4)} = 64\%$$

In a subsequent hearing in 1950 on the remedial action in the Alcoa case, the court followed a market definition that was broader than even Judge Caffey had used. Judge Knox maintained that the applicable aluminum market should not be virgin ingot, nor virgin and secondary ingot, but the market for all aluminum products: ingot as well as fabricated items. The reason given by Judge Knox for this broader market definition was the recent entry of two fully integrated aluminum producers: Reynolds Metals Company and Kaiser Aluminum and Chemical Corporation. In the words of Judge Knox,

> Thus, in the aluminum industry, competition manifests itself in the market for fabricated aluminum products rather than in that for pig and ingot. In determining the relative shares of the market among Alcoa, Reynolds and Kaiser, the integration of these producers requires the "market" to be a broad concept, unrelated to any particular aluminum product. Aluminum can be sold in the form of pig or ingot, or as a semi-fabricated or fully fabricated article. It is with reference to the totality of the markets for these products that the relative shares of the three integrated producers must be considered.[3]

THE ALCOA TEST OF MONOPOLIZATION

The *Alcoa* decision of Judge Hand is an important decision because of its emphasis on market shares rather than on abusive market practices. The decision appeared to reject the older "abuse theory," in which an illegal attempt to monopolize was inferred from predatory conduct. In its place, the Court of Appeals employed a "structure test," in which corporate size is largely the determining factor. It is questionable that the reasoning of Judge Hand, and the change in antitrust doctrine, was in fact this abrupt. Alternatively, it could be argued that Judge Hand, rather than rejecting the "abuse theory," extended the meaning of the term "abuse" to include acts which, taken alone, would generally be considered "honestly industrial," but which in the aggregate showed "no motive except to exclude others and perpetuate its hold upon the ingot market." In the words of Judge Hand,

> "Alcoa's" size was "magnified" to make it a "monopoly;" indeed, it has never been anything else; and its size not only offered it an "opportunity for abuse," but it "utilized" its size for "abuse," as can easily be shown.

THE "ABSENCE OF SPECIFIC INTENT" DEFENSE

In the *Standard Oil* case the alleged offense was an *attempt* to monopolize, since Standard Oil had not completely achieved a monopoly. Justice White sought to establish through Standard's corporate history of alleged ruthless market practices the existence of a "specific intent" to monopolize the petroleum industry. The defendant officers of Standard Oil were found to have possessed the required "specific intent," for their actions showed that they intended to commit monopolization.

In the *Alcoa* case, however, the alleged offense was not an *attempt* to monopolize but *actual* monopolization. The proof of intent was less demanding than in the *Standard Oil* case, since the acts of the defendants did not fall short of achieving an actual monopoly. The prerequisite legal intent in Alcoa was a "general intent" or a "deliberateness" to maintain its monopoly position.[4] The general intent requirement has little analytical content and is almost perfunctory in nature, since this type of intent is objectively presumed where the defendant holds an actual monopoly.

The importance of the following passage lies in the change in emphasis by Judge Hand from the concept of specific intent, which required proof of abusive market practices, to the concept of monopoly and business size taken by itself. Judge Hand thereby laid the foundation for the "structure theory" of the law of monopoly. Under this approach the intent of the defendant is de-emphasized and the market power of the defendant becomes the determining factor. According to Judge Hand,

> We disregard any question of "intent.". . . conduct falling short of monopoly, is not illegal unless it is part of a plan to monopolize, or to gain such other control of a market as is equally forbidden. To make it so, the plaintiff must prove what in the criminal law is known as "specific intent;" an intent which goes beyond the mere intent to do an act. . . . In order to fall within Sec. 2, the monopolist must have both the power to monopolize, and the intent to monopolize. To read the passage as

demanding any "specific intent," makes nonsense of it, for no monopolist monopolizes unconscious of what he is doing. So here, "Alcoa" meant to keep, and did keep, the complete exclusive hold upon the ingot market with which it started. That was to "monopolize" that market, however innocently it otherwise proceeded.[5]

The general intent required for a charge of monopolization is a conclusion based on the *deliberateness* in acquiring, maintaining, and using the monopoly power. This deliberateness is clearly shown if monopoly has been established or maintained by illegal means under Sec. 1 of the Sherman Act. However, the requisite degree of deliberateness has been found where defendant's acts were legal in themselves but nevertheless had an exclusionary effect on competitors or potential entrants.

THE "GOOD TRUST" DEFENSE

An important part of the defense presented in the *Alcoa* case was that Alcoa, even if it were a monopoly, had not abused its power. Alcoa claimed that it never received more than a "fair profit" from its activities. The District Court found that over the half century of its existence, Alcoa's profits on capital invested, after payment of income taxes, had been about ten percent.[6] Relying upon the *U.S. Steel* case, the defense argued that the absence of market abuses constituted a defense to monopoly. Judge Hand rejected this argument on the grounds that "it is no excuse for 'monopolizing' a market that the monopoly has not been used to extract from the consumer more than a 'fair' profit."[7] In the following passage the so-called "good trust" defense is rejected by the Court:

> True, it might have been thought adequate to condemn only those monopolies which could not show that they had exercised the highest possible ingenuity, had adopted every possible economy, had anticipated every conceivable improvement, stimulated every possible demand. No doubt, that would be one way of dealing with the matter, although it would imply constant scrutiny and constant supervision, such as courts are unable to provide. Be that as it may, that was not the way that Congress chose; it did not condone "good trusts" and condemn "bad" ones; it forbade all.[8]

The Defense of Monopoly "Thrust Upon"

Judge Hand stated in the *Alcoa* opinion that under some circumstances monopoly power can be innocently acquired; for example, where a change in tastes leaves only one producer remaining in the market. Since the Sherman Act condemns "monopolization" rather than "monopoly in the concrete," the antitrust laws are not violated where monopoly power is *thrust upon* the defendant. In the words of Judge Hand,

> It does not follow because "Alcoa" had such a monopoly, that it "monopolized" the ingot market: it may not have achieved monopoly; monopoly may have been thrust upon it. If it had been a combination of existing smelters which united the whole industry and controlled the production of all aluminum ingot, it would certainly have "monopolized" the market. . . . It is unquestionably true that from the very outset the courts have at least kept in reserve the possibility that the origin of monopoly may be critical in determining its legality; and for this they had warrant in some of the

congressional debates which accompanied the passage of the act. . . . This notion has usually been expressed by saying that size does not determine guilt; that there must be some "exclusion" of competitors; that the growth must be something else than "natural" or "normal;" that there must be a "wrongful intent," or some other specific intent; or that some "unduly" coercive means must be used. At times there has been emphasis upon the active verb, "monopolize," as the judge noted in the case at bar. . . . What engendered these compunctions is reasonably plain; persons may unwittingly find themselves in possession of a monopoly, automatically so to say: that is, without having intended either to put an end to existing competition, or to prevent competition from arising when none existed; they may become monopolists by force of accident.

. . . A market may, for example, be so limited that it is impossible to produce at all and meet the cost of production except by a plant large enough to supply the whole demand. Or there may be changes in taste or in cost which drive out all but one purveyor. A single producer may be the survivor out of a group of active competitors, merely by virtue of his superior skill, foresight and industry.[9]

According to Judge Hand, a defendant who survives "merely by virtue of his superior skill, foresight and industry" is not guilty of monopolization. Yet the findings given by Judge Hand for establishing the illegal monopolization of the virgin aluminum ingot market came rather close to the very factors which are considered to be within the realm of defensible monopoly. For example, is it not *foresight* to "anticipate increases in the demand for ingot and be prepared to supply them," or "to embrace each new opportunity as it opened?" Is it not *skill* to have "the advantage of experience" and the "elite of personnel?" Is it not *industry* to "double and redouble capacity?" Yet each of these factors was used by Judge Hand to establish the finding that Alcoa consciously obtained monopoly and was guilty of monopolization.

UNITED SHOE MACHINERY CASE (1953)

United Shoe successfully defended in 1918 a monopolization charge stemming from its merger with approximately 50 companies holding complementary shoe machinery patents.[10] It had been forced in 1922 to revise its leasing methods to eliminate "tying clauses" relating to supplies used in the shoe manufacturing machines.[11] Finally, in 1953 the company was unsuccessful in defending a charge that it had monopolized the shoe machinery market in violation of Sec. 2 of the Sherman Act.[12] The leases of United Shoe in 1953 took account of the judgment in the earlier case, and the mergers involved in its formation of the company were judged in 1918 to be legal. Therefore, the District Court in 1953 could not base its decision on the finding that United Shoe's conduct was an illegal restraint of trade reflecting the necessary intent for monopolization. On the other hand, the District Court was not of the opinion that United Shoe owed its monopoly *solely* to the "superior skill, foresight and industry" or to superior products, natural advantages, technological efficiency, or scientific research. United Shoe fit into an intermediate category, "where the causes of an enterprise's success were neither common law restraints of trade, nor the skill with which the business was conducted, but rather some practice which without being predatory, abusive, or coercive was in economic effect exclusionary."[13]

The record of United Shoe's performance in terms of efficient service, exceptional innovation, and absence of predatory conduct was outstanding. The company spent over $3 million annually on research and succeeded in producing several thousand patented machines. The company's market position was not attributable primarily to these patents. United did not secure a monopoly profit: it earned in the period 1925-49 about 10 percent net, after taxes, on invested capital. In finding that United Shoe's market power did not rest on predatory practices, the District Court noted that "probably few monopolies could produce a record so free from any taint of that kind of wrongdoing."[14] Nevertheless, United Shoe was found to have monopolized the shoe machinery market, in which it accounted for between 75 and 80 percent, because it maintained its market position by legal, although not economically inevitable, market practices. United Shoe was found to have engaged in market practices which would be legally permissible if practiced by a firm in a competitive market structure, but illegal if employed by a company maintaining a monopoly control of a market.

Judge Wyzanski, in a voluminous opinion, found that United Shoe engaged in a number of leasing arrangements which, although legal in themselves, tended to exclude competition. For example, United Shoe leased but did not sell its major machines; it required a ten-year lease; the lessee was obligated to use United Shoe's machinery at full capacity before using a competitive manufacturers' machine for the same operation; and service was provided at no additional charge with the result that an entrant to the industry would also have to provide servicing to remain competitive with United Shoe. Judge Wyzanski found that these practices were "honestly industrial" but nevertheless, in his words,

> . . . they are not practices which can be properly described as the inevitable consequences of ability, natural forces, or law. They represent something more than the use of accessible resources, the process of invention and innovation, and the employment of those techniques of employment, financing, production, and distribution, which a competitive society must foster. They are contracts, arrangements, and policies which, instead of encouraging competition based on pure merit, further the dominance of a particular firm. In this sense, they are unnatural barriers; they unnecessarily exclude actual and potential competition; they restrict a free market . . .
>
> The violation with which United is now charged depends not on moral considerations, but on solely economic considerations. United is denied the right to exercise effective control of the market by business policies that are not the inevitable consequences of its capacities or its natural advantages. That those policies are not immoral is irrelevant.[15]

In summary, Judge Wyzanski required a higher standard of conduct for a company possessing a monopoly or dominant market position than for a company in a more competitive market structure.

ENDNOTES

1. 148 F. 2nd 416 (2nd Cir., 1945).
2. 148 F. 2nd 416, 424 (1945).
3. 91 F. Supp. 333, 356 (1950).

4. United States, *Report of the Attorney General's National Committee to Study the Antitrust Laws*, p. 43.
5. 148 F. 2nd 416, 431-32 (1945).
6. 148 F. 2nd 416, 427 (1945).
7. *Ibid.*
8. *Ibid.*
9. 148 F. 2nd 416, 429-30 (1945).
10. *United States* v. *United Shoe Machinery Co. of New Jersey*, 247 U.S. 32 (1918).
11. *United Shoe Machinery Corp.* v. *United States*, 258 U.S. 451 (1922).
12. 110 F. Supp. 295 (D.C. Mass., 1953), affirmed *per curiam*, 347 U.S. 521 (1954). For a detailed economic analysis of the case, see C. Kaysen, *United States* v. *United Shoe Machinery Corporation*, Harvard Economic Studies No. 99 (Cambridge, Mass.: Harvard University Press, 1956). Also see L. S. Keyes, "The Shoe Machinery Case and the Problem of the Good Trust," *Quarterly Journal of Economics*, Vol. LXVIII (May, 1954), 287-304.
13. 110 F. Supp. 295, 341.
14. *Ibid.*, p. 345.
15. *Ibid.*, pp. 344-45.

THOUGHT QUESTIONS

1. Should Judge Hand have included in his market definition Alcoa's captive or "own use" production of ingot which it used to make fabricated aluminum products?
2. Should scrap aluminum have been excluded from the market?
3. Compare the "ingot market" definition of Judge Hand with the market for "ingot and fabricated products" used by Judge Knox in the remedial portion of the *Alcoa* case. Does the market definition determine the outcome of the decision or *vice versa*?
4. Why is the *Alcoa* case referred to as a "structural case" and the *Standard Oil* case as an "abuse case?"
5. What is the difference between a "specific intent" and a "general intent?"
6. If Alcoa was a monopoly, why was it unable or unwilling to earn more than a relatively low 10 percent after taxes?
7. Did aluminum compete with steel products? Should steel have been included in the market definition?
8. Debate the following proposition: "Alcoa was a model company. It developed a new product, which is now a basic raw material used throughout the world; it earned modest profits as a result of pioneering a new product against other competitive metals, and owed its success to skill, foresight and industry in anticipating increases in the demand for ingot and in building the requisite plant facilities to meet these demands."
9. In the *United Shoe* case the court found that the leasing practices of United Shoe were "honestly industrial" but exclusionary in nature.
   a) Is it fair to have the same market practice condemned if followed by a company with a large market share but permissible if engaged in by a company with a low market share?
   b) Does such a finding by a court provide certainty to businessmen in evaluating whether they should engage in a given market practice?
   c) Should we encourage restraint in the types of business practices followed by companies with large market shares?

THE CELLOPHANE CASE (1956)

In *United States* v. *E. I. DuPont de Nemours & Company* the Supreme Court faced the legal issue whether DuPont had monopolized the cellophane market in violation of Sec. 2 of the Sherman Act.[1] During the period relevant to the case, DuPont produced almost 75 percent of the cellophane sold in the United States. If the Government could prove the relevant market was cellophane, the 75 percent market share of DuPont would probably have been sufficient for establishing its monopolization charge. However, the Government failed to prove that cellophane was a distinct and separate product market. The Supreme Court held that the applicable market covered all flexible packaging materials, such as aluminum foil, glassine, Saran, and polyethylene. DuPont's share of this broader market was only 20 percent, a figure deemed insufficient for establishing monopolization.

Competition from other flexible wrapping materials was found to have prevented DuPont from possessing monopoly power over the market for cellophane. Justice Reed, writing the majority opinion of the Supreme Court, summarized the issues facing the Court as follows:

> The Government asserts that cellophane and other wrapping materials are neither substantially fungible nor like priced. For these reasons, it argues that the market for other wrappings is distinct from the market for cellophane and that the competition afforded cellophane by other wrappings is not strong enough to be considered in determining whether DuPont has monopoly power . . . The ultimate consideration in such a determination is whether the defendants control the price and competition in the market for such part of trade or commerce as they are charged with monopolizing. Every manufacturer is the sole producer of the particular commodity it makes but its control in the above sense of the relevant market depends upon the availability of alternative commodities for buyers: i.e., whether there is a cross-elasticity of demand between cellophane and other wrappings. The interchangeability is largely gauged by the purchase of competing products for similar uses considering the price, characteristics and adaptability of the competing commodities. The court below found that the flexible wrappings afforded such alternatives. This Court must determine whether the trial court erred in its estimate of the competition afforded cellophane by other materials.[2]

DEFINITION OF THE MARKET

A product market is a relative term. In the passage below, Justice Reed describes the problem of ascertaining the relevant market for cellophane:

> Determination of the competitive market for commodities depends on how different from one another are the offered commodities in character or use, how far buyers will go to substitute one commodity for another. For example, one can think of building materials as in commodity competition but one could hardly say that brick competed with steel or wood or cement or stone in the meaning of Sherman Act litigation; the products are too different. This is the inter-industry competition emphasized by some economists . . . where there are market alternatives that buyers may readily use for their purposes, illegal monopoly does not exist merely because the product said to be monopolized differs from others. If it were not so, only physically identical products would be a part of the market. To accept the Government's argument, we would have to conclude that the manufacturers of plain as well as moistureproof cellophane were monopolists, and so with films such as Pliofilm, foil, glassine, polyethylene and Saran, for each of these wrapping materials is distinguishable. These were all exhibits in the case. New wrappings appear generally similar to cellophane; is each a monopoly? What is called for is an appraisal of the ''cross-elasticity'' of demand in the trade.[3]

THE REASONABLE INTERCHANGEABILITY TEST

The use of the term "cross-elasticity" of demand by the Supreme Court marked a high point in the use of theoretical economic concepts in judicial antitrust opinions. Cross-elasticity of demand indicates the percentage of change in the quantity demanded of a particular product for a very small percentage of change in the price of another good — all other things remaining equal. The concept of cross-elasticity of demand cannot be used exclusively to define a relevant market unless price is the only important economic variable. The Supreme Court in the *Cellophane* case examined also the qualities and end-uses of products which were related or "reasonably interchangeable" with cellophane. In the words of Justice Reed,

> The "market" which one must study to determine when a producer has monopoly power will vary with the part of commerce under consideration. The tests are constant. That market is composed of products that have *reasonable interchangeability* for the purposes for which they are produced — price, use and qualities considered.[4]

The analysis of the Court of the interchangeability of cellophane in terms of price, use, and quality are examined separately below.

Price. Justice Reed agreed with the District Court that the "great sensitivity of customers in the flexible packaging markets to price and quality changes" prevented DuPont from possessing monopoly power over price. Cellophane was found to have a high cross-elasticity of demand with other flexible materials, and therefore was considered part of this broader market:

> An element for consideration as to cross-elasticity of demand between products is the responsiveness of the sales of one product to price changes of the other. If a slight decrease in the price of cellophane causes a considerable number of customers of other flexible wrappings to switch to cellophane, it would be an indication that a high cross-elasticity of demand exists between them; that the products compete in the same market.[5]

TABLE 5-1
1949 Average Wholesale Prices of Flexible Wrapping Materials

	Price Per 1000 Square Inches
1. Saran	$.061
2. Polyethylene	.054
3. Pliofilm	.038
4. Cellulose acetate	.033
5. Moistureproof cellophane	.023
6. Plain cellophane	.021
7. Aluminum foil	.018
8. Vegetable parchment	.014
9. Plain waxed sulfite	.011
10. Bleached glassine	.010
11. Bleached greaseproof	.009

In an appendix to the Supreme Court majority opinion, Justice Reed included a price list of flexible wrapping materials. The price range in 1949 was from less than one cent per 1000 square inches for bleached greaseproof paper to six cents per 1000 square inches for Saran. Both products were included by the Supreme Court in the same relevant market for flexible wrapping materials, despite the sixfold difference in price.

The dissent in the *Cellophane* case, written by Chief Justice Warren, maintained that cellophane had a low cross-elasticity of demand with other flexible wrapping materials because (1) cellophane had a considerably higher price than most of the other flexible wrapping materials, and (2) producers of these other materials did not respond with lower prices when DuPont lowered its cellophane price. In the dissenting words of Chief Justice Warren,

> . . . from 1924 to 1932 DuPont dropped the price of plain cellophane 84%, while the price of glassine remained constant. And during the period 1933-1946 the prices for glassine and waxed paper actually increased in the face of a further 21% decline in the price of cellophane. If "shifts of business" due to "price sensitivity" had been substantial, glassine and waxed paper producers who wanted to stay in business would have been compelled by market forces to meet DuPont's price challenge. . . . That producers of glassine and waxed paper remained dominant in the flexible packaging materials market without meeting cellophane's tremendous price cuts convinces us that cellophane was not in effective competition with their products. During the period covered by the complaint (1923-1947) cellophane enjoyed phenomenal growth. . . . Yet throughout this period the price of cellophane was far greater than that of glassine, waxed paper or suphite paper . . . in 1929 cellophane's price was seven times that of glassine, in 1934, four times, and in 1949 still more than twice glassine's price . . . cellophane had a similar price relation to waxed paper and . . . sulfite paper sold at even less than glassine and waxed paper. We cannot believe that buyers, practical businessmen, would have bought cellophane in increasing amounts over a quarter of a century if close substitutes were available from one-seventh to one-half cellophane's price. That they did so is testimony to cellophane's distinctiveness.[6]

The fundamental consideration in cross-elasticity of demand is the responsiveness of the sales of one product to price changes in the other. Implicit in this relationship is the *ceteris paribus* assumption that "other things remain equal." In the absence of such an assumption, it may not be possible to ascertain whether the demand for a product such as cellophane is responding to price changes in related products or is reacting on its own merits to more intensive salesmanship, promotion campaigns, general market acceptance, or a growth in the needs of its customers. The latter factor is cited in the passage below from the Supreme Court majority opinion as an explanation for the increased demand for cellophane.

> It could not be said that this immense increase in use was solely or even largely attributable to the superior quality of cellophane or to the technique or business acumen of DuPont, though doubtless these factors were important. The growth was a part of the expansion of the commodity-packaging habits of business, a by-product of general efficient competitive merchandising to meet modern demands.[7]

Since cross-elasticity of demand varies with price, a high or low cross-elasticity of demand may be a function of the level at which a monopolistic firm sets its price. A monopolist would maximize profit by raising its price up to the point where a slight additional rise would cause large-scale substitution of alternative products. At this price level cross-elasticity of demand would be high. Cross-elasticity of demand might be very low at prices equal to or slightly above normal long-run cost. Thus, cross-elasticity of demand may be limited in its usefulness in indicating the presence or absence of monopoly power since the amount of substitution of alternative products for a given change in price is dependent upon the starting price level of the product.

Only in the abstract world of economic theory can forces other than a change in the price of another product be held constant. Since the economic concept of cross-elasticity of demand presupposes such strict conditions as "other things remaining equal," it is open to the danger that standard theoretical conclusions may be drawn when the concept is utilized in examining empirical data. In contrast, the legal concept of "reasonable interchangeability," which considers other factors than price, such as quality and type of end-use, appears as a more suitable analytical tool for a court to employ in defining relevant product markets.

Quality. The Supreme Court specifically rejected in the *Cellophane* case the argument by the Government that products have to be substantially fungible or physically identical to be in the same relevant market. The proper test, stated the Court, is whether there exists "market alternatives that buyers may readily use for their purposes."

The Court found that 80 percent of the cellophane made by DuPont was sold for packaging in the food industry. A commercially suitable packaging material for fresh vegetables has to be transparent in order for a customer to visually examine the quality of a product. There must be a low permeability to gases so that the enclosed product will not be contaminated by surrounding products with strong odors; and, finally, the packaging material must have a low moisture permeability to retain freshness. Moistureproof cellophane, pliofilm, plain glassine, and Saran have the above qualities. But other flexible wrapping materials, such as aluminum foil, are completely opaque and cannot serve as an "alternative source of supply" for the packaging requirements for retailing fresh food. The degree of physical differences existing among products included in the same relevant market by the Supreme Court in the *Cellophane* case can be observed in Table 5-2, which contrasts three of the more than ten types of flexible wrapping materials included by the Court in the relevant product market.

TABLE 5-2
Physical Properties of Selected Flexible Packaging Materials

	Moistureproof Cellophane	Plain Glassine	Aluminum Foil
1. Heat sealability	Yes	Yes	No
2. Printability	Yes	Yes	Yes
3. Tear strength	Low	Good	Low
4. Bursting strength	High	Low	Low
5. Water absorption	High	High	Nil
6. Permeability to gases	Very low	Low	Very Low
7. Wrapping machine running qualities	O.K.	O.K.	O.K.
8. Dimensional change with humidity difference	Large	Moderate	None
9. Moisture permeability	Low to medium	High	Very low
10. Clarity	Highly transparent	Commercially transparent to opaque	Opaque

End-use. The relative importance of different physical characteristics can be observed from the end-uses of products. The interchangeability of flexible wrapping materials was discussed by the Court in terms of the classification of sales made by a number of converters of these materials. The sales of the converters were divided into categories, such as bakery products, candy, fresh produce, snacks, and meat and poultry. The Supreme Court summarized, in the passage below, the competition which cellophane faces:

> In determining the market under the Sherman Act, it is the use or uses to which the commodity is put that control. The selling price between commodities with similar uses and different characteristics may vary, so that the cheaper product can drive out the more expensive. Or, the superior quality of higher priced articles may make dominant the more desirable. Cellophane costs more than many competing products and less than a few. . . . It may be admitted that cellophane combines the desirable elements of transparency, strength and cheapness more definitely than any of the others . . . But, despite cellophane's advantages it has to meet competition from other materials in every one of its uses . . . cellophane furnishes less than 7% of wrappings for bakery products, 25% for candy, 32% for snacks, 35% for meats and poultry, 27% for crackers and biscuits, 47% for fresh produce, and 34% for frozen foods. Seventy-five to eighty percent of cigarettes are wrapped in cellophane. . . . Thus, cellophane shares the packaging market with others. The over-all result is that cellophane accounts for 17.9% of flexible wrapping materials, measured by the wrapping surface.[8]

In summary, the Supreme Court concluded after an examination of the price, quality, and end-use of cellophane that a reasonable interchangeability existed between this product and other flexible wrapping materials. The fact that DuPont accounted for 75 percent of the cellophane sales in the United States was not controlling. The paramount finding was that DuPont accounted for less than 20 percent of the market for flexible wrapping materials. The latter percentage was deemed insufficient by the Court to establish the requisite illegal market power for monopolization.

ENDNOTES

1. 351 U.S. 377 (1956).
2. 351 U.S. 377, 381 (1956).
3. *Ibid.*, p. 394.
4. *Ibid.*, p. 404.
5. *Ibid.*, p. 400.
6. *Ibid.*, pp. 416-18.
7. *Ibid.*, p. 385.
8. 351 U.S. 377, 395 (1956).

THOUGHT QUESTIONS

1. Criticize the following quotation in the dissent by Chief Justice Warren: "That producers of glassine and waxed paper remained dominant in the flexible packaging

materials market without meeting cellophane's tremendous price cuts convinces us that cellophane was not in effective competition with their products.'' Why did DuPont incur ''tremendous price cuts'' if it possessed a monopoly?

2. The Warren dissent also noted that, ''During the period covered by the complaint (1923-1947) cellophane enjoyed phenomenal growth . . .'' Assuming DuPont achieved economies of scale and more efficient production techniques over the twenty year span, would these changes in production cost be relevant in analyzing DuPont's pricing behavior?

3. Why does the complaint go back as far as 1923? Could a pioneer of a new product such as cellophane possess anything less than 100% of the cellophane market in 1923?

   a) Would an adverse decision against DuPont tend to discourage inventors of new products by charging them with monopoly before they even develop the market for their product?

4. As food chains and supermarkets grew in the 1940's, the individual pre-packaged portion which a customer could pick-up from a counter became increasingly important. How did this substantial increase in demand for a flexible packaging material influence the pricing of cellophane by DuPont?

5. Should the government have considered a case against DuPont for monopolizing the market for ''flexible wrapping materials used to cover cigarettes?'' DuPont accounted for 75% to 80% of the wrapping sales of cigarettes.

THE BERKEY PHOTO – KODAK CASE (1978)

In *Berkey Photo, Inc.* v. *Eastman Kodak Company* (1978) the Southern District Court in New York approved an award of damages to Berkey as a result of a jury finding that Kodak used its monopoly power in the film market to monopolize and attempt to monopolize the amateur still camera market and to restrain trade in photofinishing. A considerable portion of the evidence in the case dealt with Kodak introducing its 110 camera without prior disclosure to its competitors in order for them to have an opportunity to develop a similar competitive product. In the words of the District Court:

> The paramount strategy and goal were thus to use the film monopoly — Kodak's power in a field where its market share consistently exceeded 80% — as a lever for suddenly swelling defendant's power in the camera market, achieving there at least a temporary total monopoly of a vital new segment to be created by the system introduction. Some ''responsible persons'' within Kodak urged unsuccessfully that predisclosure concerning the new film format be given to camera competitors (as well as photofinishers and photofinishing equipment makers) so that they would not suffer in one blow the instant obsolescence of inventories and work in progress and the inability to compete at all with their cameras in the terrain of the newly announced system. The 110 announcement came substantially as a surprise, following some minimal predisclosures, for a price, two or three months earlier. And these events, it is worth mentioning, followed hard after a magicube coup in June of 1970, when Kodak gained a similar advantage of surprise and temporary exclusivity from what the jury found, and the court entirely agrees, was an unlawful combination in restraint of trade with Sylvania.

Kodak claimed that the introduction of new products without prior notice was a normal business practice and therefore could not be a basis for unlawful monopolization. The District Court rejected this argument as follows:

> Overlooking that it has been found on compelling evidence to be a monopolist in an array of markets, Kodak also overlooks that monopolies are not darlings of the antitrust laws. Whatever supposed uncertainties inhere in the standards applied to this case — and it must be conceded surely that there are some — these standards would appear to be, if anything, more lenient toward Kodak than the stringent rule of *Alcoa*, allowing a monopolist to avoid illegality only if it could show that the disfavored position of power had been "thrust upon" it as a result of its superior business acumen or skill in the relevant market. Far from approaching a showing to satisfy that standard, the evidence reveals a monopolist in one market (film) engineering that power to thrust itself into a monopoly position in a second market (cameras). The result was a world away from being "economically inevitable,". . . it is plainly avoidable, and the means Kodak chose to employ were plainly to be shunned.
>
> Kodak's complaint at root is that it faces liability for conduct which other business firms, lacking monopoly power, engage in regularly with impunity. Even if the factual premise were to be credited, the short answer is that the antitrust laws do not permit willful maintenance of monopoly power by conduct that might for a company without such power be deemed honestly industrial.

Berkey argued that the new products introduced by Kodak were not genuine improvements for the benefit of consumers but were intended primarily to injure competitors. In the words of the court:

> Berkey's thesis in this respect is that the new products were introduced so as to unbalance competition — obsoleting prior systems such as the 126, and postponing competitors' chances to compete for the sale of the new systems, rather than to give consumer's something genuinely better. The attempt to show that a new product such as Kodacolor II was not an improvement over existing products is made as a part of the effort to prove this claim. In some cases where it is not immediately apparent whether particular conduct which Berkey has complained about is exclusionary, you will be required to determine whether the conduct is primarily an effort to attract customers or primarily an effort to undermine competitors.

In the final analysis the *Kodak* case focused on injury to competitors by the practice of new product introductions. Kodak argued unsuccessfully in the District Court that "all product announcements by companies with large market positions are at risk without any legal standards to guide the businessman as to how and under what circumstances to bring out new products to market." The court dismissed this argument with the following statement directed not at the market share of Kodak, but to its absolute size:

> It is at least a little demure for defendant to describe itself as a mere company with a "large market position." Kodak is . . . a "giant," with a nearly unique agglomeration of enormous powers over adjoining markets in a huge industry.

The offense in the opinion of the District Court was not that Kodak drove Berkey out of business, but that it achieved "at least a temporary total monopoly of a vital new segment created by the system introduction."

In response to this statement one might ask what other incentive would Kodak or any other company have but to gain an edge or a headstart by introducing a new product? A *temporary* monopoly is exactly what a company should expect, and should look forward to, when it introduces a revolutionary new product. It may also explain why the company in an industry became the leader — it might have always been first on the market with the latest innovation.

The District Court's *Kodak* opinion was reversed in June 1979 by the Court of Appeals for the Second Circuit on the issue as to whether Berkey was entitled to $45,750,000 treble damages for lost profits resulting from the events surrounding the introduction of the Kodak 110 camera. Judge Kaufman concluded that Kodak did *not* have a duty to predisclose information about the 110 system to competitive camera manufacturers:

> It is the possibility of success in the marketplace, attributable to superior perform-ance, that provides the incentives on which the proper functioning of our competitive economy rests. If a firm that has engaged in the risks and expenses of research and development were required in all circumstances to share with its rivals that benefits of those endeavors, this incentive would very likely be vitiated.
>
> Moreover, enforced predisclosure would cause undesirable consequences beyond merely encouraging the sluggishness the Sherman Act was designed to prevent. A significant vice of the theory propounded by Berkey lies in the uncertainty of its application. Berkey does not contend, in the colorful phrase of Judge Frankel, that "Kodak has to live in a goldfish bowl," disclosing every innovation to the world at large. However predictable in its application, such an extreme rule would be insupportable. Rather, Berkey postulates that Kodak had a duty to disclose limited types of information to certain competitors under specific circumstances. But it is difficult to comprehend how a major corporation, accustomed though it is to making business decisions with antitrust considerations in mind, could possess the omniscience to anticipate all the instances in which a jury might one day in the future retrospectively conclude that predisclosure was warranted. And it is equally difficult to discern workable guidelines that a court might set forth to aid the firm's decision. For example, how detailed must the information conveyed be? And how far must research have progressed before it is "ripe" for disclosure? These inherent uncertainties would have an inevitable chilling effect on innovation. They go far, we believe, towards explaining why no court has ever imposed the duty Berkey seeks to create here.

A company such as Polaroid was able to enter the camera industry with a revolutionary new method of photography with instant prints. Japanese camera manufacturers have entered the U.S. market and have captured a substantial portion of the upper price range of still cameras. The variables keep changing as technology is advanced and consumer demands are altered in response to new products and different prices. There is no question that it is hard for a newcomer to keep pace with an industry leader which is continually changing and updating its products. The unanswered question of this case is whether the rate of technological progress will be slowed if we handicap the leader into being more concerned with the technological obsolescence rate of its competitors' products than in the technological advance of its own products.

THOUGHT QUESTIONS

1. One of the charges to the jury was for it to determine whether the conduct of Kodak was "primarily an effort to attract customers" or "primarily an effort to undermine

competitors.'' Since the 110 camera was a marketing success, it obviously attracted customers. Can a company attract customers without, to some extent, undermining competitors?

2. Was Kodak quietly maintaining a camera monopoly if its introduction of the 110 camera rendered its own 126 camera obsolete and thereby nullified its former market power in the 126 camera market?

3. The District Court opinion stated that the evidence against Kodak reveals a monopolist in one market (film), engineering that power to thrust itself into a monopoly position in a second market (cameras). Did Kodak really try to ''tie'' its cameras to its film, or did its high film sales simply follow in the wake of its new camera?

4. Should every leading company in an industry be required to disclose a new product?
   a) Should a new production process or ''trade secret'' also be given advance notice?
   b) Should a medium sized or smaller company also have a legal duty to disclose a revolutionary product if the market position of the dominant firm is about to be weakened or undermined?
   c) Is the intent of our patent system to offer a temporary monopoly to an inventor consistent with the District Court opinion?

5. Suppose a leading company had a sensational promotional or advertising campaign, such as a lottery. Should it have to give its smaller competitors prior notice of the advertising campaign so they can have time to print-up similar materials or lottery tickets for distribution?

6. Noting the magnitude of damages assessed against Kodak and the division of opinion between the District Court and the Circuit Court of Appeal over what otherwise might be considered ''normal business practices,'' should a leading or dominant firm soften its competitive strategies?
   a) Should the fear of treble damage suits by smaller rivals be a new variable in a corporate profit maximizing strategy?

7. Debate the following statement: The injury to competitors and the additional temporary market power achieved by new product introductions is the price to be paid for vigorous competition and technological progress.

THE FTC REALEMON OPINION (1978)

In the Matter of Borden, Inc. (ReaLemon), FTC Opinion (November, 1978), the Federal Trade Commission found that Borden, through its ReaLemon Foods, monopolized in violation of Section 5 of the Federal Trade Commission Act, the production, marketing and sale of processed lemon juice. The Commission refused to adopt the recommendation of the lower Administrative Law Judge that Borden be required on a compulsory basis to license for a period of ten years the ''ReaLemon'' name and label design to any person engaged in or wishing to enter the business of producing and marketing processed lemon juice.

The FTC ordered Borden to cease and desist from: (1) granting price reductions which result in *different net prices* among Borden's ReaLemon customers, (2) selling ReaLemon below cost or *at unreasonably low prices*, and (3) granting promotional allowances, where the effect of these practices would be ''to hinder, restrain or eliminate competition between Borden and its competitors.'' Although there is a substantial analytical distance between most initial FTC opinions and final Supreme Court opinions, the language in this recent FTC opinion suggests some of the current outer boundaries in the law of monopoly.

The principal policy question raised by the *ReaLemon* decision concerns the type of competitive behavior expected from a company which innovates a new product, develops and pushes the product until the business grows and prospers to a substantial size, and then sees new entrants copy its product and cut into its market share.

The story of ReaLemon is the dream of every small businessman with a new product idea. In the depression of the 1930's, Irvin Swartzberg had a simple idea: sell pre-squeezed lemon juice to bars, hotels and other institutional customers. The product was successful and it was clear that a consumer market existed provided the shelf life of the product could be extended. The product was changed from fresh lemon juice to a reconstituted product made from lemon juice concentrate, water and a preservative. In the 1940's the company began to use the brand name of ReaLemon.

Processed lemon juice, such as ReaLemon, is simple to manufacture. There are no secret formulas or processes involved, and the product can be made on relatively inexpensive equipment. Any plant which bottles other juices can easily pack processed lemon juice. Despite the fact that the ReaLemon product owed its existence to the substitution of its convenient product for the effort of squeezing fresh lemons, the Commission found that processed lemon juice was a separate market from fresh lemon juice. Without this finding the Commission could not have reached a finding of monopoly against ReaLemon since the processed lemon juice market is only a small percent of the combined fresh and processed lemon juice market.

The Commission predicated its finding that Borden unlawfully maintained its monopoly share on a quotation in the company's 1971 Marketing Plan:

> The spread between ReaLemon prices and those of competitors preclude any possibility of price increases to offset higher costs. By not permitting this spread to increase, at the expense of short term profits, ReaLemon anticipates maintaining its market share close to its present level. Market share is the key, since industry or total market growth will be reflected more toward ReaLemon than its competitors by virtue of ReaLemon's present 90% market share.

With respect to this Borden quotation the Commission concluded, "This document evidences Borden's intent to hold on to its monopoly share of the market by sacrificing somewhat higher prices over the short run to assure continued monopoly returns over the long haul." A completely opposite conclusion could easily be reached. It could be argued that Borden wanted to increase its prices to offset its increased manufacturing costs, but could not do so because of the price pressures of its competitors. This admission by Borden is not a statement of power and market dominance, but what Borden cannot do due to its absence of market power. Borden, because of the presence of a strong competitive fringe, was afraid — or "precluded" to use Borden's word — to raise its prices further above the price level of its competitors because it would lose sales to them. Borden also recognized that it would be better for the company if the industry continued its expansion with a wider sales base and lower prices. This is an objective entirely consistent with a competitive goal for extending output and lowering prices to the benefit of consumers.

The Federal Trade Commission also alleged that Borden sought to maintain a monopoly in ReaLemon by using geographically discriminatory promotional allowances. In 1970, Borden gave a promotional discount of approximately 5 cents a bottle. In its 1971 Marketing Plan Borden sought to increase its promotional allowances in markets where it faced strong price competition:

> In those markets where competition has been making inroads, tentative plans are to increase the size of the allowances to as much as $1.20 per case, or 10 cents per bottle . . .

Borden was in regional markets with smaller rivals pricing significantly below Borden's price, and increasing their market shares. Borden attempted to meet this competition by offering further promotions in those areas where it faced more severe competition. Retailers and consumers were given lower prices as the moves and countermoves of competition were felt in the market. The decision of the FTC was for Borden not to fight back with selective geographic price promotions because of the fear that to do so might result in injury to smaller rivals. The decision reflects the sentiment that smaller rivals should not be injured even though there may have to be softer competition. A proposed order by the FTC that Borden could no longer grant different geographic promotional allowances at the same time (unless cost justified or if they had no effects on competition) would force Borden, in the majority of instances, to lower its promotions all over the country at one time. The result of the order is that Borden will have to decrease its promotions, which in turn can be expected to increase the net prices which consumers pay for ReaLemon.

The FTC opinion justified their position as follows:

> While the short-run consequences of such actions to the consumers affected may be positive in terms of lower prices, the longer-run consequences are almost certain to be ill, because as soon as the threat of entry vanishes, and as future potential entrants come to recognize the financial disaster that will attend efforts to enter, Borden is free to raise prices back to monopolistic levels and consumers will have lost a meaningful alternative to the monopoly brand.

There is little basis in the FTC assertion that "future potential entrants will come to recognize the financial disaster that will attend efforts to enter." Minute Maid, which entered in 1975, gained, in the space of six months, approximately 18% of the dollar sales of frozen lemon juice. Instead of copying the Borden product of concentrated lemon juice, as the other small competitors had done, Minute Maid marketed a new product: *frozen* lemon juice squeezed directly from lemons without any water or preservatives added. The product had, in the opinion of many consumers, a superior taste to the concentrate ReaLemon. By the end of 1976, Borden's share had declined below 70 percent in several major cities. This new entrant, with a superior product, had no need to be scared by competitive prices or even by the previous demise of several inefficient firms.[1]

The ReaLemon brand-name had the advantage in being the originator of a product. Despite the fact that ReaLemon, in most instances, was interchangeable with other brands of reconstituted lemon juice, consumers were willing to pay more for the original and leading brand. Prior to 1970, ReaLemon was the only nationally advertised and distributed brand of processed lemon juice. Advertising was relatively minor, being under a million dollars a year. Nonetheless, ReaLemon, as the originator and leading company with a track record of quality and reasonable prices, was perceived by consumers as a "premium brand." This image required smaller rivals to offer to the consumer more than they were already getting from a perfectly satisfactory product being distributed by Borden. The only "extra" these rivals could offer for their basically fungible product was a price discount from the ReaLemon price. Minute Maid, however, was able to market their distinct frozen product at a price higher than ReaLemon. The so-called "premium price" of ReaLemon therefore disappeared once a company had something more to market than simply a copy of the existing leading product.

The FTC opinion suggested that Borden must refrain from price competition which would otherwise be deemed lawful if engaged in by a smaller company:

> As a monopolist it is obliged to refrain from the sort of retaliatory price-cutting that would be allowed a sub-monopolist.

Because of the image of a premium product, Borden was to be further burdened with the handicap that it had to take into account not only its own costs but those of its competitors. The FTC noted:

> In any event, the effect of Borden's spurious product differentiation, making it necessary for competitors to sell considerably below ReaLemon, created a circumstance where even prices above marginal cost could as the record indicates, be predatory in the sense that even equally efficient competitors could be driven from the market.

The highest price that a dominant firm believes it can charge without inducing at least one significant entrant is referred to in economic literature as the "limit price." One must second-guess a company to conclude that they should have priced their product higher after taking into consideration the future demand of the product, the growth of available substitutes, or the likelihood of future technological or product obsolescence. The so-called "limit price" of a company may also be the "competitive price" being charged by smaller rivals, rather than a price which is intended to keep out *future* entrants. In other words, to label the price of a company as a "limit price" intended to keep out potential entrants is a matter of opinion. The same price might be justified by a wide spectrum of management and marketing objectives pointing to future demand and cost developments which could be fruitful for entry. The theoretical dilemma faced by an alleged dominant firm is that it will be criticized for earning "monopoly profits" if it charges a high price and attracts entry, and will be criticized for exclusionary behavior if it charges a low price which discourages entry.[2]

Finally, the proposed order of the FTC included a provision that Borden could not sell at "unreasonably low prices" where the effect might hinder competition. To aid the management of product leaders, such as Borden, in determining an appropriate price, the FTC offered the following "advice:"

> Whether a price is "unreasonably low" must be determined by reference to Borden's own costs, its awareness of its competitors' costs, historic price differentials, and competitive conditions in the market.

This quote takes us full circle in the field of antitrust. We are back to one of the first cases in many antitrust casebooks, *United States* v. *Trenton Potteries*, 273 U.S. 392 (1927), which condemned a price-fixing conspiracy in the sale of toilet bowls. The Supreme Court in the *Trenton Potteries* decision stated its refusal to consider the reasonableness of prices which were illegally fixed:

> The reasonable price fixed today may through economic and business changes become the unreasonable price of tomorrow. Once established, it may be maintained unchanged because of the absence of competition secured by the agreement for a price reasonable when fixed. Agreements which create such potential power may well be held to be in themselves unreasonable or unlawful restraints, without the necessity of minute inquiry whether a particular price is reasonable or unreasonable as fixed and without placing on the government in enforcing the Sherman Law the burden of ascertaining from day to day whether it has become unreasonable through the mere variation of economic conditions.

The logic of the Supreme Court in the *Trenton Potteries* case with regard to price fixing is compelling: what constitutes a reasonable price changes from day to day. The FTC in the ReaLemon decision was basically advocating more government control, on a day to day basis, over the pricing and output decisions for leading companies. The FTC rather than the free enterprise system would thereby become the eye of surveillance, and the standards of performance would undoubtedly slip from the free enterprise encouragement of competitive excellence to the governmental protection of smaller rivals.

ENDNOTES

1. The fear that a new entrant or smaller firm may not survive in the competition against a firm with a major market share has resulted in a controversy as to whether the large firm should keep its prices above its average variable costs, its balance sheet full costs, or its marginal costs. There have also been suggestions for restraining the leading firm from expanding its output for a certain period in order to allow the new entrants to expand at a higher price level.   See O. Williamson, *Predatory Pricing: A Strategic and Welfare Analysis*, 87 *Yale Law Journal* 284 (1977); Reply by Areeda and Turner, *ibid.*, 1337 (1978); P. Areeda and D. Turner, Predatory Pricing and Related Practices under Section 2 of the Sherman Act, 88 *Harv. L. Rev.* 697 (1975); and F. M. Sherer, "Predatory Pricing and the Sherman Act: A Comment," 89 *Harv. L. Rev.* 868 (1976).
2. For a discussion of "limit pricing" see J. Bain, "A Note on Pricing in Monopoly and Oligopoly," *American Economic Review*, Vol. XXXIX (March, 1949), pp. 448-64; Note, *"Telex v. IBM:* Monopoly Pricing under Section 2 of the Sherman Act," *The Yale Law Journal*, Vol. 84 (1975); *Baron, Limit Pricing, Potential Entry, and Barriers to Entry*, 63 *American Economic Review* 666 (1973), and Goldberg and Moiroa, "Limit Pricing and Potential Competition," 81 *Journal of Political Economy* 1460 (1973).

THOUGHT QUESTIONS

1. The following order was unsuccessfully recommended by a lower FTC Administrative Law Judge: "Borden should be required, for a period of 10 years, to grant a license for the use of the ReaLemon name and label design to any person engaged in or wishing to enter the business of producing and marketing processed lemon juice."
   a)   Do you believe compulsory licensing is a suitable remedy?

b) Would such a remedy encourage brand proliferation of this product?

c) Would consumers be misled into thinking they were buying Borden's product?

2. If the consumer previously rejected the processed lemon juice made by smaller companies, why should they be deceived into thinking that these products are now the same as Borden's?

a) What protection is afforded to the consumer that the same quality of concentrated lemon juice used by Borden will be used by the licensee?

b) Suppose the product name was "Borden's Processed Lemon Juice," as in the case of Kellogg's Corn Flakes, would the compulsory licensing remedy have to extend to the company's name?

c) Would the testimony in the *ReaLemon* case that smaller competitors were adulterating their product affect your answer?

3. The FTC opinion stated that Borden "as a monopolist is obliged to refrain from the sort of retaliatory price-cutting that would be allowed a sub-monopolist." Do you believe that "meeting a competitive price" should be included in the same group of lawful, yet not economically inevitable practices, such as leasing in *United Shoe*, new capacity in *Alcoa* and prior notice of new product innovations in *Berkey-Kodak*?

4. The proposed order of the FTC included a provision that Borden could not sell at "unreasonably low prices." The FTC defined such a price with reference to not only Borden's own costs, but "its awareness of its competitors' costs." How is Borden to determine its competitors' costs?

a) Should Borden consider any technological improvements in making processed lemon juice which will lower its costs substantially?

b) Is the FTC asking Borden to maintain an "umbrella price" which is high enough for the survival of all competition?

c) Would a successful industry wide price fixing conspiracy produce a similar result?

5. Considering the large number of multi-billion dollar food companies in the United States, discuss the FTC assertion that the long run consequences of strong price competition and failure of some firms will be that "future potential entrants will come to recognize the financial disaster that will attend efforts to enter." Why was Minute Maid not afraid to enter?

THE MEMOREX-IBM CASE (1978)

The Memorex suit against IBM for monopolizing or attempting to monopolize various segments of the computer industry is one of a large number of antitrust proceedings against IBM, including one brought by the United States Government.[1] The Memorex case was tried in front of a jury which was asked to decide whether IBM monopolized or attempted to monopolize various markets in the computer industry. The trial lasted five months, during which 87 witnesses were called whose testimony filled more than 19,000 pages of transcript. More than 2,300 exhibits were introduced in evidence. After deliberating for 19 days, the jury reported itself hopelessly deadlocked, and the court declared a mistrial. Thereafter, the court wrote a directed verdict in favor of IBM and denied the request of Memorex for another jury trial. The court noted that the jury was having trouble grasping the concepts that were being discussed by expert witnesses, most of whom had doctorates in engineering or economics. Only one of the jurors had even limited technical education. The judge noted that while he was appreciative of the effort the jurors put into deciding the case,

> . . .it is understandable that people with such backgrounds would have trouble applying concepts like cross-elasticity of supply and demand, market share and market power, reverse engineering, product interface manipulation, discriminatory pricing, barriers to entry, exclusionary leasing, entrepreneurial subsidiaries, subordinated debentures, stock options, modeling, and etc.[2]

In response to a question by the judge as to whether a case of this type should be tried to a jury, the foreman of the jury said, "If you can find a jury that's both a computer technician, a lawyer, an economist, knows all about that stuff, yes, I think you could have a qualified jury, but we don't know anything about that."

THE DEFINITION OF COMPUTER MARKETS

The broadest market Memorex attempted to define was the "general purpose computer systems market." IBM offered evidence to show that an alternative to a central processing unit was a series of mini-computers. Leasing companies, which purchase computer equipment from manufacturers and lease it to users, were another source of computer equipment. Finally, service bureaus that sell computer time offer an alternative method for data processing. The court found these were reasonable alternative products and services which disproved the existence of a "general purpose computer systems market."

Memorex further attempted to prove the existence of three "IBM plug compatible" markets for peripheral devices: disk drives, disk drive control units and communications control units. An IBM plug compatible device could plug directly into an IBM central processing unit without the need of further engineering or interfacing. IBM contended that these three plug compatible markets were too narrowly defined since they excluded other data storage devices such as tape drives and main memory, and comparable peripheral devices for use on non-IBM systems. IBM demonstrated at the trial that non-IBM products could be interfaced into the IBM central processing unit without considerable engineering difficulty.

The court found that tape drives and memory units were competitive media for the storage of data. Potential competition was also found to exist from non-IBM plug compatible products which could be converted or interfaced into IBM compatible peripherals. Finally, the court recognized that peripherals account for the major portion of most computer systems with the result that the higher the price of IBM peripherals, the greater the cost of an IBM computer system. Competition between computer systems was therefore considered an important restraint on IBM's prices for its peripherals such as disk drives and communication control units. For these reasons, the court held that Memorex had not satisfied its burden of proving that the markets it had defined were relevant markets or submarkets for antitrust purposes. This failure of proof by Memorex on market definition resulted in the court dismissing the *monopolization* charge against IBM. The court then addressed the *attempt to monopolize* claim of Memorex against IBM.

The Pricing of IBM

Memorex tried to prove its *attempt to monopolize* charge by challenging as "predatory" the prices IBM charged for its peripherals. IBM argued that prices may be predatory only when they are below marginal or average cost, and that it reduced its prices primarily to meet the lower prices of its competitors.

The *Memorex* opinion cited as a basis for its predatory pricing tests the case of *Hanson* v. *Shell Oil Co.*,[3] which held that Shell Oil did not engage in predatory pricing since there was no evidence that Shell's prices were below its marginal or variable costs.

The court in the Memorex case quoted with approval the following passage from the *Hanson* opinion:

> There is some question, however, whether pricing below a profit maximizing point which is still above marginal and average variable costs should be considered predatory; it only discourages inefficient new entrants who must have higher prices to survive. . . . If its prices were above its costs, and nevertheless Shell's did drive Hanson out of business, this can only be because Hanson was so inefficient that at prices at which Shell could make a reasonable profit he could not. The antitrust laws were not intended, and may not be used, to require businesses to price their products at unreasonably high prices (which penalize the consumer) so that less efficient competitors can stay in business. The Sherman Act is not a subsidy for inefficiency.[4]

The court interpreted the *Hanson* case as establishing two tests of predatory pricing: (1) pricing below marginal or average variable costs, and (2) pricing above marginal or variable costs but below the short run profit-maximizing price where barriers to entry are high. Since Memorex did not offer any evidence that IBM's prices were below its marginal or average variable costs, it could not establish the first test of illegality. With regard to the second test, the court found that barriers were not high in the plug compatible peripheral market since a large number of manufacturers, including both companies manufacturing just peripherals and those manufacturing complete systems, were able to enter these markets with relative ease and compete with IBM.

The court found that the prices for the plug compatible disk drives and other peripherals in the case were at a level established not by IBM, but by Memorex and the other plug compatible manufacturers. IBM reduced its prices to meet the lower prices of its competitors. In dismissing the claim of Memorex that IBM *attempted to monopolize* various computer markets, the court held that IBM should not be liable for predatory pricing if it was only meeting the lower prices of Memorex:

> A company should not be guilty of predatory pricing, regardless of its costs, when it reduces prices to meet lower prices already being charged by its competitors. To force a company to maintain non-competitive prices would be to turn the antitrust laws on their head.[5]

Predatory Pricing and Marginal or Average Cost

Customers will tend to continue with a leading supplier which has shown a history of knowledge, experience, service and quality. The newcomer, which has not established an equal reputation, must offer an actual or equivalent lower price by providing more service, higher specifications or some extra performance to match the reputation of the established firm. A lower price is the traditional competitive means for challenging the leader. The leading company in an industry with high barriers to entry must weigh the likelihood that meeting the prices of smaller companies may result in their business failure and expose the company to a treble damage suit of a staggering amount. Memorex sought $306 million and Telex sought $352 million in damages against IBM.

There has been considerable controversy in antitrust over the subject of predatory pricing. The measurement of cost is considerably subjective in cost accounting. Assumptions of future output levels, variances and budgets are necessary before standard costs can be calculated. There are very few companies that have knowledge of their marginal costs, namely, the cost associated with an incremental unit of output. Marginal costs are below average costs for the initial levels of output and tends to be above average costs as the plant approaches its full capacity level. See Appendix B, Fig. B-1. The use of average cost as a proxy for marginal cost is correct only at the point of intersection of the two curves. However, there appears to be no ready alternative to the use of average cost since that is basically the only cost data companies keep.

A major economic policy issue in predatory pricing cases is whether we want to forbid, like a *per se* rule, the pricing below some arbitrary cost level, such as a marginal or average cost curve, or below some output level such as a short term profit maximizing position. And, in the event we do decide such a *per se* rule is required, can we enforce such a rule within due process standards if companies are not sure what their marginal cost curve looks like, the current status of their average cost curve, or their short-run profit maximizing level of output?

When a company determines its costs, it generally constructs "standard costs" which are estimates of the expected costs of the raw materials and labor costs in their major products based on the estimated purchase cost of their raw material components, their expected labor costs including anticipated increases from collective bargaining, and expected output levels of the finished product. For example, a candy or beverage manufacturer will have to estimate a per pound "standard cost" for sugar used in its product. The refined sugar may be obtained from a combination of current or spot market purchases with delivery within a few weeks, future long term requirement contracts with delivery at a fixed or spot market price in a period frequently ranging from six to twelve months, plus some of its own in-house inventory which may be valued on a current market price (LIFO: Last In and First Out), or on a basis of original cost (FIFO: First In and First Out). An adjusted cost basis may also result from an extraordinary gain or loss from the reevaluation of its inventory. The products being sold from finished inventory are frequently made from raw materials purchased at widely different costs and points of time.

The estimated or standard costs in large companies may be prepared six months in advance in order to be approved by a series of management budget meetings. Since a company cannot be expected to recalculate its cost position every day, it should be allowed to rely on reasonable estimates and variances which can be corrected at various appropriate intervals for assumed cost levels for raw materials. Salesmen in the field generally have very little knowledge of the current state of the spot market for the component raw materials, or the relative weights accorded these component costs in the calculation of the final product costs. Only the current standard costs which are based on budgets and estimates are known, not by the marketing department, but by the executives in the operating management of a company. Consequently, there are very few sales divisions or marketing departments which will know the current position of a marginal cost curve, average cost curve or short term profit maximizing ouput level.

A company will know its current costs only after the fact: when all the data is in, its books are closed for the quarter or the year, its earnings per share are calculated, the saving or run-overs from budgets and variances are known and a new set of future cost estimate schedules are being introduced. It is questionable whether a precise point on a cost curve, or the intersection of a marginal cost curve and marginal revenue curve, can be established as a rule of law if few defendants can be reasonably expected to have current knowledge of the critical point.

Consider a number of alternative situations in which the arbitrary application of the average or marginal cost rule would be anti-competitive. A leading company with a rapidly declining market share may want to run a promotion at a lower price for a product, such as a peripheral, to promote its complete system or full line of products. The temporary price reduction may be below its average cost for the period of the promotion, if the only cost examined is for the peripheral. However, the cost for the computer system as a whole may be above its average cost. Alternatively, the company may sell as a promotion only one peripheral, but get its foot in the door with the knowledge that customers will need additional peripherals of the same kind if they are satisfied with the product. If these expected future sales are taken into account in the calculation of the current average costs, the company would not appear to be selling below average cost.

In a classic article on the subject of predatory pricing, Professors Donald Turner and Philip Areeda have noted the importance of expected future costs:

> An average variable cost rule, like a marginal cost rule, should be flexible enough to allow a defendant to demonstrate that its price was equal to or above a reasonably anticipated average variable cost. A firm may legitimately determine its price and output levels according to expected future costs rather than historical accounting costs. Of course, historical costs may be the best approximation of costs for the near future, but a defendant should be permitted to show why it anticipated lower costs in the future.[6]

The same problem of expectations is applicable to defining a demand curve and its derivative marginal revenue curve. This marginal revenue curve must be calculated under the second *Memorex* and *Hanson* tests which refer to the "pricing below the short-run profit-maximizing price where barriers to entry are high." The profit maximizing price must theoretically be determined from the expectations or future anticipated conduct from potential buyers. A demand curve represents "a series of simultaneous alternative maximum bids for quantities associated with each price." As the late Professor Oskar Morgenstern noted, "This means that each point is valid to the exclusion of all other stated bids at the same or immediately following point of time."[7]

As soon as a transaction occurs, an entirely new demand curve is reconstituted which may be the same or different than the preceding curve. The customer which has purchased the product no longer has the previous need for it, incomes have changed and there exists a different set of customers. Thus, as Professor Morgenstern observed, a time interval exists for the successive trading or reconstitution of a demand curve. In the case of the individual, "his maximum bids are the products of a plan which is established (a) by his (anticipated) wants — which may be short or long run, periodic or not periodic at all — and (b) by (his past) income, which in the majority of cases is periodic."[8] Evidence of this type, showing the expectations underlying supply and demand curves, transforms the apparent precision of a point on the marginal cost or revenue curve into a range of values dependent on the financial astuteness of accountants, the budgets of marketing departments, the variances of corporate controllers, and the vagaries of competition. In the *Memorex* case the judge noted that "courts should not get involved in second guessing engineers." The court would have had to second guess more than engineers if they had actually tried to ascertain whether IBM's pricing was below its "short run profit-maximizing price, where barriers to entry are high." Instead, the court avoided the problem by noting that Memorex had introduced no data with regard to IBM's marginal and average costs, and the barriers to entry in the computer industry were not high.

THE ECONOMIC RIGHT TO MATCH A LAWFUL COMPETITIVE CASE

The difficult problem with predatory pricing is its "visual similarity to healthy business rivalry."[9] The primary reason for encouraging new entrants is to lower the price which a dominant firm may be charging. The price competition of the new entrant is expected to force the leading company to reduce its prices or watch its market share erode. At the early growth stages of the new entrant, the leading firm has more to lose in reduced revenue by lowering its price than by allowing the new entrant to nibble at its market share. If the new entrant, such as Memorex, continues to grow, a point will be reached when the leading company can no longer afford to lose its market position. The fact that peripheral manufacturers, such as Telex and Memorex, were suing for hundreds of millions of dollars in damages shows that these companies had reached financially significant proportions. Their success was dependent upon the market developed by IBM with its central processing units. That these companies reached their present size suggests that IBM did not block their original entry. At what point in the growth of these companies should IBM be able to match their prices even though it may be below some type of cost curve or short-run profit-maximizing position?

Some authorities, such as Professors Turner and Areeda, believe that the leading company should generally *not* be allowed to meet the lower prices of rivals if that price is below the marginal cost of the leading company: "We would not permit a monopolist to price below marginal cost in order to meet the lawful price of a rival."[10] As a consequence of this position, a leading or dominant company will be foreclosed from competing against smaller rivals where its price may, in the opinion of a relatively uneducated jury or a judge with a limited accounting background, be below some estimated marginal cost curve or possibly a short run profit maximizing position.

Once the smaller rival determines the marginal or average cost level of the larger company, it will know at what price it can sell without facing competitive bids from the larger rival. The smaller rival with less overhead and research and development costs may well have lower average costs over a significant range of output than the larger rival. After the leading company has lost a number of its major accounts, its average costs may rise as its output level declines and it loses some of its former economies of scale. Furthermore, additional advertising and promotion expenses will be required to retrieve its lost customers. The leading company may find it impossible to match the prices of the smaller rival without falling below its average or marginal cost curve.

The arguments over predatory pricing reduce in the end to the familiar battles of *per se* versus rule of reason standards, and "protection of competition" versus the "protection of competitors." But there is one additional note in this controversy. Economic liberties, such as the freedom of a company to meet a competitive price, are important ingredients in a free enterprise system. A company should not be denied the right to compete anymore than an individual should be denied the right to speak. Rather, our legal system should encourage the defense of economic liberties, and insure the right for all companies to match a lawful competitive price, regardless of the size or cost structure of the company.

ENDNOTES

1. The *Memorex-IBM* case is cited as part of the companion cases, *ILC Perpherals Leasing Corp.* v. *International Business Corp.*, and *Memorex Corp.*, *MRX Sales and Service Corp.* v. *International Business Machines Corp.* (D.C. Calif., 1978), 1978-2 *Trade Cases*, para. 62,713. Other major cases brought against IBM include the decade long Department of Justice proceeding against IBM, *Telex Corp.* v. *IBM*, 510 F. 2d 894 (1975), which was settled in 1975; *California Computer Products, Inc.* v. *IBM* (CA-9, 1979), 1979-1 *Trade Cases*, Para. 62,713; *Transamerica Computer Co., Inc.* v. *IBM* (DC Calif., 1979), 1979-2 *Trade Cases*, Para. 62,989; and *Greyhound Computer Corp., Inc.* v. *IBM*, 559 F. 2d 488 (1977), cert. denied *U.S.* (1978).
2. 1978-2 *Trade Cases*, Para. 62,713.
3. 541 F. 2nd 1352 (9th Cir., 1976), cert. denied, 429 U.S. 1074 (1977).
4. *Ibid.*
5. 1978-2 *Trade Cases*, Para. 62,713.
6. Philip Areeda and Donald F. Turner, "Predatory Pricing and Related Practices Under Section 2 of the Sherman Act," *Harvard Law Review*, Vol. 88 (1975), p. 697; F. M. Scherer, "Predatory Pricing and the Sherman Act: A Comment," *Harvard Law Review*, Vol. 89 (1976), p. 869; and O. E. Williamson, "Predatory Pricing: A Strategic and Welfare Analysis," *Yale Law Journal*, Vol. 87 (1977), p. 284.
7. O. Morgenstern, "Demand Theory Reconsidered," *Quarterly Journal of Economics*, (February, 1948), pp. 165-201, at p. 168.
8. *Ibid.*, p. 183.
9. K. Elzinga, "Predatory Pricing: The Case of the Gunpowder Trust," Journal of Law & Economics, Vol. 223 (1970). Also see J. McGee, "Predatory Price Cutting: The Standard Oil (N.J.) Case," 1 *Journal of Law & Economics*, Vol. 137 (1958).
10. See footnote 6.

THOUGHT QUESTIONS

1. In *Hanson* v. *Shell Oil*, the Court made the following statement as a test of predatory pricing: "pricing above marginal or variable costs but below the short run profit-maximizing price where barriers to entry are high." Discuss whether the subjective, expected demand implicit in the theoretical definition of a demand curve, the alternative methods of allocating costs, and finally, the subjective budget elements in standard costs undermine the existence of a "short run maximizing price."

2. Assume that Memorex and IBM both had the choice of lowering its price or introducing an innovation which would make its improved product more desirable at the same price.
    a) If neither company introduces the innovation, are either at their short term profit maximizing price?
    b) If IBM does and Memorex does not, should IBM's action be deemed as "tantamount to a price reduction?" If so, could such conduct be characterized as "predatory?"
    c) If Memorex made the product innovation and IBM did not, but lowered its price slightly below Memorex, would this be predatory?
    d) Suppose IBM lowered its price to clear its inventory of machines in preparation for introducing a new line of equipment. Would this conduct be predatory?
3. Discuss the following statement from the text: Expectations underlying supply and demand curves transform the apparent precision of a point on the marginal cost or revenue curve into a range of values dependent on the financial astuteness of accountants, the budgets of marketing departments, the variances of corporate controllers, and the vagaries of competition."
4. If the primary reason for encouraging new entrants is to lower the price that the dominant firm is charging, why should we discourage the dominant firm through treble damage suits from lowering its price, at least down to its marginal costs?

6

PRICE FIXING CASES

INTRODUCTION ON PROOF OF CONSPIRACY

The mutual awareness and often identical movement by oligopolists has not been treated by the courts as a contract or conspiracy in restraint of trade under Sec. 1 of the Sherman Act.[1]

In *Theater Enterprises, Inc.* v. *Paramount Film Distributing Corp.*[2] the Supreme Court refused relief in an action for treble damages brought by a suburban theater owner against motion picture producers and distributors for violating the antitrust laws by conspiring to restrict "first run" pictures to downtown Baltimore theaters. Suburban theaters could therefore only exhibit subsequent runs. The Court found that the conduct of the defendants, despite its uniformity, could be adequately explained by *independent business justification*. The suburban theater owned by the party bringing the action was located in a small shopping center with an audience drawing ability of less than one-tenth of a downtown area. The downtown theaters were found to "offer far greater opportunities for the widespread advertisement and exploitation of newly released features, which is thought necessary to maximize the overall return from subsequent runs as well as first-runs." The *Theater Enterprises* case established that uniform business conduct is not sufficient in and of itself to establish a conspiracy. In the words of the Court,

> But this Court has never held that proof of parallel business behavior conclusively establishes agreement or, phrased differently, that such behavior itself constitutes a Sherman Act offense. Circumstantial evidence of consciously parallel behavior may have made heavy inroads into the traditional judicial attitude toward conspiracy; but "conscious parellelism" has not yet read conspiracy out of the Sherman Act entirely.[3]

Business behavior is admissible as circumstantial evidence from which an agreement may be inferred or a conspiracy implied. For instance, in *Eastern States Retail Lumber Dealers Association* v. *United States*[4] the Supreme Court found a conspiracy in restraint of trade by the concerted actions of a trade association which systematically circulated among its members reports naming wholesalers that sold directly to consumers. Upon receipt of these notices from the trade association, retailers generally refused to do business with the offending wholesalers. The Court noted that "It is elementary . . . that conspiracies are seldom capable of proof by direct testimony and may be inferred from the things actually done. . . ."[5] Similarly, in *Interstate Circuit, Inc.* v. *United States*[6] the Supreme Court found, absent direct testimony of an agreement among eight film distributors, a conspiracy might be implied by their signing similar contracts with the same theater chain operator. The contracts fixed the admission charges and provided that the movies could not be subsequently run on a double bill. Although there was no evidence that the film distributors spoke or communicated among themselves, each knew that the other distributors were asked to participate. Therefore, the Court concluded:

> Acceptance by competitors, without previous agreement, of an invitation to partici-
> pate in a plan, the necessary consequence of which, if carried out, is restraint of
> interstate commerce, is sufficient to establish an unlawful conspiracy under the
> Sherman Act.[7]

The cases involving implied conspiracy and conscious parallelism demonstrate that in antitrust the means adopted for a course of action are as important as the ends accomplished. Identity of price may be encouraged by the statistical reporting activities of trade associations, by the historic conduct of a price leader initially recognizing changes in market conditions, by direct price fixing schemes or by a resale price maintenance program. From a legal viewpoint, the means by which one arrives at the identity of prices are more important than the result. Mere uniformity of competitors' prices in the sale of a product is not in itself evidence of a violation of the Sherman Act.[8] Proof of an agreement, express or implied, must be shown for the establishment of a conspiracy under the antitrust laws.[9]

DIRECT PRICE-FIXING AGREEMENTS

In February 1961, General Electric, Westinghouse, Allis Chalmers, and a number of other electrical equipment producers pleaded guilty to collusive price fixing in violation of Sec. 1 of the Sherman Act.[12] As a result of this illegal price-fixing conspiracy, approximately 2000 treble damage suits were brought against the defendants by companies which had purchased electrical equipment at allegedly higher price levels than would have existed had there been no price-fixing agreements.

In *Ohio Valley Electric Corp.* v. *General Electric Co.*[13] two electric utility companies sued General Electric and Westinghouse under Sec. 4 of the Clayton Act for treble damages amounting to $16 million. The defendants were alleged to have conspired to establish uniform book prices and to keep order prices as close as possible to their published list or "book prices." The utility companies sought to establish the price they would have paid for 11 steam turbines purchased in 1952 if there had not existed a price-fixing conspiracy between the defendants.

The theory of damages advanced by Ohio Valley was a comparison of the actual discount off-book prices received in 1952, amounting to 11 percent, with the substantially larger discounts, amounting to 25 per cent, given by the defendant companies after 1959 when the conspiracy was exposed. The District Court found that the 1952 and postconspiracy discounts off-book prices were comparable, since in both periods defendants considered the book prices as realistic anticipated sales prices.

The equipment manufacturers argued that even if there was a price-fixing conspiracy in 1952 it had no effect on the prices paid by Ohio Valley. The defense introduced in evidence the testimony of two economists to show that a "reconstructed competitive unit price," which was based on extensive calculations of average costs and rates of utilized capacity, was higher at the time of purchase than the price actually paid by Ohio Valley for the steam turbines. The District Court judge noted that an acceptance of the economic testimony as to the "reconstructed competitive unit price" would be tantamount to a finding that "the conspirators were completely wasting their time at these meetings."

The District Court refused to conclude that the conspiracy in the *Ohio Valley* case was ineffective. However, the changes in discount from book prices after 1959 were found to be not entirely a result of the termination of the conspiracy. The District Court found that the postconspiracy period included the presence of foreign competition for the first time, an increase in the manufacturers' capacity to produce steam turbine generators which caused an over-supply, a lessening of ordinary growth in demand, and a drop in manufacturing cost which allowed defendants to offer their products at lower prices. Accordingly, the District Court reduced the claim for damages of Ohio Valley by 30 per cent to take account of changes in the estimated price level that would have prevailed in the absence of the price conspiracy.

PRICE REPORTING PLANS

Trade associations generally provide their members with industry data or information concerning at least one of the following subjects: sales, production, planned or actual capacity, credit worthiness of individual members, cost accounting, quality standards, innovation, and research developments. Trade association activities which serve to encourage better products, to avoid waste and inefficiency, and to promote better relations with labor, the public, or government are not inimical to the antitrust laws. Such activities do not hamper the independent decision-making functions of members with respect to price policies and levels of production. However, activities of trade associations which tend to fix or raise prices, restrict output, allocate territories or markets, or standardize products with the aim of achieving uniform prices have been found illegal.

In *The Sugar Institute, Inc.* v. *United States*[14] the Supreme Court held illegal under the Sherman Act a trade association price-filing plan which required members to announce their prices publicly in advance of sales, and to adhere to these prices until they publicly announced changes. The fifteen defendant companies, all members of the Sugar Institute, refined practically all imported raw sugar processed in the United States, and supplied approximately 80 per cent of the sugar consumed here. The Institute was formed primarily to stop secret concessions and price discriminations granted by ten so-called "unethical" sugar refiners to principally large buyers. It was estimated that at least 30 per cent of the sugar sold before the Sugar Institute was formed carried secret concessions of some kind. Other secondary purposes for forming the Institute included (1) the supplying exclusively to the fifteen members accurate trade statistics regarding production, deliveries, and stocks on hand, (2) the elimination of wasteful practices, (3) the creation of a credit bureau, and (4) the institution of an advertising program to increase consumption, lagging in part because of a public "slimness campaign."

The Supreme Court found that the sugar industry, before the Institute was organized, was in a "demoralized state which called for remedial measures;" but the steps taken by the sugar refiners were held to have gone too far. Since the formation of the Sugar Institute there were fewer price changes for refined as compared to raw sugar, and the price level for refined sugar remained relatively higher as compared to the price for raw sugar. The Institute brought a "friendly cooperative spirit" to the sugar industry, since each refiner was given the assurance that "he need meet only the prices, terms, and conditions announced by his competitors in advance of sales." The trial court found, and the Supreme Court agreed, that any unfair method of competition caused by the secret concession system could have been prevented by immediate publicity given to the prices and conditions in all closed transactions. The basis of illegality was in the requirement that the defendant trade association members adhere to the publicly announced prices:

> For the question, as we have seen, is not really with respect to the practice of making price announcements in advance of sales, but as to defendants' requirement of adherence to such announcements without the deviations which open and fair competition might require or justify.[15]

The Supreme Court found of paramount importance two facts: (1) the relative industry position of the fifteen defendants, *i.e.*, they refined practically all the imported raw sugar processed in the United States, and (2) the standardized product of the defendant. Even though domestic refined sugar competes with beet sugar and imported refined sugar (called "off-shore refined"), the Court found that "the maintenance of fair competition between the defendants themselves in the sale of domestic refined sugar is manifestly of serious public concern." Furthermore, because sugar is a standardized commodity, sold largely on price, there is a "strong tendency to uniformity of price," which, in the words of the Court, "makes it the more important that such opportunities as may exist for fair competition should not be impaired."

In *Tag Manufacturers Institute* v. *Federal Trade Commission*,[16] an action was brought under Sec. 5 of the Federal Trade Commission Act to enjoin as an "unfair method of competition" the publication and filing of price lists and off-list prices made by members of the Tag Manufacturers Institute. The members of the trade association sold approximately 95 per cent of the tag products purchased in the United States. The members agreed to report to the Institute by the close of the next business day any changes in their price lists, as well as the prices, terms, and conditions of each sale of any tag product. The trade association mailed to the members daily bulletins or "pink sheets" recording all off-list transactions. The "pink sheets" showed the name of the seller, description of the tag product, quantity, list price, actual price of the particular off-list transaction, and the state where the customer was located. The name of the buyer was not disclosed.

The Court of Appeals found that (1) approximately 80 per cent of the business was custom made-to-order tags, with an almost unlimited variety of features; (2) only past prices were submitted to the Institute; (3) the published reports of the Institute could be subscribed to by interested purchasers of tag products and were also available for public inspection in the New York City office of the Institute; (4) no actual or implied agreement existed among members to adhere to the prices submitted to the Institute, and most importantly, (5) approximately 25 per cent of the dollar volume of the aggregate total sales of all subscribing manufacturers had been at off-list prices. Upon these findings, the Court of Appeals held that the reporting activities of the Institute did not constitute an "unfair method of competition."

In *U.S.* v. *Container Corp. of America*[17] the government brought an action against the eighteen leading manufacturers of corrugated boxes charging a price-fixing agreement in violation of Section 1 of the Sherman Act. There was an exchange of price information, but unlike the *Sugar Institute* case, there was no agreement to adhere to a price schedule. In the words of the Court:

"Here all that was present was a request by each defendant of its competitor for information as to the most recent price charged or quoted, whenever it needed such information and whenever it was not available from another source. Each defendant on receiving that request usually furnished the data with the expectation that it would be furnished reciprocal information when it wanted it."

The Court found that there was over-capacity in the corrugated box industry, prices had drifted downward for the past eight years and the industry continued to expand in the Southeast from 30 manufacturers with 49 plants in 1955 to 51 manufacturers with 98 plants in 1963. An abundance of raw materials and machinery made entry into the industry easy with an investment of $50,000 to $75,000. The Court concluded that the occasional exchange of price information concerning specific customers had the effect of "keeping prices within a fairly narrow ambit. The inferences are irresistible that the exchange of price information has had an anticompetitive effect in the industry, chilling the vigor of price competition."

Three justices of the Supreme Court dissented in the *Container* case. The dissenting opinion held that "it is just as likely that price competition was furthered by the exchange as it is that it was depressed." The dissent noted,

"In all cases, the information obtained was sufficient to inform the defendants of the price they would have to beat in order to obtain a particular sale. Complete market knowledge is certainly not an evil in perfectly competitive markets. This is not, however, such a market, and there is admittedly some danger that price information will be used for anticompetitive purposes, particularly the maintenance of prices at a high level . . . However, I do not think it can be concluded that this particular market is sufficiently oligopolistic, especially in light of the ease of entry, to justify the inference that price information will necessarily be used to stabilize prices. Nor do I think that the danger of such a result is sufficiently high to justify imposing a *per se* rule without actual proof."[17]

In 1978 the issue of price verification between competing sellers was again presented to the Supreme Court in *U.S.* v. *United States Gypsum*, which involved the criminal indictments of several major gypsum board manufacturers. Gypsum board is a laminated type of wall board composed of paper, vinyl or other specially treated coverings over a gypsum core. The product has substantially replaced wet plaster on interior walls. Gypsum board is essentially fungible. Differences in price, credit terms and delivery services largely dictate the purchasers' choice between competing suppliers. Demand, which is a function of construction activity, is only marginally affected by price fluctuations. The eight largest companies in the industry accounted for 94% of national sales in 1973.

The focus of the government's price fixing case at trial was the practice of interseller price verification whereby one gypsum board manufacturer would call a competitor to determine the price currently being offered to a specific customer. The defendants maintained that those exchanges of information which did occur were for the purpose of documenting a competitive price in order to establish a Section 2(b), "meeting competition defense," under the Robinson-Patman Act. The defendants also argued that they were trying to avoid being fraudulently tricked into giving a customer a lower price to match a fictitious price of a competitor.

The government argued that the "effects only" of the price verification program were controlling. If the effect of verification was to raise, fix, maintain or stabilize prices, the purpose or intent of the defendants to comply with the Robinson-Patman Act was irrelevant. The Supreme Court held that since this was a criminal case the requisite intent had to be shown and the "effects only" test was inappropriate. A defendant's purpose in complying with the Robinson-Patman Act would in certain limited circumstances "constitute a controlling circumstance excusing Sherman Act liability." The Supreme Court concluded that the trial court was in error in not having the jury examine the element of intent by the defendants in exchanging price information:

> "The imposition of criminal liability on a corporate official, or for that matter on a corporation directly, for engaging in such conduct which only after the fact is determined to violate the statute because of anticompetitive effects, without inquiring into the intent with which it was undertaken, holds out the distinct possibility of overdeterrence; salutary and procompetitive conduct lying close to the borderline of impermissible conduct might be shunned by businessmen who chose to be excessively cautious in the face of uncertainty regarding possible exposure to criminal punishment for even a good-faith error of judgment. . .For these reasons, we conclude that the criminal offenses defined by the Sherman Act should be construed as including intent as an element."

An important and unanswered question raised in the price verification cases concerns whether we want to strive for a goal of total information as suggested by a model of perfect competition. Data concerning all possible buyers or sellers of a particular product at a particular point of time might be displayed on a computer terminal in the future. Buyers could then easily find the best price from alternative suppliers. If time was a factor, a buyer could find the closest supplier with a particular product in inventory. Delivery could be synchronized with other industries or competitors in order to avoid cross-hauling the same product in opposite directions. The efficient matching of the product demands of buyers with the product availability of suppliers would provide a better allocation of limited resources. But it is not clear that the antitrust laws want to encourage these types of efficiency if the opportunity for collusion is enhanced.[18] The trend in information technology is clear: more rather than less information will become available as domestic and international communication systems continue their rapid advance.

A public policy against illegal collusive price fixing will have to be weighed against the economic costs for buyers not being able to shop around easily for the lowest price or the most suitable product, or sellers not having an opportunity to match a lower price, an earlier delivery date or a superior product specification.

NOTE APPENDIX C: OLIGOPOLY MODELS

ENDNOTES

1. *The Theory of Monopolistic Competition*, 7th ed., p. 31.
2. 346 U.S. 537 (1954).
3. 346 U.S. 573, p. 541. For selected views on conscious parallelism, see Heflebower, "Parallelism and Administered Prices," pp. 88-116; United States, *Report of the Attorney General's National Committee to Study the Antitrust Laws*, pp. 36-42, A. Phillips, "Policy Implications of the Theory of Interfirm Organization," *American Economic Review*, Vol. LI (May, 1961), pp. 245-52; R. A. Givens, "Parallel Business Conduct Under the Sherman Act," *Antitrust Bulletin*, Vol. V (May-June, 1960), p. 273; A. Phillips and G. R. Hall, "The Salk Vaccine Case: Parallelism, Conspiracy and Other Hypotheses," *Virginia Law Review*, Vol. XLVI (1960), p. 717; M. Conant, "Consciously Parallel Action in Restraint of Trade," *Minnesota Law Review*, Vol. XXXVIII (1954), p. 794; L. Schwartz, "New Approaches to the Control of Oligopoly," *University of Pennsylvania Law Review*, Vol. CIX (1960), p. 31; W. H. Nicholls, "The Tobacco Case of 1946," *American Economic Review*, Vol. XXXIX (1949), pp. 284-96; and Markham, "The Nature and Significance of Price Leadership," pp. 891-905.
4. 234 U.S. 600 (1914).
5. *Ibid.*, p. 612.
6. 306 U.S. 208 (1939).
7. *Ibid.*, p. 227. Also see *United States* v. *Masonite Corp.*, 316 U.S. 265, 275 (1942); *American Tobacco Co.* v. *United States*, 328 U.S. 781 (1946); *United States* v. *Paramount Pictures, Inc.* 334 U.S. 131 (1948); *Federal Trade Commission* v. *Cement Institute*, 333 U.S. 683 (1948); *National Lead Co.* v. *Federal Trade Commission* 227 F. 2nd 825, 832-34 (7th Cir., 1955), reversed on other ground 352 U.S. 419 (1957).
8. *Pevely Dairy Co.* v. *United States*, 178 F 2nd 363 (8th Cir., 1949), *certiorari denied* 339 U.S. 942 (1950). Cf. *C-O-Two Fire Equipment Co.* v. *United States*, 197 F. 2nd 489 (9th Cir., 1952), *certiorari denied*, 344 U.S. 892 (1952).
9. United States, *Report of the Attorney General's National Committee to Study the Antitrust Laws*, p. 39.
10. 273 U.S. 392 (1927). For a discussion of direct price-fixing agreements see G. W. Stocking and M. W. Watkins, *Monopoly and Free Enterprise* (New York: Twentieth Century Fund, 1951), *Cartels or Competition?* (New York: Twentieth Century Fund, 1948), and *Cartels in Action* (New York: Twentieth Century Fund, 1946). Also see Phillips, *Market Structure, Organization and Performance*; and J. Rahl, "Conspiracy and the Antitrust Laws," *Illinois Law Review*, Vol. XLIV (1950), p. 743.
12. *City of Philadelphia* v. *Westinghouse Electric Corp.*, 210 F. Supp. 483 (E. D. Penn, 1962). See P. Neal and P. Goldberg, "The Electrical Equipment Cases: Novel Judicial Administration," *American Bar Association Journal*, Vol. L (1964), pp. 621-28; and R. A. Smith, "The Incredible Electrical Conspiracy," *Fortune* (April, 1961), p. 132 and (May, 1961), p. 161.
13. 244 F. Suppl. 914 (S.D.N.Y., 1965). Also see W. M. Sayre, "Developments in Multiple Treble Damage Act Litigation — Introduction," *N.Y. State Bar Association Antitrust Law Symposium* (New York: Commerce Clearing House, 1966), pp. 46-54; W. L. Kaapcke, "Proof and Measure of Damages in Antitrust Cases," *ibid.*, pp. 143-68.
14. 297 U.S. 553 (1936).
15. *Ibid.*, p. 582.
16. 174 F. 2nd 452 (1st Cir., 1949).
17. 393 U.S. 333 (1969).
18. See Bock, B., "Antitrust and Emerging Information Technology," *The Conference Board Record* (November, 1970), p. 30: "The critical question here is not whether we can approximate some of the elements of 'perfect' markets, but whether we want to approximate them."

THOUGHT QUESTIONS

1. In the electrical conspiracy cases in the 1960's, there was extensive testimony given that the purpose of the conspiracy was to keep the weaker companies, such as Allis Chalmers, in business. When business is bad, and price wars are driving a company into bankruptcy, it may weaken in integrity and resort to illegal activities to survive. If losses, rather than profits, are related to collusive activities, can high profits be related with logical consistency to collusion?

2. Consider a "game theory" example of two companies attempting to fix prices. Both are, by assumption, immoral and dishonest in willfully violating the law. Neither can be expected to trust each other. Each asks the other to call a truce by stopping the excessive price discounting. Both agree, with the expectation that if the other company raises its price and they do not, their market share will increase. Both lie to each other and prices do not change. Discuss the testimony of one of the witnesses: "I did not fix prices nor conspire to fix prices. I just tried to make the others think I was going along with the price rise. I wanted to encourage them to raise their prices so that I could get their customers with my same old price."

3. Discuss the testimony of another witness: "I am the president of one of the smallest companies in my industry. The other companies are tenfold larger than my company. If I did not attend the price fixing meeting, the large companies would all drop prices in my small region and put me out of business. They made the market and I nibbled at their customers. I attended the meeting out of fear and without the intent to follow their prices."

4. Should we allow U.S. companies to meet in order for jointly submitting a bid for foreign construction projects, such as off-shore drilling platforms, where the other foreign bidders will be collaborating?

5. Consider the following sequence. 1) Company A calls a competitor, Company B, and asks if Customer X has paid its bills and is a good credit risk. 2) Company B says Customer X is not, and they are planning to cut-off his credit. 3) Company A replies, "We will too." Company A then asks 4) "What price are you charging Customer X?" 5) Upon hearing the price, Company A states that it will more than match the price to the customer and hangs up the phone. Discuss the possibilities of illegal conduct and the competitive and non-competitive effects of the interchange of information.

6. With reference to the preceding question, discuss the comment in the dissent of the Container case that "it is just as likely that price competition was furthered by the (information) exchange as it is that it was depressed."

7. Price fixing is generally classified as a "per se" antitrust offense. However, the litigation of these cases includes voluminous evidence of costs, profit margins, discounts, changes in average prices, and the relationship between price increases and the wholesale and consumer price index. Most of this evidence is introduced under the question of the "intent" of the defendant. Do you agree with the liberal rule toward evidence in a criminal case?

8. A defendant justifies an industry increase in list prices by 5% with an industry labor contract increase at approximately the same time. Should this evidence be allowed if there is also evidence of meetings and possible collusion? Discuss whether the defendant is arguing that the price is "reasonable" or that the conduct of a joint price increase by industry members can be explained by independent external factors.

9. In *Catalano, Inc.* v. *Target Sales, Inc.* (U.S. Supreme Court, 1980), a group of beer wholesalers in California agreed among themselves that they would sell to retailers only if cash payment were made in advance or upon delivery. In 1980 the Supreme Court considered whether this agreement to stop giving interest free credit was

tantamount to an agreement to eliminate discounts and should fall within the *per se* rule against price fixing. What did the Court decide?

a)   Would the elimination of free credit merely force the invoice price down to correct for any implicit discount without any effect on the seller's net price?

b)   Would an agreement to charge extra for formerly "free delivery" be tantamount to a *per se* price fixing agreement?

c)   Would an agreement not to extend credit to any dealer overdue in payment for six months be *per se* illegal?

d)   Would an agreement to no longer send free baseball tickets to the dealers be *per se* illegal?

7

VERTICAL INTEGRATION CASES

The vertically integrated firm, by virtue of its multiple operations in production and distribution, may be able to use its market strength at one level of competition to further its interests at another. In recent years there have been several bills introduced and considered in Congress which would limit or prevent the major oil companies from owning refineries, pipelines and retail gasoline stations. Although the attack of these bills has been more against the major oil companies rather than at vertical integration as such, the arguments advanced by the proponents of these bills stress the apparent advantages of vertical integration as a source of market power.

In metal fabricating industries, a vertically integrated firm may charge an unduly high price for a raw material, such as aluminum ingot, which is purchased by non-integrated customers who fabricate it into sheets and other finished products. The nonintegrated fabricators can be caught in a "price squeeze" if the vertically integrated firm charges them a high price for ingot and then meets these same customers in the market for finished sheet where the vertically integrated firm undercuts the prices of the non-integrated competitors.

In other market structures the vertically integrated firm may make purchases from the same companies to which it sells. A firm may sell raw materials to a fabricator and also purchase fully fabricated products from the same company. Such a firm might resort to the practice of reciprocity, whereby it would use its position as a buyer of fabricated products to encourage or force its sales of raw materials to independent fabricators. The anticompetitive effects of these types of market practices associated with vertically integrated firms are analyzed in this chapter.

THE FORECLOSURE OF SUPPLIERS

Complete or absolute foreclosure of competing suppliers by a firm employing either exclusive requirements contracts or vertical integration is present when a

94

supplier obtains all outlets in a particular product market in order to deny competing nonintegrated suppliers any access to the market. In Fig. 7-1 there are four suppliers (A, B, C, and D) and one outlet. Since no firm is assumed to have any priority in the distribution of competing goods through the one outlet, the market structure reflects a total absence of the foreclosure of suppliers.

FIG. 7-1. Absence of Foreclosure of Suppliers

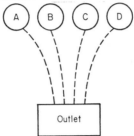

The diametrically opposite market structure appears in Fig. 7-2. Firm A, through an exclusive requirements contract or vertical acquisition, preempts the business of the outlet and forecloses the competing market suppliers (B, C, and D) from any access to the *sole* outlet. This absolute foreclosure of competitors is denoted by the straight line *F*. Given the market structure of four suppliers and one outlet, the absolute foreclosure of all competitors by a given firm will unquestionably violate the present antitrust laws.

FIG. 7-2. Absolute Foreclosure of Suppliers

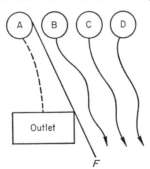

In *United States* v. *Maryland and Virginia Milk Producers Assn.*,[1] an association of milk dealers was required by the Supreme Court to divest the previously acquired assets of its leading competitor in the distribution of milk. The decision has been described as presenting "an unambiguous leverage problem, i.e., the use of power at one level — distribution — to secure or strengthen power at another level — production."[2]

The defendant milk association (square X) in Fig. 7-3 accounted for approximately 86 per cent of all sales of fluid milk to all twelve of the milk dealers in the Washington metropolitan area. Embassy Dairy (square Y) was an independent concern not buying from the defendant association, but procuring its supply directly from farmers refusing to sell to the defendant association. Embassy accounted for 10 per cent of the fluid milk sales in the above market.

FIG. 7-3. Foreclosure of Competing Suppliers

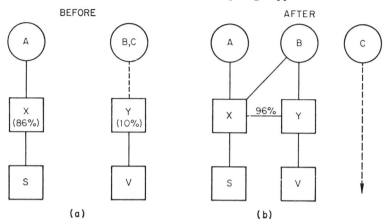

The association, by gaining control of Embassy, achieved 96 per cent of the Washington fluid milk market. This market position allowed the association not only to stop most of the inflow of lower-priced milk, but to use its apparent monopoly control over the retail market as leverage in forcing the remaining independent farmers, who formerly sold milk to Embassy, to join the association.

The independent dairy farmers, such as B and C in Fig. 7-3, had the choice after the acquisition of joining the association and having their milk sold in the Washington area, or refusing membership in the association and being forced to ship milk to other markets such as Baltimore, Maryland. The diagonal line in Fig. 7-3 connects some of the formerly independent farmers (circle B) with the association (square X). A few farmers, such as C, shipped their milk to other markets rather than accept membership in the association.

THE "SQUEEZING" OF INDEPENDENT FABRICATORS

In the *United States* v. *Aluminum Co. of America*[3] the sole domestic producer of virgin aluminum also engaged, along with several other manufacturers, in the fabrication operation of rolling aluminum ingots into sheets. The offense committed by Alcoa was the subsidization of sheet manufacturing, which was performed at a near loss, by the profits made at the higher level of ingot production. The Court of Appeals segregated the various technological levels of the integrated firm and treated each level as an independent operation, in an accounting sense, for estimating "fair price" and "fair profit."

Subsidization by Alcoa of some levels of operations by the profits or returns made at other levels was referred to as the act of "squeezing" independent fabricators. Figure 7-4 shows Alcoa as circle A, its manufacturing or rolling operation as square X, and finally its outlet or retail level as the square V. The other manufacturers of sheet who had to purchase ingots from Alcoa are represented by the square Y. These manufacturers sold rolled sheets through their outlets, square S, in competition with the Alcoa outlet, square V. Alcoa charged the competing fabricators a high price for ingots and, thereby, raised their raw material cost base. Alcoa also sold sheets through its own outlets at an exceptionally low price in competition with the other independent fabricators.

FIG. 7-4. Squeezing Non-integrated Fabricators

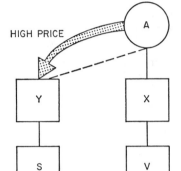

Since Alcoa was alleged to have set both the ingot and sheet prices, it had the power to determine for its competitors the profit spread between the raw material and the finished product. Alcoa was "squeezing" when it set the ingot price so high and the sheet price so low that its fabricating customers had great difficulty surviving.

Alcoa was alleged to be using its profits from ingot sales to subsidize its fabricating operations until, presumably, its fabricating competitors went under. Alcoa's defense that it could not determine until the end of an accounting period whether it had made a profit or loss was rejected by the court.

Theoretically, one might argue that if Alcoa had a pure monopoly it could sell ingots at an unusually high price and maximize its profits without entering the fabrication field. Alternatively, Alcoa could split this profit between ingots and fabrication.

However, the Court of Appeals suggested that these alternative methods for making profits may be unlawful:

> . . . that it was unlawful to set the price of "sheet" so low and hold the price of ingot so high, seems to us unquestionable, provided, as we have held, that on this record the price of ingot must be regarded as higher than a "fair" price. True, this was only a consequence of "Alcoa's" control over the price of ingot, and perhaps it ought not be considered as a separate wrong . . .[4]

The offense of Alcoa was not simply the charging of a high price for ingots nor the coordinated charging of a low price for sheets. Rather, the offense was the continuation of this pricing policy *after* it had been put on notice that the survival of independent sheet rollers was in danger. Only when the existence of independent or nonintegrated firms is at stake do the practices of subsidization or squeezing become open to question as tending to lessen competition.

THE SQUEEZING DILEMMA

In *Federal Trade Commission* v. *Standard Oil of Indiana*,[5] a price squeeze existed which was almost the reverse of that found in the *Alcoa* case. Instead of following the Alcoa pattern of selling raw materials at a high price to customers, and attempting to undersell them at the outlet level, Standard Oil sold gasoline at a high price to its own retailers, and sold at a low price to wholesale jobbers. In Fig. 7-5 Standard Oil is represented by circle A, its own retailers by square V, and competing wholesalers by square X.

FIG. 7-5. The Squeezing Dilemma

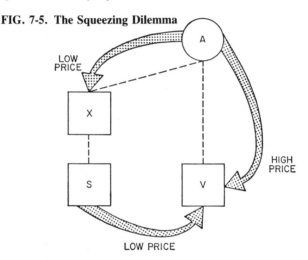

LOW PRICE

The Federal Trade Commission charged that Standard Oil violated the provisions of the Robinson-Patman Act against price discrimination in granting lower prices exclusively to four jobbers in the Detroit area. The Commission maintained that the lower prices to the four jobbers were injurious to retail dealers in Detroit who were buying directly from Standard Oil. The retailers who were able to buy at lower prices from these four jobbers could undercut retailers buying at higher prices directly from Standard Oil.

The Commission, in trying to enforce a decree compelling Standard Oil not to sell to its retail customers at a price higher than that charged its wholesale customers, was in effect ordering Standard to put a price squeeze on its integrated wholesale customers (square X).[6] Standard Oil faced the dilemma of either continuing its present pricing pattern, which was putting a price squeeze on its retail customers, or complying with the Commission's request and changing its pricing pattern into an Alcoa-type squeeze on wholesale customers. Standard Oil was able to avoid the Commission's order by proving that the lower prices granted to the four jobbers were made in good faith to meet the competition of other gasoline suppliers who were quoting the same or lower prices to the four jobbers.[7]

THE TOTAL SQUEEZE

The District Court in *United States* v. *Bethlehem Steel Corp.*[8] considered the position of fabricators who purchase their raw materials of *rope wire* from Youngstown, twist it, and then sell back to Youngstown the fully fabricated product of *wire rope*. Since Bethlehem fabricated wire rope, and could reasonably be expected in the future to sell large quantities to Youngstown, the District Court found that the merger of Bethlehem and Youngstown would tend to place the independent nonintegrated firm at a competitive disadvantage.

Youngstown is represented in Fig. 7-6 by circle *Y*, Bethlehem by circle *B*, and the two firms after the merger by circle *B-Y*. At first glance the independent fabricators, such as *Z*, appear to be threatened by an Alcoa-type price squeeze if the proposed merger is consummated. The source of supply for *Z* would change from a noncompetitor (Youngstown) to a vertically integrated competitor (Beth-lehem-Youngstown). Bethlehem-Youngstown could charge the independent fabri-cators a high price for rope *wire*, the basic raw material, and then undersell the independents with a low price for wire *rope*, the finished product. In the words of the District Court:

> . . . the opportunities for a price squeeze on the independent are enhanced, since the supplier may shift his profit between rope wire and wire rope in such a manner as to narrow or eliminate the independent's margin or profit on wire rope. As to this latter disadvantage, for several years prior to the trial and at the same time of the trial the price of rope wire (the raw material) had been raised several times while the price of wire rope (the ultimate product) remained virtually constant. . . . The evidence established that the independents were caught in a price squeeze.[9]

FIG. 7-6. The Total Squeeze

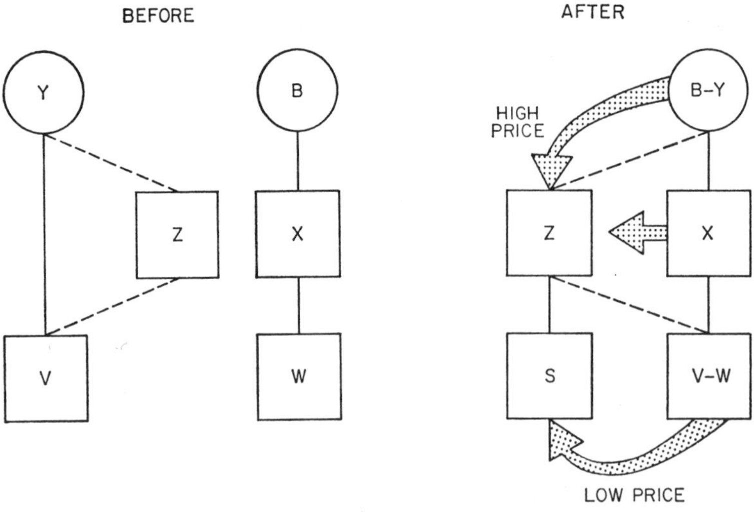

Unlike the price squeeze in the *Alcoa* case, where an integrated firm had almost complete control over the raw material supply for fabricators, the combination of Bethlehem-Youngstown did not have exclusive control over the raw material of rope *wire*.

The independent fabricators could purchase their supplies of rope *wire* from a number of other steel firms. However, Youngstown was one of only six companies in the United States which sold the raw material of rope *wire* without also fabricating wire *rope*. Youngstown was therefore one of the few suppliers which could not squeeze the independent fabricators of wire rope. The District Court concluded that "to remove Youngstown as a source of supply would render even more hazardous the competitive position of independents and might well mean the difference between their continued existence and their extinction."[10]

Youngstown, as a *seller* of the raw material rope wire, accounted for 12.5 per cent of the total rope *wire* shipments in 1955 consumed by companies which manufacture wire *rope* but do not produce their own wire. In the same year, Youngstown, as a *buyer*, purchased approximately 1.3 per cent of the shipments of the finished product of wire *rope*. Thus, Youngstown appeared to have an advantage in the rope *wire* market before its proposed merger with Bethlehem: It could use its position as a buyer of fabricated wire rope to influence its sales of wire to fabricators. This practice, known as "reciprocal buying," will be discussed in the next section.

Another competitive advantage of the proposed merger involved the loss of a significant customer to the independent fabricators. If Youngstown switched its purchases away from the independent fabricators and over to Bethlehem, the independents would be deprived of a significant customer. Since Bethlehem is a substantial producer of wire *rope*, a reasonable probability existed, in the opinion of the District Court, that Bethlehem would attempt to foreclose the independent fabricators from supplying the Bethlehem-Youngstown outlets with wire rope.

The elimination of Youngstown as a potential market for wire *rope* fabricated by independents is depicted in Fig. 7-6 by the arrow between squares X and Z. Before the merger, the independent fabricator Z supplied the Youngstown outlets V. After the merger, Youngstown outlets would be combined with the Bethlehem outlets (square V-W). The amount of sales between the independent fabricator Z and the integrated outlet V-W would tend to decrease as the independent fabricators were excluded. These vertical features of the case contributed to the finding by the District Court that the proposed merger between Bethlehem and Youngstown would tend to lessen competition substantially and violate Sec. 7 of the Clayton Act.

BUSINESS RECIPROCITY

Business reciprocity may be present where companies encounter each other in the dual capacities of buyer and seller. Reciprocal buying, for instance, covers an arrangement between firms that "We will buy from you, if you will buy from us."[11] The willingness of each company to purchase from the other is conditioned on the expectation of reciprocal purchases.

Basically, all economic transactions in a society involve a degree of reciprocity. A barter economy operates exclusively under a system of reciprocity, whereby every seller must of necessity be a buyer. In antitrust the practice of reciprocity generally includes an element of coercion: an involuntary conditioning of the sale of one product on the purchase of another.

In *Federal Trade Commission* v. *Consolidated Foods Corp.*[12] the Federal Trade Commission ordered the divestiture by Consolidated Foods, a large diversified processor and seller of food products, of the assets of an acquired company, Gentry, which was primarily engaged in the production of dehydrated onion and garlic. The Supreme Court found that the effect of the acquisition may be substantially to lessen competition in violation of Sec. 7 of the Clayton Act.

Since Consolidated was a substantial purchaser of the products of food processors, who in turn purchased dehydrated onion and garlic for use in preparing and packaging their foods, the opportunity for reciprocal buying was made possible by the acquisition. Gentry, prior to the acquisition by Consolidated, had 32 per cent of the total sales of the dehydrated garlic and onion industry. In dehydrated onion sales, Gentry's market share rose after its acquisition from 28 per cent in 1950 to 35 per cent in 1958. In dehydrated garlic sales, Gentry's market share fell during the same period from 51 per cent to 39 per cent of the industry total. The production of each of these two products more than doubled in the eight-year period following the acquisition.

The Federal Trade Commission rejected the argument made by Consolidated Foods that the decline in its share of the dehydrated garlic market proved the ineffectiveness of any practice of reciprocity. In the words of Commissioner Elman,

> We do not know that its share would not have fallen still farther, had it not been for the influence of reciprocal buying. This loss of sales fails to refute the likelihood that Consolidated's reciprocity power, which it has shown a willingness to exploit to the full, will not immunize a substantial segment of the garlic market from normal quality, price, and service competition.[13]

The Supreme Court agreed with the Federal Trade Commission that the acquisition may tend substantially to lessen competition as a result of the opportunity for reciprocity.

> We hold at the outset that the "reciprocity" made possible by such an acquisition is one of the congeries of anticompetitive practices at which the antitrust laws are aimed. The practice results in "an irrelevant and alien factor," . . . intruding into the choice among competing products, creating at the least "a priority on the business of equal prices."[14]

FIG. 7-7. Reciprocal Buying

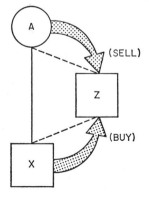

The *Consolidated Foods* case is depicted in terms of its vertically integrated market structure in Fig. 7-7. Circle *A* is the Gentry Division, which supplies dehydrated seasonings. Square *Z* is the independent food processor which purchases its seasoning requirements from Gentry, and then resells the processed item to Consolidated Foods, which acts as a distributor (square *X*).

The market setting in *Consolidated Foods* was different from that found in the *Bethlehem* case. First, the input of seasoning used by the processor *Z* was a small percentage of the total output cost of canned or packaged items. The supplier *A* could not squeeze the fabricator *Z* out of business, as alleged in the *Bethlehem* case, because the cost base of seasoning is but a minor part of the total cost base of the processed food items.

Second, the barriers to entry in the steel industry are not present in the dehydrated garlic and onion industry. In the *Bethlehem* case the independent wire rope fabricators could not be expected to undertake the construction of a steel mill in order to produce their own rope wire. There was evidence in the *Consolidated Foods* case that barriers to entry did not exist in the dehydrated spice industry. A new firm, Gilroy Foods, entered the industry during the litigation of the case. Even though there were only a few suppliers of these seasonings, no one of these suppliers could raise its prices unduly high without encouraging the large food processors to enter the industry and manufacture their own dehydrated spices.

The market practice of reciprocal buying is closely related to tying arrangements. In a tying arrangement a powerful seller in the market for the tying good may use its strength in this market to coerce a buyer to accept the tied good. In contrast, the act of reciprocal buying consists of a market for the "tying good" which is dominated by a purchaser, rather than a seller. But the "tied good" continues in the same posture as part of a seller's market. Consolidated Foods allegedly used its leverage as a strong buyer of food products to coerce its weak suppliers (such as small processors) to purchase their requirements for dehydrated seasoning from its Gentry Division. In view of the large number of firms and vast size of the food distribution industry, it may be questioned whether Consolidated Foods had a dominant position sufficient to coerce suppliers to purchase from its Gentry division.

TERRITORIAL RESTRICTIONS ON DEALERS

In *Continental T.V., Inc.* v. *GTE Sylvania, Inc.*, 433 U.S. 36 (1977), the Supreme Court was asked to review the practice of GTE-Sylvania, a manufacturer of television sets, in restricting its franchised dealers to sell Sylvania products only from locations at which it had a franchise. Continental T.V. had a franchise in California from GTE for its San Francisco store and asked for another franchise for a new store to be located in Sacramento. GTE denied the request on the grounds that the Sacramento area was already adequately served by another dealer. Continental then transferred some of its Sylvania sets, which were destined for its franchised San Francisco location, to its unfranchised Sacramento store. Sylvania terminated the franchise relationship for the San Francisco store and sued to collect monies owed to it by Continental. Continental defended the case by arguing that GTE-Sylvania violated Section 1 of the Sherman Act by "restraining trade" through its franchise agreements with dealers that limited sale of the products to specified franchise stores.

The Supreme Court held for GTE-Sylvania on the grounds that the restriction was a reasonable limitation for a manufacturer to impose on its dealers. In reaching this conclusion, the Supreme Court overruled its earlier decision, *U.S. v. Arnold, Schwinn & Co.*, 388 U.S. 365 (1967) which held that once title to a product passed from a manufacturer to a dealer, the manufacturer could not restrict the territory in which the product could be sold. Any such restrictions were deemed *per se* illegal. The one exception to the Schwinn rule was where a manufacturer was vertically integrated or held title and bore the risk of the goods in question. This exception was not present in GTE-Sylvania since title had clearly passed to Continental. The Court believed a more flexible rule was needed. In overruling Schwinn, the Court in *GTE-Sylvania* held that pure territorial restrictions, without any constraints on prices, should be analyzed under the rule of reason.

There are a number of factors which should be considered in a rule of reason analysis of non-price vertical restraints. First, the market power of the company imposing the restraint should be analyzed. Second, the effect on "*inter*brand competition" among various manufacturers; and third, the effect on "*intra*brand competition" among retailers selling products of the same manufacturer with the same brand name. In contrast to the Schwinn case where the defendant was the leading manufacturer of bicycles, *GTE-Sylvania* had a market share of only 2% and the industry leader, RCA, had a share of 60%-70%. Sylvania phased out its wholesalers and began a policy of selling only to a select group of franchised retailers. Sylvania argued that the territorial restrictions allowed it to attract more competent and aggressive retailers. However, the company retained the discretion to increase the number of retailers in an area in light of the success or failure of existing franchised retailers in developing their market. The marketing strategy was apparently successful since Sylvania was able to increase its national market share from 2% to approximately 5% in 1965. To the extent that these vertical constraints on territories improved the quality of franchised retailers, there was more "*inter*brand competition" for a marginal manufacturer, such as Sylvania, against larger manufacturers, such as RCA. The price, however, for the strengthened "*inter*brand competition", was a reduction in "*intra*brand competition" among retailers selling Sylvania products.

The *GTE-Sylvania* decision reflects a number of traditional concerns by the Supreme Court. The strict *per se* rule of Schwinn created an incentive for the vertical integration of manufacturers into the distribution system in order to space out competing retailers of their products. A marginal manufacturer, such as Sylvania, could not afford to integrate forward into retailing or to maintain company operated service centers. The rule of reason of the *GTE-Sylvania* case permitted evidence to be introduced which showed the position of a manufacturer was improved to the extent that stronger retail dealers were obtained. Similarly, the position of franchised retailers were improved to the extent that they were insulated from nearby stores selling the same product. Both from the point of view of the weak manufacturer or the vulnerable retailer, the theme of *GTE-Sylvania* is protectionism and, paradoxically, it is done in the name of competition. Namely, the Supreme Court implicity accepted the proposition that unless some vertical territorial constraints were allowed, there will be fewer retailers and manufacturers surviving in the long run.

NOTE APPENDIX D: ECONOMIC THEORY OF VERTICAL INTEGRATION

ENDNOTES

1. 362 U.S. 458 (1960).
2. F. Kessler and R. H. Stern, "Competition, Contract, and Vertical Integration," *Yale Law Journal*, Vol. LXIX (November, 1959), p. 73.
3. 148 F. 2nd 416 (2nd Cir., 1945). Also see 91 F. Supp. 333 (S.D.N.Y., 1950) for the remedial part of the case.
4. 148 F. 2nd 416, 438 (1945).
5. 340 U.S. 231 (1951). See J. McGee, "Price Discrimination and Competitive Effects: The Standard Oil of Indiana Case," *University of Chicago Law Review*, Vol. XXIII (Spring, 1956), pp. 398-473; and Note, *Harvard Law Review*, Vol. LXVII (December, 1953), pp. 294-317.
6. F. Rowe, *Price Discrimination Under the Robinson-Patman Act*, (Boston: Little, Brown & Company, 1962), pp. 217-219, 544; G. A. Birrell, "The Integrated Company and the Price 'Squeeze' under the Sherman Act and Section 2(a) of the Clayton Act, As Amended," *Notre Dame Lawyer*, Vol. XXXII (December, 1956), p. 21; A. E. Sawyer, *Business Aspects of Pricing Under the Robinson-Patman Act*, Trade Regulation Series (Boston: Little, Brown & Company, 1962); and H. Taggart, *Cost Justification* (Ann Arbor, Mich.: University of Michigan Press, 1959).
7. *Federal Trade Commission* v. *Standard Oil*, 355 U.S. 396 (1958). Section 2(b) of the Robinson-Patman Act, which covers the good faith "meeting competition" defense, provides in part: ". . .that nothing herein contained shall prevent a seller from rebutting the prima-facie case thus made by showing that his lower price or the furnishing of services of facilities to any purchaser or purchasers was made in good faith to meet an equally low price of a competitor, or the services or facilities furnished by a competitor."
8. 168 F. Supp. 576 (S.D.N.Y., 1958). Also see M. A. Adelman, "Economic Aspects off the Bethlehem Opinion," *Virginia Law Review*, Vol. XLV (June, 1959), p. 684; and L. S. Keyes, "The Bethlehem-Youngstown Case and the Market Share Criterion," *American Economic Review*, Vol. LI (September, 1961), p. 653.
9. 168 F. Supp. 576, p. 612.
10. *Ibid.*, p. 613.
11. B. Bock, "Mergers and Reciprocity," *Conference Board Record*, Vol. II (July, 1965), pp. 27-36; C. Edwards, "Conglomerate Bigness as a Source of Power," in *Business Concentration and Price Policy*, Universities-National Bureau Committee for Economic Research (Princeton, N.J.: Princeton University Press, 1955), especially pp. 342-45; J. Ferguson, "Tying Arrangements and Reciprocity: An Economic Analysis," *Law and Contemporary Problems*, Vol. XXX (Summer, 1965), pp. 552-580; M. Handler, "Gilding the Philosophic Pill — Trading Bows for Arrows," *Columbia Law Review*, Vol. LXVI (January, 1966), pp. 1-11; and G. Stocking and W. Mueller, "Business Reciprocity and the Size of Firms," *Journal of Business*, Vol. XXX (April, 1957), pp. 73-95.
12. 380 U.S. 592 (1964).
13. Docket No. 7000, Opinion of the Commission (November 15, 1962), p. 19 of the mimeographed text.
14. 380 U.S. 592, 594 (1964).

THOUGHT QUESTIONS

1. If the vertically integrated company follows a quota system in times of shortages based on prior year purchases, what provision should be made for new entrants in the industry or for new customers? Must the vertically integrated firm put its own subsidiaries and outlets on a similar quota system?
2. Suppose a vertically integrated company decides as a marketing strategy to lower the price of its final product in order to increase substantially its output and lower its per unit costs of production. If the expected increase in demand is not forthcoming, and therefore its per unit cost of production is not lowered, should the company be charged

with deliberately selling its product below its average cost? If the company held a dominant position, would your answer be different?

3. In the *Alcoa* case, do you believe that Alcoa was lowering its prices for aluminum sheet to destroy aluminum fabricators or was it meeting the competitively low prices being charged by these fabricators? Does it make sense that Alcoa was trying to destroy its ingot customers by undercutting them in the sheet market if Alcoa really had the easier alternative of simply raising the ingot price?

4. In the *Alcoa* case, the Court suggests that otherwise lawful practices of Alcoa became unlawful once Alcoa was put on notice that the survival of independent sheet rollers were in danger. Is the Court suggesting that Alcoa should not compete "too hard;" and that Alcoa should keep its sheet prices high so that all the independent fabricators can earn healthy profit margins?

5. Do you believe Alcoa's policy of keeping fabricated product prices low and earning a low rate of return was a result of competition from steel, or a result of a corporate policy not to maximize profits?

6. There have been no cases brought involving reciprocity for almost a decade. Do you believe that the practice has, on balance, been more pro-competitive than anti-competitive? Is "reciprocity" an example of good public relations and reciprocal forms of appreciation?

7. Do you believe the effect of the *GTE-Sylvania* case was to raise the price of TV sets to consumers by stopping nearby stores from selling the same brand product?

8. Discuss whether the existence of territorial restrictions on dealers is a national waste of gasoline since consumers have to travel farther to find a dealer in another territory who may offer a lower price.

9. Discuss whether the practice of a vertically integrated firm undercutting the price being charged by independent fabricators is not a reflection of vertical integration but only of the disparate size of the two companies?

10. Discuss whether some independent fabricators may have lower production and marketing costs than the larger vertically integrated firms with more expensive offices, higher executive salaries and extra burdens, such as corporate jet planes.

8

TYING ARRANGEMENTS

ECONOMIC RATIONALE FOR TYING ARRANGEMENTS

Tying arrangements are among the most elementary market practices whereby a firm operates simultaneously in more than one market for the purpose of increasing its aggregate profit. The practice is, therefore, a useful starting point for analyzing the behavior of multiple product firms. The typical tying arrangement either conditions the sale of one commodity (tying good) on the sale of another (tied good), or conditions the lease of a machine on the use of supplies or services furnished by the lessor. The practice of tying goods together is implicit in other business practices, such as full-line forcing, where a seller presses his complete line of different products on a buyer predominantly interested in only a given product.

PRICE EVASION

A prominent motive for employing tying arrangements during war years, when administrative price controls were imposed, was the evasion of price ceilings. Ceiling prices on rationed items prevented manufacturers and retailers from setting an otherwise higher profit-maximizing price. However, buyers could be coerced often to purchase under a tying arrangement an unregulated item. The portion of "lost profit" due to the ceiling on the tying good could be recouped by the higher price on the tied good.[1] Analogously, a firm not wanting to upset an oligopoly price structure in one market might employ a tying arrangement as an alternative to changing its price.[2]

PROTECTION OF GOODWILL

A manufacturer may tie a service contract, including repair parts, with the sale or lease of its machines in order to preserve the goodwill associated with its product. For example, a manufacturer of electronic equipment used on antenna sites of television stations tied the servicing of its equipment in the contract of sale, and offered as a justification of the tying arrangement that the industry was new and the equipment was so specialized that anyone not trained by the company and familiar with the particular equipment could cause tremendous damage to the whole antenna site.[3,4] However, IBM was not allowed to tie the requirement for the purchase of its own tabulating cards with the leases of its computers.[5] The Supreme Court held that the company could adequately safeguard its goodwill by conditioning its leases on the use of cards that met reasonably high specifications.[6]

ECONOMIES OF PRODUCTION OR DISTRIBUTION

Economies of production through tying arrangements include almost all assembled products. A radio, for example, is theoretically a tying arrangement of semi-conductors and resistors. However, the functional necessity for all the parts excludes the radio from the tying arrangement nomenclature.[7,8]

PRICE DISCRIMINATION[9]

In two early patent cases the courts were faced with a patented machine licensed practically at cost with a restriction that the machine be used only with supplies furnished by the patent holder.[10] The patent holder made almost his entire profit not from the machine but from the *unpatented* supplies, which were buttons in one case, and mimeograph ink and paper in the other. Customers using the machines more intensively required a greater quantity of supplies, and thereby allowed the owner to derive a greater profit from them through the sale of supplies, which were priced above their marginal costs. Thus, the tying arrangement in effect required these customers to pay a higher price. In the words of Professor Burstein, "the tied good in these cases serves very much as a counting or metering device; the tying arrangement results in streams of payments flowing from the users of the machine to its seller (or lessor) with the rates of flow being directly proportional to the intensity of use of the machine. Those using the machine more intensively are paying more; *price discrimination* is being achieved."[11] The courts have rejected generally the defense that there exists no alternative profitable means for marketing a patented machine other than a tying arrangement.[12]

ECONOMIC LEVERAGE

"The essence of illegality in tying arrangements," in the words of the Supreme Court, "is the wielding of monopolistic leverage; a seller exploits his dominant position in one market to expand his empire into the next."[13] A firm by virtue of a tying arrangement increases its share of the tied-good market and gains the power to set the price of the tied product with respect to those customers purchasing its tying product. But the firm does not necessarily obtain the power to set the price in the general market for the tied product, which includes purchasers not accepting the tying arrangement. Therefore, the courts speak of a "limited" or "partial" monopoly in the tied good market.[14]

Professor Bowman makes the distinction between leverage as a revenue-maximizing device and leverage as a monopoly-creating device. "The first involves the use of existing power. The second requires the addition of new power. . . . If the tying seller is maximizing his return on the tying product and the same output of the tied product can still be produced under circumstances consistent with competitive production of the tied product, no additional or new monopoly effect should be assumed."[15] The finding by both Professors Bowman and Burstein, that tying arrangements do not necessarily extend the tying product monopoly into a second monopoly over the tied-good market, is instrumental in their reaching substantially the same conclusion, namely, that the law should favor tying arrangements in certain cases where only incidental effects exist in the market for the tied product.

In the *Motion Picture Patents* case[16] the plaintiff held a patent covering a mechanism used in motion picture projectors for feeding film at a smooth and uniform rate. Projectors with this mechanism had a notice attached to them restricting the use of the machine to motion pictures obtained from a licensee of the patentee. The plaintiff-patentee was denied relief against the defendants, who were manufacturing motion pictures and exhibiting them in projectors embodying the plaintiff's patented feeding mechanism. The Supreme Court held that "it is not competent for the owner of a patent, by a notice attached to its machine, to, in effect, *extend the scope of its patented monopoly* by restricting the use of it to materials necessary in its operation, but which are no part of the patented invention. . ."[17]

Although the plaintiff's argument was unsuccessful in the *Motion Picture Patents* case, it is important in the analysis of leverage and tying arrangements. The Court summarized the plaintiff's argument as follows:

> It is argued as a merit of this system of sale under a license notice that the public is benefited by the sale of the machine at what is practically its cost, and by the fact that the owner of the patent makes its entire profit from the sales of the supplies with which it is operated. This fact, if it be a fact, instead of commending, is the clearest possible condemnation of the practice adopted, for it proves that under color of its patent, the owner intends to and does derive its profit, not from the invention on which the law gives it a monopoly, but from the unpatented supplies with which it is used, and which are wholly without the scope of the patent monopoly, . . .[18]

Justice Holmes, in his dissent from the majority decision in the *Motion Picture Patents* case, contended that since the law gives the patentee the right to withhold his invention unconditionally from the public, he should be allowed the less severe alternative of *conditionally* withholding his patent. A typical condition would be that the patented machine can only be used in conjunction with unpatented supplies purchased from the patentee. Justice Holmes maintained that the tying arrangement allowed the patentee to obtain what he was rightfully entitled to under the patent law:

> But there is no predominant public interest to prevent a patented teapot or film feeder from being kept from the public, because, as I have said, the patentee may keep them tied up at will while his patent lasts. Neither is there any such interest to prevent the purchase of the tea or films that is made the condition of the use of the machine. The supposed contravention of public interest sometimes is stated as an attempt to extend the patent law to unpatented articles, which of course it is not, and more accurately as a possible domination to be established by such means. But the

108

domination is one only to the extent of the desire for the teapot or film feeder, and if the owner prefers to keep the pot or the feeder unless you will buy his tea or films, I cannot see in allowing him the right to do so anything more than an ordinary incident of ownership, . . .[19]

The arguments of the majority and dissenting opinions in the *Motion Picture Patents* decision are presented in Fig. 8-1. Case I suggests a tying arrangement in which the firm earns no more profit from the tying product (II_a) and the tied product (II_b) than it could have earned by selling these products separately. Case II shows a tying arrangement in which the firm decides to take all profit in the tied-good market and sell the tying good at cost. The firm earns the same profit in the tied product B market ($II_a + II_b$) as it formerly earned on a combined basis in the product A market (II_a) and the product B market (II_b). Case III shows a firm earning by virtue of a tying arrangement additional profit (II_*) that it could not have earned if the products were sold separately.

FIG. 8-1. Manipulation of Profit Between the Markets for the Tying and the Tied Goods

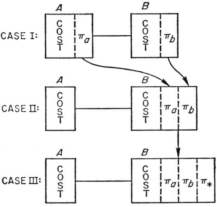

If the tying and tied products are sold in *fixed* proportions, such as one unit of product A always being tied to one unit of product B, the division of the joint demand into separate demand curves for the tying and tied products is not meaningful. It makes no difference to a purchaser of a pair of gloves to know that the left glove is the same price or more expensive than the right one. Consequently, demand analysis of the case of fixed proportions is more appropriately considered on an aggregate basis. However, in the case of *variable* proportions the demands for the tying and tied goods should be considered separately. The firm will increase its profits from the sale of the tied good; by raising its price for this product above the competitive rate, but the firm will suffer a reduction of profits from the sale of the tying good. The tying arrangement will be an economically rational mode of conduct, provided the decrease in profits from the sale of the tying good is more than compensated by increased profits from the sale of the tied good.

The term "leverage," in the words of Professor Bowman, "specifically describes the establishment of a new or second monopoly. The existence of such leverage depends upon the effect of the tying arrangement on the output of the tied product. If the tying seller is maximizing his return on the tying product, and the same output of the tied product can still be produced under circumstances consistent with competitive production of the tied product, no additional or new monopoly effect should be assumed.''[20] In the case of complements used in variable proportions, the output of the tied good for use with the tying good will be less than it would be if the tied good were sold competiti el. This restriction on the supply of the tied good is deemed an exercise of economic leverage.

The power held over a tied good in the complementary demand case can be seen as an incident of the monopoly of product A, which carries a certain amount of power over product B for its uses with Product A. The additional profits (II_*) earned by the firm in tying together products with complementary demands used in variable proportions, giving monopoly in the tied-good market only to the extent of the desire for the tying-good. The position of Justice Holmes is that the holder of a tying-good monopoly is entitled, as an incident of his ownership, to *all* the additional II_* profit resulting from complementarity with a tied good. In recent antitrust law cases, the contrary position is generally the rule: the tying monopolist is entitled to *none* of the additional II_* profits of the tied good which was gained by the extension of its power over the tying good.

THE *PER SE* RULE FOR TYING ARRANGEMENTS

The Supreme Court summarized the present standard of *per se* illegality applying to tying arrangements in the *Northern Pacific* case,[21] which involved a railroad company's "preferential routing" clause requiring lessees of its land to ship over its railroad all commodities produced on the land provided that its rates were equal to those of competing carriers:

> They are unreasonable in and of themselves whenever a party has sufficient economic power with respect to the tying product to appreciably restrain free competition in the market for the tied product and a 'not insubstantial' amount of interstate commerce is affected.

The Court appears to be stating the following equation for finding tying arrangements *per se* violations of the antitrust laws.

(1) Economic power in the market for the tying goods, *plus*

(2) substantial commerce in the tied goods, *equals*

(3) a *per se* violation of the antitrust laws.

When this apparently straightforward *per se* equation is applied by courts to cases involving tying arrangements, a brief answer is seldom forthcoming. Indeed, the evidence required for part (1) of the equation suggests a discussion of the available economic evidence in what might appear to be a *rule of reason* approach.

In the extreme form of the *per se* doctrine, there is no need to examine the purpose or justification for the actions of the defendant. In the words of Justice Black,

> . . . there are certain practices which because of their pernicious effect on competition and lack of any redeeming virtue are conclusively presumed to be unreasonable and therefore illegal without elaborate inquiry as to the precise harm they have caused or the business excuse for their use. This principle of *per se* unreasonableness not only makes the type of restraints which are proscribed by the Sherman Act more certain to

the benefit of everyone concerned, but it also avoids the necessity for an incredibly complicated and prolonged economic investigation into the entire history of the industry involved, as well as related industries, in an effort to determine at large whether a particular restraint has been unreasonable — an inquiry so often fruitless when undertaken.[22]

The tying arrangement is classified by Justice Black as an example of *per se* unreasonableness. Therefore, it might be concluded that once a contract containing tying clauses is introduced and accepted in evidence, a *per se* violation of the antitrust laws is established. But the courts are following a different standard of illegality, since there invariably is made an inspection of both the degree of market power over the tying good, and the substantiality of commerce affected in the market for the tied good.[23]

INDICIA OF ECONOMIC LEVERAGE

One concept is fundamental to an economic analysis of tying arrangements: leverage cannot be wielded over the market for the tied good without the existence of substantial economic power over the tying-good market. Courts must look at economic evidence for the empirical content of words such as "dominance," "exploitation," "leverage," or "market," which appear in the previously discussed Supreme Court rule that,

> . . . the essence of illegality in tying arrangements is the wielding of monopolistic leverage; a seller exploits his dominant position in one market to expand his empire into the next.[24]

The following indicia of economic power over the market for the tying good are useful in determining whether there exists a "wielding of monopolistic leverage." These indicia also illustrate the breadth of evidence present in tying arrangement cases.

MARKET DOMINANCE

The phrase "market dominance" is described by the Supreme Court as referring to "some power to control price and to exclude competition."[25] The presence of dominance in the market for the tying goods forebodes almost certain illegality for the practices of the defendant, provided a substantial amount of commerce is affected in the tied-good market. However, the prerequisite economic power over the tying-good market for illegality can be considerably less than market domination. "Even absent a showing of market dominance, the crucial economic power may be inferred from the tying product's desirability to consumers or from the uniqueness in its attributes."[26]

DESIRABILITY OF THE TYING GOOD

Since customers will seldom purchase a product which appears undesirable to them, the equating of economic power with the desirability of a product is a circular way of invariably finding the crucial market power in the tying good. For example, in *United States* v. *Jerrold Electronics Co.*,[27] which permitted, for a temporary period of time, a tying arrangement of service contracts with community television antenna systems, the District Court stated:

> Jerrold's highly specialized head end equipment for antennas was in great demand — in fact it was the only equipment available which was designed to meet all of the varying problems arising at the antenna site. This placed Jerrold in a strategic position and gave it the leverage necessary to persuade customers to agree to its service contracts. This leverage constitutes "economic power" sufficient to invoke the doctrine of *per se* unreasonableness.[28]

UNDESIRABILITY OF THE TIED GOOD

The "coercion theory" of tying arrangements focuses on the comparative bargaining power of the parties. In the usual tying arrangement a customer is required to take a product or brand which he does not necessarily want in order to secure one which he desires.[29] "By conditioning his sale of one commodity on the purchase of another, a seller coerces the abdication of buyers' independent judgment as to the 'tied' product's merits . . ."[30]

The case of a dealer being subjected to a tying arrangement can be distinguished from the consumer facing a tying arrangement involving a trivial expenditure. In *Standard Oil Co. (Calif.)* v. *United States*, commonly referred to as *Standard Stations*,[31] there were 5,937 gasoline stations, constituting 16 per cent of the relevant market, which entered into exclusive requirements contracts with Standard Oil of California. Since the lease of a gas station generally commits the average proprietor to a substantial amount of his savings, it would be unwise for him to risk his whole business by not complying with the tying arrangements imposed by the lessor-supplier. A related area involves the sale of tires, batteries, and accessories (TBA) to dealers by the major oil companies.[32] The coercion exerted on a lessee or franchise holder is of far greater magnitude than the pressure found in the consumer tying arrangements, such as where an individual is required to purchase an undesirable cologne with a favorite shaving lather.

The coercion theory is also suggested by the Supreme Court's analysis in the *Loew's* case.[33] Large distributors of feature motion pictures were found to have violated Sec. 1 of the Sherman Act by their practice of block booking. The gist of the offense was seen as the forcing of small independent television stations into acceptance of inferior films along with desirable pictures.

In contrast, the Supreme Court in the *Tampa Electric* case[34] allowed a long-term requirements contract for one million tons of coal annually for a period of 20 years. Both parties were extremely large concerns, and there was evidence that the contract was negotiated at the customer's behest to insure a sufficient supply of coal for a newly constructed electric power plant. Although the Court did not rest its conclusion solely on this finding, and the case did not involve a tying arrangement, the attention paid to the relative strength of the parties indicates that the "coercion theory" is part of the prerequisite analysis for the broader category of exclusive arrangements.

The undesirability of the tied product to the buyer is sometimes obvious from the initial facts. In these cases the Court presumes the existence of economic power over tying goods.[35]

BARRIERS TO ENTRY

One of the first cases to be brought under Sec. 3 of the Clayton Act raised the issue of barriers to entry as a factor to be considered in tying arrangements. In *Federal Trade Commission* v. *Sinclair Refining Co.*,[36] the Supreme Court allowed Sinclair as well as thirty other refiners to continue the practice of leasing underground tanks to gasoline stations at a minimal rental, upon the condition that the equipment should be used only for the storage of gasoline supplied by the lessor. The Court was impressed by the lowering of barriers to entry at the retail level. The practice of leasing allowed an individual to open a gasoline station with a comparatively small capital investment.

Barriers to entry have been viewed by some writers as the principal evil of tying arrangements. In the words of Professors Turner and Kaysen:

> A tie-in always operates to raise the barriers to entry in the market of the tied good to the level of those in the market for the tying good: the seller who would supply the one, can do so only if he can also supply the other, since he must be able to displace the whole package which the tying seller offers. Developing a substitute for the tying product may be very difficult, if not impossible. Thus tying tends to spread market power into markets where it would not otherwise exist: for example, few firms are prepared to supply machines like those of IBM, whereas many may be prepared to supply punch cards.[37]

The lowering of barriers to entry is one of the few exceptions to the general proscription against tying devices. In *Brown Shoe Co.* v. *United States*[38] the Supreme Court stated, "unless the tying device is employed by a small company in an attempt to break into a market, . . . the use of a tying device can rarely be harmonized with the strictures of the antitrust laws, which are intended primarily to preserve and stimulate competition."

PATENTS, TRADEMARKS OR COPYRIGHTS COVERING THE TYING GOOD

The courts have condemned any attempt by the patentee to extend a patent beyond his invention into markets for unpatented goods. The patentee is seldom attempting to monopolize the market for the tied good, and in some instances, appears to be sacrificing some of his potential profit from the tying-good market and making it up in the market for the tied good. Consequently, neither monopoly power nor profits are necessarily increased by the patentee tying unpatented goods to his patent.

Tying arrangements between patented and unpatented items are presumed to be illegal under present antitrust decisions. This presumption grew out of the doctrine holding that a patentee who utilizes tying arrangements to sell supplies and related machinery would be denied relief against infringement of his patent.[39] Implicit in the presumption is the belief that since a patent or copyright is a statutory monopoly, it follows that each must also be a market monopoly. But all patents do not confer substantial or even significant market power. Nevertheless, the law today is that the "requisite economic power is presumed when the tying product is patented or copyrighted."[40]

In *Siegel* v. *Chicken Delight, Inc.*, 448F. 2d. 43 (1971) the Court of Appeals held that the franchisees of the fast-food chain were entitled to damages against their parent company requirement that they purchase a specified number of cookers, fryers, packaging supplies and mixes from Chicken Delight as a condition for being licensed to use the Chicken Delight trademark. Since Chicken Delight charges its franchisees no fee, its profit was based on the percentage mark-up on supplies which it sold to them. Consequently, the franchisees could obtain comparable supplies from outside sources at lower prices. Chicken Delight, on the other hand, would be denied compensation for its marketing concept, the specification for its mixes and the know-how for the preparation of the chicken. The Court of Appeals held that the presumption of illegality that exists in the case of patents and copyright should also apply to the trademark.

Chicken Delight was not allowed to tie the supplies, such as cooking machinery, and dip and spice mixes, to the use of its licensed trademark. A jury in the District Court found that the specifications for seasoning and equipment could be obtained from outside sources by the licensees without loss of quality control by Chicken Delight. The trademark related not to what was used (the mixes and spices), but the formula and how the supplies were used in the preparation of the finished product. Therefore, the supplies and the trademark were held as not constituting an inseparable product being sold as originating from the parent, Chicken Delight.

In contrast to the *Chicken Delight* case, a Chevrolet dealer would not be permitted to substitute engines not manufactured by General Motors in a Chevrolet. However, the dealer could substitute lesser accessories, such as radios or tires which are not an integral part of the unit designed and manufactured and being claimed as originating from General Motors. Whether General Motors has the flexibility to switch engines itself among different models was open to question, and privately settled, when a large number of customers objected to having engines from different General Motor models substituted in their cars.

THE REQUIREMENT FOR TWO PRODUCTS

The early tying arrangement cases involved two physically distinct products, generally a patented machine and unpatented supplies used in the machine. In more recent tying arrangement cases, there have been questions raised as to whether there are two products involved, or alternatively, different aspects or components of one product. In the *Chicken Delight* case, the defendant-franchisor argued, unsuccessfully, that its trademark was not separate from its spices, mixes and cooking equipment.

IBM provided until 1969 free software to customers leasing their computers. Initially, customers were reluctant to purchase a computer without obtaining the extensive programming required to make the computer operate as a system. The bundling of the software and hardware could be justified as a necessity for a pioneer to enter a fledgling industry. The tied product was not forced upon customers but demanded by most of them. As the computer market grew, the availability of software consultants expanded as well as the internal programming staffs of companies. Smaller computer manufacturers of hardware complained of the handicap in having to provide free software to be competitive with the leading companies. The free software provided by leaders, such as IBM, was "unbundled'' from the hardware. Software also became recognized by the U.S. Patent Office as an item which could be covered by a copyright. This further encouraged the commercial development of a software industry. Thus, in the early development of an industry a tying arrangement may not be an exercise of leverage, but a complementary service or product required for the initial entry, development and operation of a system.

In the *Telex* case the issue was raised as to whether IBM was free to change the design of its computers in such a manner that it would be impossible for competing manufacturers of peripherals, such as discs and tape drives, to be plugged into the central processing units of certain IBM computers.[41] The issue in the Telex case was raised in the context of the intent of IBM to monopolize a segment of the computer industry. But the fundamental question is still what constitutes a necessary system design versus separable components. An analysis is required of the changing market in terms of availability of supply, quality standards and concern for the survival of smaller companies. The definition of what constitutes a single product in a tying arrangement correspondingly may have to change with its economic environment.

THE FORTNER CASES (1969; 1977)

In one of the more contradictory cases in antitrust law, the Supreme Court considered whether the availability of a low interest financial loan was a tie-in with the sale of a product. In *Fortner Enterprises, Inc.* v. *U.S. Steel Corp.*, (1969) and (1977),[42] the Supreme Court wrote two separate opinions concerning the question whether U.S. Steel engaged in a tying arrangement by lending a small housing developer mortgage money at 6% interest with which to build prefabricated homes with materials sold by a subsidiary of U.S. Steel. The developer, in 1960, purchased only $190,000 in prefabricated houses from U.S. Steel and defaulted on the loan. From 1960 to 1977, U.S. Steel had to litigate whether its actions constituted a tying arrangement or merely a reduction in the price of prefabricated houses which it was finding difficult to sell without ancillary financing. In the 1969 opinion, Justice Black, who also wrote the *Northern Pacific* opinion ten years earlier, found that the conduct challenged ''involved a tying arrangement of the traditional kind.'' The tied product was the prefabricated houses and the tying good was the inexpensive development loan. The Supreme Court held that the case should go to trial in the lower court on the issue as to whether U.S. Steel had some ''special economic power in the credit market.'' Justice Black found ''no basis for treating credit differently in principle from other goods and services.'' The Court noted,

> If the larger companies have achieved economies of scale in their credit operations, they. . .should not, any more than economies in other lines of business, be used to exert economic power over other products that the company produces no more efficiently than its competitors.

Two separate dissenting opinions found no evidence of market power by U.S. Steel over the tying product, namely, the credit market. U.S. Steel was not selling credit in any general sense as a banking institution. The financing provided was solely for the sale of prefabricated houses. The cutting of prices on loans was not a reflection of market power in the credit market, but of weakness in the market for prefabricated homes. In the words of the dissent written by Justice White,

> Cutting prices in the credit market is more likely to reflect a competitive attempt to offset the market power of others in the tied product than it is to reflect existing market power in the credit market. Those with real power do not offer uniquely advantageous deals to their customers; they raise prices.

In 1977 the Supreme Court in a unanimous opinion agreed with the earlier dissenting opinions in 1969 that there was no tying arrangement and only one product. The loan was an integral part of the sale of the prefabricated house and its low rate was functionally equivalent to a reduction in the price of the prefabricated houses sold. This conclusion by the Supreme Court in 1977 may appear to be somewhat obvious. A discouraging part of the case was the fact that Fortner Enterprises was a dormant corporation in 1960 with a $16,000 deficit, and was not even authorized to engage in building or the real estate business. It was owned entirely by one person who, not surprisingly with these facts, had difficulty obtaining financing. U.S. Steel extended credit to this company in order to sell their prefabricated homes. Fortner Enterprises defaulted on the loan and, in another action, U.S. Steel sought to obtain a judgment against Fortner, and foreclose its mortgage on the prefabricated homes.[43] It is a sad commentary that the judicial system had to witness 17 years of litigation and bear the cost of two Supreme Court decisions for Fortner to argue whether he was liable for paying U.S. Steel $190,000 for the receipt of materials purchased on credit.

ENDNOTES

1. Bowman, "Tying Arrangements and the Leverage Problem," *Yale Law Journal*, Vol. LXVII (November, 1957), pp. 19-36.
2. M. L. Burstein, "A Theory of Full-Line Forcing," *Northwestern University Law Review*, Vol. LV (February, 1960), p. 67. For a mathematical treatment of tying arrangements see Burstein, "The Economics of Tie-In Sales," *Review of Economics and Statistics*, Vol. XLII (February, 1960), pp. 68-73. Subsequent references to Burstein are to the former article.
3. *United States v. Jerrold Electronics Co.*, 187 F. Supp. 545 (E.D. Pa., 1960), *affirmed per curiam*, 365 U.S. 567 (1961). The service contracts were allowed for several years until outside technicians were trained by the company.
4. *Pick Mfg. Co. v. General Motors Corp.*, 80 F. 2nd 641 (7th Cir., 1935), *affirmed per curiam*, 299 U.S. 3 (1936).
5. Hale and Hale, *Market Power: Size and Shape Under The Sherman Act.*, p. 273.
6. *International Business Machines Corp. v. United States*, 298 U.S. 131 (1936). Also see United States, *Report of the Attorney General's National Committee to Study the Antitrust Laws* (Washington, D.C.: Government Printing Office, 1955), p. 139.
7. D. Turner, "The Validity of Tying Arrangements Under the Antitrust Laws," *Harvard Law Review*, Vol. LXXXII (November, 1958), 50-75. Compare *Mercoid Corp. v. Mid-Continent Investment Co.*, 320., U.S. 661 (1944).
8. Bowman, "Tying Arrangements and the Leverage Problem," p. 29.
9. For a general discussion of price discrimination see Robinson, *The Economics of Imperfect Competition*, pp. 179-202; and Machlup, "Characteristics and Types of Price Discrimination," pp. 397-435.
10. *Heaton Peninsular Button-Fastener Co. v. Eureka Specialty Co.*, 77 F. 288 (6th Cir., 1896) and *Henry v. A. B. Dick*, 224 U.S. 1 (1912). These decisions, which were rendered before the

enactment of the Clayton Act in 1914, allowed the patentee to restrain another individual (called a contributory infringer) from selling unpatented supplies to its licensees. The decisions were later repudiated by the courts. See *Motion Picture Patents Co.* v. *Universal Film Mfg. Co.*, 243 U.S. 502 (1917), which overruled the *A.B. Dick* case, *supra*. The patent misuse doctrine, first stated in the *Motion Picture Patents* case, denies protection against direct and contributory infringement where the patentee employs a tying arrangement as a means for restraining competition in the unpatented product or supplies. Note *Morton Salt Co.* v. *Suppiger*, 314 U.S. 488 (1942); and *Attorney General's Report*, pp. 250-259.

11. Burstein, "A Theory of Full-line Forcing," pp. 64-65. Also see A. Director and E. H. Levi, "Law and the Future: Trade Regulation," *Northwestern University Law Review*, Vol. LI (May-June, 1956), 281-92, at p. 291; and G. W. Hilton, "Tying Sales and Full-Line Forcing," *Weltwirtschaftliches Archiv*, Vol. LXXXI (1958), 265-76.

12. *B.B. Chemical Co.* v. *Ellis*, 314 U.S. 495 (1942).

13. *Times-Picayune Publishing Co.* v. *United States*, 345 U.S. 594, 611 (1953).

14. Burstein, "A Theory of Full-line Forcing," pp. 63-64, discards "the simple and natural view, so favored by the courts, that full-line forces and tie-in sales are primarily for the purpose of extension of monopoly into new markets," because, he argues, *full* monopolies seldom exist in the tied-good market. He asks, "Can it sensibly be accepted that G.S. Suppiger Co. tied salt to its salt dispensing machinery as part of a scheme to monopolize the American salt market? Did Morgan Envelope Co. tie its toilet paper to its dispenser as part of a grand scheme to monopolize the American bathroom tissue market? Why do we see again and again in the court reports cases involving the tying of rivets, staples, windshield wipers, repair parts, varnish, etc. when the tying monopolist's share of the market for the tied product remains miniscule? The game is afoot, and the extension-of-monopoly hypothesis is surely a rusty flintlock!" (footnotes omitted). References in the quotation are to *Morton Salt Co.* v. *Suppiger Co.*, 314 U.S. 488 (1942) and *Morgan Envelope Co.* v. *Albany Perforated Paper Co.*, 52 U.S. 425 (1893).

15. Bowman, "Tying Arrangements and the Leverage Problem," pp. 19-20.

16. *Motion Picture Patents Co.* v. *Universal Film Mfg. Co.*, 243 U.S. 502 (1917).

17. *Ibid.*, p. 516 (italics added).

18. *Ibid.*, pp. 516-17.

19. *Ibid.*, p. 520.

20. *Ibid.*, p. 20. Reprinted by permission of the Yale Law Journal Company and Fred B. Rothman & Company. Footnotes omitted from quotation.

21. *Northern Pacific Railway Co.* v. *United States*, 356 U.S. 1, 6 (1958).

22. *Northern Pacific Railway Co.* v. *United States*, 356 U.S. 1, 5 (1958).

23. Cf. W. L. Baldwin and D. McFarland, "Some Observations on 'Per Se' and Tying Arrangements," *Antitrust Bulletin*, Vol. VI (July-December, 1961), 433-39, and "Tying Arrangements in Law and Economics," *ibid.*, Vol. VIII (September-December, 1963), pp. 743-80. Also see J.C. Stedman, "Tying Arrangements," *American Bar Association Section of Antitrust Law*, Vol. XXII (April, 1963), 64-73; Phillips, *Market Structure, Organization, and Performance*, pp. 199-242; and W. B. Lockhart and H. R. Sacks, "The Relevance of Economic Factors in Determining Whether Exclusive Arrangements Violate Section 3 of the Clayton Act," *Harvard Law Review*, Vol. LVX (April, 1952), 919-42.

24. *Times-Picayune Publishing Co.* v. *United States*, 345 U.S. 594, 611 (1953).

25. *United States* v. *Loew's Inc.*, 371 U.S. 38, 45 (1962).

26. *Ibid.*, p. 45. Also see Turner, "The Validity of Tying Arrangements Under the Antitrust Laws," pp. 50-75.

27. 187 F. Supp. 545, 555 (E.D. Pa., 1960), *affirmed per curiam*, 365 U.S. 567 (1961).

28. *Ibid.*, p. 567.

29. Hale and Hale, *Market Power, Size and Shape Under the Sherman Act*, pp. 44-58 and 267-74.

30. *Times-Picayune Publishing Co.* v. *United States*, 345 U.S. 594, 604 (1953).

31. 337 U.S. 293 (1949). The decision is also noteworthy for the controversy which arose over its doctrine of "quantitive substantiality." See United States, *Report of the Attorney General's National Committee to Study the Antitrust Laws,*, pp. 141-49.

32. See *Osborn* v. *Sinclair Refining Co.*, 286 F. 2nd 832 (4th Cir., 1960), *cert. denied,*, 366 U.S. 963 (1961) and *Goodyear Tire & Rubber Co.* v. *Federal Trade Commission*, 331 F. 2nd 394 (7th Cir., 1964), *affirmed* 381 U.S. 357 (1964).

33. *United States* v. *Loew's Inc.*, 371 U.S. 38 (1962).

34. *Tampa Electric Co.* v. *National Coal Co.*, 365 U.S. 220 (1961).

35. See the dissenting opinion of Justice Harlan in *Northern Pacific Railway Co.* v. *United States*, 356 U.S. 1, 16 (1958).

36. 261 U.S. 463 (1923).
37. Reprinted by permission of the publishers from Carl Kaysen and Donald F. Turner, *Antitrust Policy* (Cambridge, Mass.: Harvard University Press), copyright 1959 by the President and Fellows of Harvard College, p. 157.
38. 370 U.S. 294, 330 (1962).
39. See *Motion Picture Patents Co.* v. *Universal Film Mfg. Co.*, 243 U.S. 502 (1917).
40. *United States* v. *Loew's, Inc.*, 371 U.S. 38, 45 (1962).
41. 510 F. 2d 894 (1975).
42. *Trade Cases*, Para. 72,757 (1969) and Para. 61,294 (1977-1).
43. *Trade Cases*, Para. 72,576 (1967).

9

ROBINSON-PATMAN CASES

PRICE DISCRIMINATION UNDER SECTION 2(A)

Legal and Economic Definitions of Price Discrimination. A prerequisite for a finding of illegal price discrimination under Sec. 2(a) of the Robinson-Patman Act is a *price difference* resulting from sales by an individual seller of the same kind of goods at a lower price to one purchaser than to another. Section 2(a) of the Robinson-Patman Act provides in part:

> That it shall be unlawful for any person engaged in commerce . . . to discriminate in price between different purchasers of commodities of like grade and quality . . . where the effect of such discrimination may be substantially to lessen competition or tend to create a monopoly in any line of commerce . . .

Unless a price differential between two customers is established, a court will not consider the further legal issue of whether the price discrimination may injure competitors, or tend to lessen competition substantially or tend to create a monopoly.

Economic discrimination may occur even in the absence of a price differential. If two buyers of the same kind of goods are charged identical prices by a single seller, but the seller incurs different transportation, selling, or production costs in serving them, economic discrimination exists.[1] Thus, in order to know when there is price discrimination in an economic sense between two buyers, it is necessary to have information concerning not only the prices charged, but also the costs incurred by the seller.

Primary-Line and Secondary-Line Competition. The Robinson-Patman Act was enacted in response to the complaints of independent wholesalers that chain stores were obtaining unwarranted lower prices, greater advertising and promotion allowances, and special discounts. These concessions could not be justified by lower costs as a result of the large volume purchases by the chain stores. Consequently, the independent wholesalers had to pay higher prices for their goods and operated under a competitive handicap. This plan of competition among *buyers* is referred to as "secondary-line" competition.

The Supreme Court has held that the Robinson-Patman Act is also applicable to "primary-line" competition, where *sellers* are injured by the discriminatory pricing practices of one of their competitors.[2] In *Federal Trade Commission* v. *Anheuser-Busch, Inc.*[3] the defendant was charged with violating Sec. 2(a) of the Robinson-Patman Act for lowering the price of its premium beer, Budweiser, to the same price level as regional beers in St. Louis, Missouri.[4] Budweiser, as a premium beer, is generally priced higher than beers of regional and local breweries. As a result of the promotional price cut, Budweiser sales advanced over 200 per cent during several months as compared to a similar period in the preceding year. There was no discrimination by Anheuser-Busch among its buyers within the St. Louis area. All the buyers were offered the same lower promotional price. The Supreme Court found, however, that Anheuser-Busch maintained higher prices for customers outside the St. Louis area, while charging lower prices for customers within St. Louis. Although there was no competition between the customers in these geographically distinct markets, the Supreme Court nevertheless held that Anheuser-Busch had discriminated in price when it charged different prices in the separate geographic areas.[5] This same concept of discrimination, which has reference to a price differential between separate geographic markets, is at the crux of the delivered price system cases, which are considered next.

Delivered Price Systems. There are several types of delivered price systems. Under a single basing point system, a buyer is charged a price that includes both the cost of a good at a geographic location designated the basing point *plus* the transportation charges from the basing point to the buyer's place of business. In contrast, a company that does not engage in a delivered price system generally sells its product under an "f.o.b. mill price system." Each plant or mill quotes a price for its product "free on board" (f.o.b.) a carrier, such as a truck or railroad car, which is at or nearby the seller's plant. The seller bears the cost of loading its product from its door to the adjacent carrier, but the buyer bears the transportation costs from there on.

In the period 1905 to 1924 the steel industry in the United States followed a single basing point system entitled "Pittsburgh-plus." This delivered price system established Pittsburgh as the single basing point, U.S. Steel's price for steel products in that city as the *base* price, and the transportation costs from Pittsburgh to any customer as the "plus" element. A customer was charged the Pittsburgh base price plus the railroad transportration charge from Pittsburgh, even though the steel product was delivered from a plant not located in the Pittsburgh area. If the buyer was located in Chicago and received delivery from a Chicago steel mill, he paid a delivered price that included "phantom freight" from Pittsburgh. The result of this delivered price system was that a steel buyer would be quoted an identical price, regardless of his location, by any steel supplier in the United States.

After 1924, as a result of a Federal Trade Commission suit against U.S. Steel, the steel industry abandoned the "Pittsburgh-plus" system, and established a *multiple* basing point system with Chicago, Birmingham, and Pittsburgh as the new bases.[6] Steel buyers in the East were still quoted a "Pittsburgh-plus" price; but buyers in the South were quoted a "Birmingham-plus" price, since Birmingham was a nearer basing point; buyers in the West took advantage of a "Chicago-plus" delivered price. In 1951 the members of the steel industry consented to a

Federal Trade Commission order barring them from agreeing to refuse to sell and deliver any steel products at an f.o.b. mill price.[7]

A variant of multiple basing point pricing is called the "freight equalization system."[8] The most favorably located seller's mill to a given buyer generally serves as the basing point from which the actual freight to the buyer's plant is added. Any seller in the industry may "equalize" his delivered price with the base price plus freight charged by the competing seller nearest the buyer. Thus, by absorbing freight costs, a more distant supplier can match the price of the seller nearest the buyer, but the buyer faces identical delivered prices from different geographically located suppliers.

In "zone pricing" the country is divided into a number of geographic areas and all buyers within a single zone receive the same delivered price; delivered prices may differ between zones.[9] If a seller is located in the center of a zone, those buyers on the periphery of the zone will have the benefit of the seller absorbing part of their freight costs; those near the center will bear more than the actual transportation costs from the seller's mill.

From the point of view of the buyers within a delivered pricing zone, there is no price differential between the delivered prices they pay and those that their competitors within the same zone pay. But from the seller's side, there exists a wide variation in the net receipts resulting from sales to buyers at different distances from the seller's mill. The "mill net return," or the amount the seller receives for his product after deducting from the delivered price his transportation expenses, will be greater where the buyer pays a delivered price that includes "phantom freight" and less where the seller must absorb part of the freight costs. If the term "price" in Sec. 2(a) of the Robinson-Patman Act is construed as the seller's "mill net return," a delivered price system with freight absorption or "phantom freight" reflects the necessary price differential, even though all customers pay identical delivered prices regardless of their distance from a supplying mill. The prevailing view, however, is to interpret price as the actual amount the buyer must pay, i.e., the delivered price, rather than the "mill net return" received by the seller.[10]

The discriminatory aspects of a single basing point delivered price system under Sec. 2(a) of the Robinson-Patman Act were considered by the Supreme Court in *Corn Products Refining Co.* v. *Federal Trade Commission*,[11] and the companion case, *Federal Trade Commission* v. *A. E. Staley Mfg. Co.*[12]

In the *Corn Products* case the defendant operated a plant in Chicago which produced glucose used by candy manufacturers. When the company opened a new plant in Kansas City, it continued to maintain Chicago as its basing point. Both plants sold only at delivered prices, computed by adding to a base price at Chicago the published railroad rate to the point of delivery. The Supreme Court found that candy manufacturers located near Kansas City had to pay "phantom freight" from Chicago even though they received their glucose shipments from the new Kansas City plant. Since the Kansas City customers were found to be competitors of the Chicago customers, the discrimination was held to be unlawful.

In the *Staley* case, a smaller glucose manufacturer located in Decatur, Illinois, which was two hundred miles from Chicago, followed the "Chicago-plus" basing point system of Corn Products. When Staley sold glucose to candy manufacturers in Chicago, it absorbed the freight from Decatur to the Chicago basing point; however, Staley gained "phantom freight" when it sold its product to customers situated closer to Decatur than Chicago. Basically, Staley accepted Corn Products at the glucose price leader and followed its prices in all markets. The Court held that Staley could not justify the adoption of a competitor's basing point price system under Sec. 2(b) as a good faith attempt to meet the latter's equally low price.

The Supreme Court found that the single basing point system followed by Staley and Corn Products was illegal under Sec. 2(a) of the Robinson-Patman Act. Price discrimination resulted because the basing point was different from the point of production. Customers paid different delivered prices, and these discriminatory prices were found to result in competitive injury between customers purchasing from the Chicago plant and those purchasing from the Kansas City plant.

If the candy manufacturers located near Kansas City had no alternative source of supply for glucose than Chicago, Corn Products could charge a high f.o.b. price at their Kansas City plant. The candy manufacturers near Kansas City were not necessarily entitled to the cost savings resulting from Corn Products locating a new plant in Kansas City. Neither was the public necessarily entitled to lower candy prices resulting from lower raw material costs, if Corn Products chose to pass on its cost savings to the candy maker, who, in turn, chose to pass on these cost savings to consumers. Rather, it can be argued, a company constructing a new plant or warehouse should receive, in the short run, the resulting profit from cost savings.

Consider the position of the candy manufacturers located nearby Kansas City *before* Corn Products built its new plant. The candy manufacturer had a higher raw material cost for glucose than a company located in Chicago. Therefore, if the candy manufacturer wanted to sell its product primarily in Chicago, it should have located near its source of supply and major market. However, a candy manufacturer desiring to sell its product primarily in Kansas City would have to choose between locating near its source of supply (Chicago) or near its sales outlet (Kansas City). If the company decided to locate in Kansas City, it would have to bear the cost of having glucose shipped from Chicago, but the company would save on transportation costs in shipping finished candy to its customers in Kansas City.

Consider the market structure in the *Corn Products* case *after* the Kansas City plant was constructed. If Corn Products continued to use a Chicago-plus delivered pricing system, the candy manufacturers would not be any worse off than they were before the Kansas City plant was constructed. Of course, if the Kansas City candy makers could get glucose at a lower price, they could extend the geographic area of their sales and meet more effectively the competition from Chicago candy manufacturers. Or, alternatively, the Kansas City candy makers could maintain the same price and sales volume for their candy and earn higher profits resulting from lower costs for glucose. There is no obvious reason why the Kansas City candy makers are entitled to a lower cost base for glucose and the resulting higher profits in preference to Corn Products which built the new plant that made these cost differentials possible.

The later delivered pricing cases were brought by the Government also under Sec. 5 of the Federal Trade Commission Act as "unfair methods of competition." In the *Cement Institute* case[13] the Supreme Court found an industrywide multiple basing point system in the sale of cement a twin violation of Sec. 5 of the Federal Trade Commission Act and Sec. 2(a) of the Robinson-Patman Act. Under the auspices of the Cement Institute, a trade association, a concerted program of reprisals and boycotts was established for enforcing strict adherence to the delivered price system. The focus in delivered pricing cases changed from price discrimination to a theory that the concurrent use by competing companies in an industry of a delivered price system is partial, if not conclusive, evidence of concerted action that unfairly restrains trade.

THE MEETING COMPETITION DEFENSE UNDER SEC. 2(B)

The Meeting Competition Proviso as an "Absolute" Defense. The *Federal Trade Commission* v. *Standard Oil of Indiana* 340 U.S. 231 (1951) decision established that the good-faith meeting of a competitor's price was an absolute defense under 2(b) of the Robinson-Patman Act, to a charge of price discrimination, irrespective of findings as to competitive injury.

Section 2(b) provides in part:

> That nothing herein contained shall prevent a seller from rebutting the prima-facie case thus made by showing that his lower price or the furnishing of services or facilities to any purchaser or purchasers was made in good faith to meet an equally low price of a competitor . . .

The Supreme Court held that once the defendant was able to show that his lower price did not undercut competitors, but merely met their equally low price, he would be excused, regardless of the competitive effects of his lower price.

In the earlier proceedings of the *Standard Oil of Indiana* case, the Federal Trade Commission took a contrary position. Once it was established that the discriminatory prices charged by Standard Oil were competitively injurious to retail dealers who bought from Standard directly, a violation of the Robinson-Patman Act should be conclusively established. But the Supreme Court refused to follow the opinion of the Federal Trade Commission that injury to competitors should be avoided, and held that encouraging competition is paramount, regardless of the effects of the lower price.

Retaining versus Obtaining New Customers. In *Sunshine Biscuits, Inc.* v. *Federal Trade Commission*[14] the Federal Trade Commission argued that the defense of meeting competition under Sec. 2(b) of the Robinson-Patman Act should be limited to a seller acting in self-defense against competitive price attacks, and should *not* apply to a seller reducing prices to obtain new customers.

This particular issue did not arise in the preceding *Standard Oil of Indiana* case, since the lower prices granted were made only to retain existing customers. The Circuit Court held in the *Sunshine Biscuit* case that the meeting competition defense should not be limited to defensive cuts in price to retain old customers:

> . . . (if) sellers could grant good faith competitive price reductions only to old customers in order to retain them, competition for new customers would be stifled and monopoly would be fostered.[15]

The Federal Trade Commission declined to seek Supreme Court review of the Circuit Court decision that set aside its order.

Meeting Prices of the Seller's Competitors or His Customers' Competitors. In

Sun Oil v. *Federal Trade Commission*[16] the Supreme Court rejected the meeting competition defense raised by Sun Oil. Sun Oil lowered its price only to McLean, one of a number of independent dealers operating Sunoco service stations in Jacksonville, Florida. Sun Oil made the discriminatory price to McLean in order to enable him to meet the lower price of a competitive private brand gasoline, Super Test, sold by an independent retail dealer.

The defense argued that McLean was merely a "conduit" in marketing the products of Sun Oil. Therefore, as a practical matter Sun Oil was competing at the retail level with Super Test. The Supreme Court disagreed, holding that the lower price which must be met refers to the price of a competitor of the seller who grants the discriminatory price (such as another refiner-supplier). It does not refer to the price of a competitor (such as Super Test) of the buyer who receives the discriminatory price allowance. If Sun Oil as a wholesale supplier reduced its price to McLean when another wholesale supplier attempted to obtain McLean as a retail customer, the meeting competition defense would be allowed. However, when Sun Oil lowered its price to McLean sufficiently to allow McLean to reduce his price to meet a competitive retail price of Super Test, a gasoline station located across the street, the meeting competition defense was not allowed, since Sun Oil was not meeting the price of one of its own competitors.

In the *Sun Oil* case the Supreme Court assumed, contrary to the Circuit Court, that Super Test was engaged solely in retail operations and that it was not the beneficiary of any enabling price cut from its own supplier: "Were it otherwise, *i.e.*, if it appeared either that Super Test were an integrated supplier-retailer, or that it had received a price cut from its own supplier — presumably a competitor of Sun — we would be presented with a different case, as to which we neither express nor intimate any opinion."[22]

The economic effects that were alleged as inevitable, if discriminatory price concessions such as Sun Oil made to McLean were not permitted, are noteworthy. Sun Oil argued that the Court's interpretation of the Robinson-Patman Act would harm rather than protect small independents such as McLean:

> . . . the limited resources available to McLean bar his survival in a gasoline price war of any duration. McLean's small margin of profit, his relative inability to lower his retail price because (it is) a direct function of the price he pays his supplier, here Sun, and other factors make his continued independent existence in a present-day price war wholly dependent upon receipts of aid — in the form of a price reduction — from his supplier.[18]

Second, the Commission maintained that the nearby Sunoco service stations would be injured by virtue of McLean's discriminatory price concession. The Commission found that neighboring Sunoco dealers were able to identify customers who, apparently retaining a preference for Sun Oil products, shifted their patronage from the competing stations to McLean. The defense asserted "that the harm to the competitors of McLean must be suffered as a consequence of the very competition which is the pervasive essence of our overall antitrust policies."[19] The Supreme Court was, therefore, faced with a dilemma:

> . . . the mere recognition that harm sometimes may be a by-product of competition is the beginning, not the end, of analysis. Whatever the result here, someone may be hurt — to allow Sun to pursue its discriminatory pricing policy will, as has been indicated, harm other Sun dealers who compete with McLean; to prevent Sun from

making discriminatory price allowances, it is asserted, will injure the McLeans of the competitive world.[20]

Third, the Court noted that there would be economic effects on the pricing behavior of gasoline dealers if Sun Oil were not permitted to grant a discriminatory price concession to its customer McLean. In the words of the Court,

> While allowance of the discriminatory price cut here may provide localized and temporary flexibility, it inevitably encourages maintenance of the long-range and generalized price rigidity which the discrimination in fact protects. So long as the wholesaler can meet challenges to his pricing structure by wholly local and individual-ized responses, it has no incentive to alter its overall pricing policy. Moreover, as indicated, the large supplier's ability to "spot price" will discourage the enterprising and resourceful retailer from seeking to initiate price reductions on his own. Such reasoning may be particularly applicable in the oligopolistic environment of the oil industry.
> We see no reason to permit Sun discriminatorily to pit its greater strength at the supplier level against Super Test, which so far as appears from the record, is able to sell its gasoline at a lower price simply because it is a more efficient merchandiser, particularly when Super Test's challenge as an "independent" may be the only meaningful source of price competition offered the "major" oil companies, of which Sun is one.[21]

Finally, Sun Oil argued that if it were denied the meeting competition defense, it would be forced vertically to integrate further into the retail distribution of gasoline to the detriment of the very independent retail operators whom the Robinson-Patman Act was intended to preserve and protect.

KNOWINGLY INDUCING AND RECEIVING DISCRIMINATORY PRICES UNDER SECTION 2(f)

In *Great Atlantic & Pacific Tea Co., Inc. (Borden)* v. *Federal Trade Commission*, 1979-1 Trade Cases Para. 62,475, the Supreme Court found that a major food chain, A&P, was not liable under Section 2(f) for knowingly inducing and receiving a discriminatory price from a major dairy company, Borden. A&P refused Borden's first price and encouraged Borden to bid again in order to meet a lower bid from a competitor. Borden unknowingly submitted a second price that was lower than necessary to meet the competitor's price. A&P accepted the Borden bid and did not inform Borden that its price was lower than the competitive bid. The case is noteworthy in considering the amount of disclosure required of a buyer during contract negotiations involving competitive bidding.

In 1965, A&P asked Borden to give it a bid for supplying its Chicago area stores with milk sold under the A&P private label. Previously, Borden supplied A&P with milk sold under the Borden label. Borden had just expended over $5 million dollars on its milk facility at Woodstock, Illinois which supplied the A&P stores. A&P was Borden's largest account and the loss of this customer raised the real possibility that Borden would be forced to close its Woodstock plant. After receiving competitive bids from several Chicago dairies, A&P told Borden that its bid was "so far out of line, it is not even funny. You are not even in the ball park."

A&P allowed Borden to submit a second bid but refused to disclose to Borden the amount of the lowest bid. Borden, of course, could not speak to its competitors to find out the amount of their bids without risking a Sherman Act violation such as occurred in the *Gypsum* case. Nor could Borden risk, from a business standpoint, the loss of the A&P account without having to take a substantial loss of millions of dollars in having to close its dairy plant. Borden therefore submitted a substantially lower bid to A&P.

Unknown to Borden was the fact that its bid to A&P was $83,000 lower than the previous low bid submitted by Bowman Dairy. A&P did not inform Borden that it had beaten the Bowman low bid. The case raised the question whether A&P had an affirmative duty to tell Borden that its second bid was not just "meeting competition" but was substantially lower than its competitor's bid it was trying to meet.

The Supreme Court held that A&P did not have to disclose to Borden that the second bid of Borden was lower than necessary. Since Borden's conduct was innocent in attempting to meet a competitive bid, the "meeting competition" defense was available to Borden. The Court concluded there could be no violation for illegally inducing and receiving a price discrimination by a buyer, A&P, since the seller, Borden, had a justified meeting competition defense.

The Court did not consider whether they would have reached the same result if the buyer had lied about the competitive bid. For example, in the earlier *Kroger Co. v. Federal Trade Commission*, 438 F.2d 1378 (1971) *cert. denied* 404 U.S. 871 (1971), the Court of Appeals held that Kroger was liable under Section 2(f) because it lied to its milk supplier that it had received a lower price offer when it really had not. Kroger's milk supplier was innocent in submitting a second bid which beat the competitive lowest bid. Even though the innocent supplier was entitled to a meeting competition defense, the Court of Appeals held Kroger was liable under Section 2(f) for inducing lower discriminatory prices by lying about receiving lower bids. The Court of Appeals in the *A&P (Borden)* case found no difference between "affirmative misrepresentations," such as occurred in the *Kroger* case, and passive silence, which produced the same result of an offer below the "meeting competition" price. The Court of Appeals stated:

> "The rule that the 'meeting competition' defense must be looked at from the buyer's perspective where the buyer is charged under Section 2(f) is a salutary and correct one, whether the buyer lies or merely keeps quiet about the nature of the competing bid it has already been offered."

The Court of Appeals decision is consistent with the basic purpose of the Robinson-Patman Act to curtail abuses by large buyers, such as food chains. Nevertheless, the Supreme Court overruled the Court of Appeals and held that the buyer who did not lie, but merely invited a seller to meet a competitor's price and then fortuitously obtained a lower bid, should be allowed to accept the lower bid which beat a competitor's price without facing liability under Section 2(f).

The *A&P (Borden)* case was one of the longest antitrust cases litigated. Voluminous briefs were filed by the FTC, Borden and A&P. The critical fact related to a telephone conversation in 1965 concerning whether Borden was "in the ballpark" on its bid. The litigation began in 1970 at the Federal Trade Commission when memories and records were already five years old. By 1979, when the Supreme Court heard the argument in this case, the critical telephone conversation was fourteen years old, Borden had lost A&P as a customer, and the Woodstock plant had been closed for several years. Nevertheless, in a concurring and dissenting opinion, Justice White suggested the case should be remanded back to where it all began, namely, at the Federal Trade Commission.

> "Because it was thought the issue was irrelevant where the buyer knows that the price offered is lower than necessary to meet competition, neither the Commission nor the Court of Appeals decided whether Borden itself would have had a valid meeting-competition defense. The Court should not decide this question here but should remand to the Commission whose job it is initially to consider such matters."

The majority did not follow Justice White's suggestion, and one can only speculate whether another decade of litigation would be required. In perspective, the case involved a bid by Borden in 1965 which was $83,000 lower than a competitor's bid. The cost to the government, A&P and Borden to litigate this case involved millions of dollars. The legal principle involved in terms of antitrust law is relatively minor. The ethical conduct of business negotiations was more at issue than the technical provisions of the Robinson-Patman Act.

The Supreme Court noted the finding that A&P's usual practice was to allow only one bid to a seller. If A&P would have followed its usual practice and simply awarded the contract to the lowest bidder (Bowman Dairy), there never would have been a lawsuit. But A&P deviated from its usual practice and offered Borden the opportunity to bid again. A&P did not ask Bowman Dairy for another bid, which in terms of fair business conduct one might expect. A&P was clearly using the Bowman bid as a tool to drive down Borden's price. Borden asked A&P what price they were to meet under the "meeting competition" defense to the Robinson-Patman Act. This request by Borden was reasonable and is often confirmed in writing in order for the seller to be protected from a Robinson-Patman price discrimination charge. A&P refused this request by Borden. Borden had the choice of walking away from the A&P business and closing its Woodstock plant, which was heavily dependent on the A&P business, or submitting another bid without knowledge of the price to match.

The FTC believed that A&P should have told Borden what the price was which Borden was to match. The Supreme Court disagreed and held that A&P did not have a legal duty to tell Borden what the lowest price was which had to be met. The fine point of morality turns on whether the buyer, as in the *Kroger* case, tricked the seller by "lying" through affirmative misrepresentations into granting a bid below that required to meet a competitive bid; or whether the buyer, as A&P in this case, achieved the same result by simply remaining silent.

The Supreme Court's opinion basically has a logical flaw. If the buyer's liability (A&P) depends on that of the seller (Borden), then absent seller liability, such as when the seller unknowingly grants a discriminatory low price, it logically follows that the buyer's unethical conduct and bad faith are irrelevant since the seller is innocent. An alternative solution to the case might have been for A&P to refund Borden $83,000 in return for the Federal Trade Commission dropping the case.

ENDNOTES

1. Rowe, *Price Discrimination Under the Robinson-Patman Act*, p. 29.
2. The courts have consistently found a violation of Sec. 2(a) of the Robinson-Patman Act in cases where a company maintained a substantially lower price in one locality while charging higher

prices elsewhere, for the obvious predatory purpose of driving a specific competitor out of business. See *Moore* v. *Mead's Fine Bread Co.*, 348 U.S. 115 (1954); *E.B. Muller & Co.* v. *Federal Trade Commission*, 142 F. 2nd 511 (6th Cir., 1944); *Maryland Baking Co.* v. *Federal Trade Commission*, 243 F. 2nd 716 (4th Cir., 1957); and *Atlas Building Products Co.* v. *Diamond Block & Gravel Co.*, 269 F. 2nd 950 (10th Cir., 1959), cert. denied 363 U.S. 843 (1959).

3. 363 U.S. 536 (1960). Compare to *Utah Pie Co.* v. *Continental Baking Co.*, 386 U.S. 685 (1967).

4. A problem arises when a price reduction of a "premium" image product matches a rival's price of a nonpremium good, so that in a marketing sense, the latter price is undercut. This aspect of the *Anheuser-Busch* case can be found in 54 FTC 277 (1957). Also see *United States* v. *The Borden Company*, 383 U.S. 637 (1966).

5. The Supreme Court, after deciding that price discrimination existed, remanded the case to the Circuit Court to consider whether the requisite injury to competition also existed for a finding of *illegality* under Sec. 2(a). The Circuit Court found that the sharp increase in sales by Anheuser-Busch during the price promotional resulted in only a temporary improvement in its market position in St. Louis. Therefore, the Circuit Court concluded, there was no injury to competition, and dismissed the action against Anheuser-Busch. See *Anheuser-Busch, Inc.* v. *Federal Trade Commission*, 289 F 2nd. 835 (7th Cir., 1961).

6. 8 FTC (December 1, 1924).

7. Federal Trade Commission Order No. 5508 (August 16, 1951).

8. See *Bond, Crown & Cork Co.* v. *Federal Trade Commission*, 176 F. 2nd 974 (4th Cir., 1949).

9. *Milk and Ice Cream Can Institute* v. *Federal Trade Commission*, 152 F. 2nd 478 (7th Cir., 1946).

10. *In the Matter of National Lead Co.*, 49 FTC 791 (1953); *In the Matter of Chain Institute, Inc.*, 49 FTC 1041 (1953); and United States, *Report of the Attorney General's National Committee to Study the Antitrust Laws*, pp. 216-17.

11. 324 U.S. 726 (1945).

12. 324 U.S. 746 (1945). For a discussion of these companion cases, see Neale, *The Antitrust Laws of the U.S.A.*, pp. 254-58.

13. *Federal Trade Commission* v. *Cement Institute*, 333 U.S. 683 (1948). Also see *Federal Trade Commission* v. *National Lead Co.*, 352 U.S. 419 (1957).

14. 306 F. 2nd 48 (7th Cir., 1962). Also see *Standard Motor Products, Inc.* v. *Federal Trade Commission*, 265 F. 2nd 674 (2nd Cir., 1959), *cert. denied*, 361 U.S. 826 (1959).

15. *Ibid.*, p. 52. Also see J. W. Markham, "Antitrust Trends and New Constraints," *Harvard Business Review*, Vol. XLI (May - June, 1963), 84-92.

16. 371 U.S. 505 (1963).

17. *Ibid.*, p. 512.

18. *Ibid.*, p. 518.

19. *Ibid.*, p. 519.

20. *Ibid.*

21. *Ibid.*, p. 523 (footnote omitted).

THOUGHT QUESTIONS

1. The cost of mailing a postcard anywhere in the U.S. is the same. Is this price discrimination?

2. Assume that before the Robinson-Patman Act was passed independent wholesalers operated under a competitive handicap in not receiving prices as low as those paid by chain stores. Would it have been a better public policy to encourage these independent wholesalers to merge, or to form cooperative buying associations, rather than prevent the chain from exacting lower prices from food manufacturers and passing these lower prices on to consumers?

3. In the final analysis, did the Supreme Court's opinion in the *Anheuser-Busch* case encourage the defendant to lower its suburban prices for beer to the level of prices being charged in the city of St. Louis, or to raise its city prices to the higher suburban price level?

   a) Should beer price wars for national brands, as against local or regional brands, being encouraged or discouraged?

4. An isolated mill charges its nearby customers the same price as the next closest competitor plus a "phantom freight" surcharge equal to the cost of shipping the product from the competitor to the customer. The mill argues that it does not charge "phantom freight" but simply charges the most it can get for its product, and is limited only by the price it must meet from its competitor. Discuss whether "phantom freight" does not involve freight costs but merely competitive pricing.

    a) Should an isolated country store be entitled to charge a price premium for its products to local summer hikers?

    b) Is the higher profit earned by the store "phantom freight"?

5. Many of the leading cases concerning the Robinson-Patman Act involve the distribution of petroleum products to service stations before the Arab oil embargo. Discuss the effect of economic shortages and conservation of natural resources on the application of the Robinson-Patman Act to the oil industry.

6. In the *A&P - Borden* case, A&P did not inform Borden that its second bid was *below* the lowest competitive price. Since the Supreme Court held A&P had no duty to inform Borden of this fact, there existed an information gap on what constituted the lowest competitive price. In the questions below, assume no agreement regarding a specific price is made between any two dairies.

    a) Could the dairies agree to submit bids to chain stores only at a public auction?

    b) Would such an agreement be conspiratorial or in violation of the antitrust laws?

    c) Could the dairies have hired a common broker to represent them independently and to negotiate the final price based on sealed bids?

    d) Could the dairies agree only to bid independently at a "Dutch auction" where the price starts at a very high level and the first and highest bid wins?

7. In the *A&P - Borden* case, do you believe there is a moral or legal difference between a buyer tricking a seller into granting a lower price by lying about a competitive bid, or a buyer asking for a second bid and remaining silent with regard to the fact that it is below the lowest competitive first bid?

8. In the *A&P - Borden* case, should A&P have allowed Borden to submit to them a second bid? Did the opportunity to submit a second bid which A&P gave Borden make a sham of the bidding process? Is there a difference between a buyer being given an opportunity to submit a second, third or fourth bid and simple price negotiation?

10

MERGER CASES

A. DETERMINATION OF THE RELEVANT MARKET

The legality of a merger covered by Sec. 7 of the Clayton Act rests in most cases on the following critical language of this Act: "where in any line of commerce in any section of the country, the effect of such acquisition may be substantially to lessen competition, or tend to create a monopoly." The phrase "in any line of commerce" has reference to a particular product market. The phrase "in any section of the country," has reference to a selected geographic area. In order to judge whether or not a merger will "substantially lessen competition," a court must reach a definition of a *relevant market* which takes into account both product and geographic factors.

DEFINING PRODUCT MARKET BOUNDARIES

The boundaries of a product market are determined by the reasonable interchangeability of end-use, or the cross-elasticity of demand, between a product and its substitutes. The courts examine such factors as (1) the product's peculiar characteristics and uses, (2) unique production facilities, (3) distinct customers, (4) distinct sellers, and (5) industry or public recognition.

The Brown Shoe Case (1962). In *Brown Shoe Co.* v. *United States*,[1] the Supreme Court found illegal the acquisition by Brown Shoe Company, the fourth largest shoe manufacturer, of the G. R. Kinney Company, the nation's largest family-style retail shoe chain and twelfth largest shoe manufacturer. The Court held that the relevant lines of commerce encompassed by the acquisition were men's, women's, and children's shoes because (1) the public recognizes these product lines as separate, (2) each line is manufactured in separate plants, (3) each has peculiar characteristics which render it noncompetitive with the others, and (4) each line is directed to a distinct class of customers.

132

The Court rejected the argument of Brown Shoe that the predominantly medium-priced shoes that it manufactured occupied a product market different from the predominantly lower-priced shoes that Kinney sold. Medium-priced shoes were held to compete with lower-priced shoes. "It would be unrealistic," in the words of the Court, "to accept Brown's contention that, for example, men's shoes selling below $8.99 are in a different product market from those selling above $9.00"[2]

Brown Shoe was also unsuccessful in its argument that the product market definition of children's shoes should take account of age and sex differences. For example, Brown argued that "a little boy does not wear a little girl's black patent leather pump." Brown contended that "infants' and babies'" shoes, "misses' and children's" shoes, and "youths' and boys' shoes" should each be considered a separate line of commerce. The Court could find no advantage for Brown Shoe if these finer product definitions were employed:

> Brown manufactures significant comparable quantities of virtually every type of nonrubber men's, women's, and children's shoes, and Kinney sells such quantities of virtually every type of men's, women's, and children's shoes. Thus whether considered separately or together, the picture of this merger is the same.[3]

The Continental Can (Hazel-Atlas) Case (1964). In *United States* v. *Continental Can Co.*[4] the Supreme Court held illegal a merger between the second largest manufacturer of metal containers (Continental Can) with the third largest manufacturer of glass containers (Hazel-Atlas). The District Court found that glass and metal containers constituted separate lines of commerce, since the containers had different characteristics that could disqualify them from particular uses; the machinery necessary to pack in glass is different from that employed when cans are used; and the users of glass or metal cans do not shift back and forth as relative prices for these containers change. The Supreme Court noted that metal containers and glass containers were separate industries, but held that the inter-industry competition between the manufacturers of these two types of containers brought both metal and glass containers under one combined product market for judging the merger. The Court found that both types of containers are used to pack baby food, soft drinks, beer, and other products. Furthermore, metal cans were penetrating a number of traditional glass container markets, such as carbonated soft drinks. Continental Can had been a major factor in promoting the entry of metal cans into the former domain of glass containers in a number of product categories. In the words of the Court,

> Thus, though the interchangeability of use may not be so complete and the cross-elasticity of demand not so immediate as in the case of most intra-industry mergers, there is over the long run the kind of customer response to innovation and other competitive stimuli that brings the competition between these two industries within Sec. 7's competition-preserving proscriptions.[5]

A dissenting opinion was written in the *Continental Can* decision by Justice Harlan. The dissent contended that the majority opinion was a "travesty of economics," since the Court provided "its own definition of a market, unrelated to any market reality whatsoever." Justice Harlan believed that the metal container industry and glass container industry were separate lines of commerce. The grouping of metal and glass containers into one product market, or a combined line of commerce was, in the words of Justice Harlan, "completely fanciful."

> The bizarre result of the Court's approach is that market percentages of a non-existent market enable the Court to dispense with "elaborate proof of market structure, market behavior and probable anticompetitive effects."[6]

It is interesting to note that the Government did not suggest that "glass and metal containers" constituted a separate line of commerce until submitting their brief to the Supreme Court. Furthermore, the Government deliberately omitted mention of market shares, since "those traditional yardsticks are generally unavailable to measure the full consequences which an inter-industry merger would have on competition."[7] Thus, it can be argued that if a market does not exist for "glass and metal containers," *market shares* cannot be meaningfully compiled.

Continental Can argued that the purpose of its merger with Hazel-Atlas was to diversify into the related glass container field. The District Court held that the case involved a "conglomerate merger" between a manufacturer of metal containers and a manufacturer of glass containers. As shown in Table 9-1A, Hazel-Atlas accounted for 9.6 per cent of the total shipments of glass containers, and Continental Can accounted for 33 per cent of the metal container shipments in the United States.

TABLE 10-1A
Percentage of Metal and Glass Container Shipments Accounted for by Continental Can and Hazel-Atlas, 1955

	Continental Can	Hazel-Atlas	Continental Can and Hazel-Atlas Combined
Glass Containers	None	9.6	9.6
Metal Containers	33.0	None	33.0
Glass and Metal Containers	21.9	3.1	25.0

The Supreme Court majority opinion held, in effect, that Continental Can had not moved into a separate market by its merger with Hazel-Atlas, but had fortified its position in the combined metal and glass container market. Continental, with 21.9 per cent of the shipments, ranked second in this product market, and Hazel-Atlas, with 3.1 per cent, ranked sixth. In the words of the Court,

> By the acquisition of Hazel-Atlas stock Continental not only increased its own share more than 14% from 21.9% to 25%, but also reduced from five to four the most significant competitors who might threaten its dominant position. The resulting percentage of the combined firms approaches that held presumptively bad in *United States* v. *Philadelphia National Bank* . . .[8]

Justice Harlan, in his dissenting opinion, objected to the comparison with the *Philadelphia National Bank* case, which involved the merger of the second and third largest banks in the metropolitan Philadelphia area. Both banks were clearly in the same product market, commercial banking, which was a market "sufficiently inclusive to be meaningful in terms of trade realities." In the *Continental Can* case the product market definition was not clear. In such a context, Justice Harlan believed that the presumptively illegal market share approach taken by the majority in *Continental Can* was inappropriate:

> When a merger is attacked on the ground that competition *between* two distinct industries, or lines of commerce, will be affected, the shortcut "market share" approach developed in the *Philadelphia Bank* case . . . has no place.[9]

The Alcoa (Rome Cable) Case (1964). In the *Alcoa* (Rome Cable) case,[10] decided by the Supreme Court in the same year as Continental Can, the District Court's definition of the relevant product market was also reversed. The District Court held that the acquisition of Rome Cable by Alcoa did not violate Sec. 7 of the Clayton Act. In both *Alcoa* (Rome Cable) and *Continental Can* (Hazel-Atlas), the Supreme Court found the acquisitions to be illegal. In *Alcoa* (Rome Cable) the Supreme Court severed the product market determined by the District Court. In *Continental Can* the Supreme Court joined into one product market the separate lines of commerce found by the District Court.

Both the District Court and the Supreme Court in the *Alcoa* (Rome Cable) case agreed that bare aluminim conductor was a product submarket; it had virtually displaced copper in overhead lines used to carry electric power from generating plants to consumers. The courts disagreed on whether bare aluminum conductor and insulated aluminum conductor could be joined into one product market, namely, aluminum conductor.

The District Court found that insulated *aluminum* conductor could not be treated as a separate line of commerce from insulated *copper* conductor, since both are functionally interchangeable by the users; the conductor industry does not differentiate between copper and aluminum insulated products; both may be produced interchangeably on the same fabricating machinery; and neither has distinct customers or specialized vendors.

The Supreme Court found that despite the competition existing between insulated aluminum and insulated copper conductors, insulated aluminum could be treated as a separate line of commerce. The Court noted that the price of most insulated aluminum conductor is 50 to 60 per cent of the price of insulated copper conductor of the same size. Furthermore, the growth of insulated aluminum conductor in the market for insulated overhead lines, from less than 10 per cent in 1950 to over 75 per cent in 1959, reflected advantages for this product.

Having found that insulated conductor constituted a line of commerce, the Supreme Court went on to hold that aluminum conductor (bare and insulated) constituted the relevant product market. This was, in the words of the majority of the Court, merely "a logical extension of the district court's findings." The dissent could find little justification for grouping bare and insulated aluminum conductor together. The combination was not recognized by the industry as a separate line of commerce, and different equipment and engineering skills were required for their manufacture and sale. Thus the dissent concluded:

> But even if insulated aluminum conductor is a proper line of commerce, there is no basis in logic, or in the competitive realities of the conductor industry, for lumping together in one line of commerce bare and insulated aluminum conductors.[11]

Diversification was the avowed purpose of the mergers in both the *Alcoa* (Rome Cable) and *Continental Can* (Hazel-Atlas) cases. Continental Can, a producer of metal containers, merged with Hazel-Atlas in order to enter the field of glass containers. Alcoa, a fully integrated aluminum producer, acquired Rome Cable in order to enter the insulated copper conductor market and broaden its insulated aluminum conductor line.

The District Court in the *Alcoa* (Rome Cable) case found that Alcoa "lacked the 'know-how' to manufacture the more complicated types of insulated wire and cable for which there was a growing demand." Alcoa believed that the time required to obtain such competence from its own organization, and the expense involved necessitated the acquisition of a company that already had this ability in the insulating field. At the time of the merger, Alcoa was the leading producer of primary aluminum ingot (38.6 per cent) and the leading fabricator of bare aluminum conductor (32.5 per cent). Alcoa produced no copper conductor cable or wire.

Rome was predominantly a copper manufacturing company. In 1958 Rome was one of the ten largest manufacturers of copper conductor in the United States. Its share of the bare aluminum conductor market was insignificant (0.3 per cent). As shown in Table 9-2A, the combined Alcoa-Rome share of the combined aluminum and copper conductor, bare and insulated, was 3.2 per cent. Their combined share of the total insulated copper and aluminum market was 1.6 per cent. The District Court found that the market shares of Alcoa and Rome in these broad product markets were insufficient for a lessening of competition as a result of the merger.

TABLE 10-2A
Percentage of Aluminum and Copper Conductor Market Accounted for by Alcoa and Rome Cable in 1958

	Alcoa	Rome	Combined
Aluminum conductor	27.8	1.3	29.1
Bare	32.5	0.3	32.8
Insulated	11.6	4.7	16.3
Total alumnium and copper conductor	1.8	1.4	3.2
Bare	10.3	2.0	12.3
Insulated	0.3	1.3	1.6

The Supreme Court, by treating aluminum conductor as the relevant market, was able to achieve more substantial market shares. The Court held that Alcoa by acquiring Rome Cable was able to add 1.3 percentage points to its already leading share (27.8 per cent) of the aluminum conductor field. This increment of 1.3 percentage points was sufficient to make it reasonably likely that the merger would produce a substantial lessening of competition within the meaning of Sec. 7 of the Clayton Act. There was no mention of the finding by the District Court that Alcoa's share of the aluminum conductor was steadily declining for the past decade, and continued to decline after the merger. The Alcoa-Rome share of aluminum conductor fell 4.3 percentage points from 29.1 per cent in 1958, the year preceding the merger, to 24.8 per cent in 1961. Thus, in the aluminum conductor market, Alcoa increased its share by 1.3 percentage points in 1959 by the acquisition of Rome Cable, but lost this amount plus an additional 3 percentage points by 1961.[12]

DEFINING GEOGRAPHIC MARKET BOUNDARIES

The geographic market boundaries in which the competitive effects of a merger are judged are normally the area or "section of the country" in which the acquired and acquiring companies can be expected to conduct business. The coverage of a geographic market is not confined to political subdivisions such as states or cities. But the availability of data often requires a particular region, state, or metropolitan area to be selected as an approximation to a more accurate area of effective competition.

The Brown Shoe Case (1962). In *United States* v. *Brown Shoe Co.*[13] the Supreme Court found that the relevant geographic market at the *manufacturing* level was the entire nation. "The relationships of product value, bulk, weight and consumer demand enable manufacturers to distribute their shoes on a nationwide basis, as Brown and Kinney, in fact, do." However, for judging the effect of the acquisition at the *retail* level, the relevant geographic market was held to cities "with a population exceeding 10,000 and its immediate contiguous surrounding territory in which both Brown and Kinney sold shoes at retail through stores they either owned or controlled."

The Supreme Court rejected the contention by Brown Shoe that the relevant geographic market for retailing should in some cases include only the central business districts of large cities, and in others, should encompass "standard metropolitan areas" within which smaller suburban communities are found. Brown Shoe was, in effect, arguing that the relevant geographic market should in some cases be small enough to separate center-city shoe markets (where Brown Shoe's outlets were primarily located) from the surrounding suburban shoe markets (where Kinney's stores were primarily located).[14] The Supreme Court found that shoe stores in the outskirts of cities compete effectively with stores in the central downtown areas. Therefore, the relevant geographic market was held to include both downtown and suburban areas:

> Such markets are large enough to include the downtown shops and suburban shopping centers in areas contiguous to the city, which are the important competitive factors, and yet are small enough to exclude stores beyond the immediate environs of the city, which are of little competitive significance.[15]

The Philadelphia Bank Case (1963). In *United States* v. *Philadelphia National Bank*[16] the Supreme Court held that the proper question to ask in determining the appropriate geographic relevant market is "not where the parties to the merger do business or even where they compete, but where, within the area of competitive overlap, the effect of the merger on competition will be direct and immediate."[17] In applying this test the Court found that the relevant geographic market for judging the economic effects of the proposed acquisition by Philadelphia Bank of Girard Trust was the four-county Philadelphia metropolitan area (Philadelphia, Montgomery, Bucks, and Delaware counties) in which the merging banks were permitted under state law to operate branches, and from which the bulk of their business originated.

The Supreme Court rejected the finding of the lower court that the relevant geographic market consisted of the northeastern United States, or at least New York City and the entire Delaware Valley (*i.e.*, Philadelphia, Bucks, Montgomery, Delaware, and Chester counties in Pennsylvania; and in New Jersey, Burlington, Camden, and Gloucester counties). The Supreme Court noted that large borrowers and depositors in the four-county area did considerable business with New York City banks, and were in need of a large bank in the Philadelphia area to avoid going to other cities for major financing. In contrast, the smaller bank customers are influenced by convenience and generally confine their banking activities to local banks. Therefore, the Court observed in a footnote: "the four-county area remains a valid geographic market in which to assess the anticompetitive effect of the proposed merger upon the banking facilities available to the smaller customer — a perfectly good 'line of commerce'. . ."[18]

The El Paso Case (1964). In *United States* v. *El Paso Natural Gas Co.,*[19] the Supreme Court found illegal the acquisition between the sole company licensed by the Federal Power Commission to distribute natural gas from out of state into the state of California (El Paso) and the only other important interstate pipeline company licensed to operate west of the Rockies (Pacific Northwest Pipeline). Pacific Northwest operated a pipeline from the San Juan Basin, New Mexico, to the state of Washington, and was authorized to receive large quantities of Canadian gas.

Prior to the acquisition, Pacific Northwest had attempted unsuccessfully to obtain a license to distribute natural gas into the rapidly expanding California market. Pacific northwest also entered into negotations with the Southern California Edison Company for the sale of natural gas which would be delivered at a point on the California-Oregon border. Edison, which was the largest industrial user of natural gas in Southern California, used El Paso gas, which it purchased through a distributor on a low-priority "interruptible" basis, *i.e.*, subject to interruption during periods of peak demand. Upon learning of the negotiations between Pacific Northwest and Edison, El Paso succeeded in getting one of its distributors to give Edison a contract on a noninterruptible basis. A few months later El Paso acquired control of Pacific Northwest.

The Supreme Court held that Pacific Northwest, though it had no pipeline into California, was a substantial factor in the California market at the time it was acquired by El Paso. "We would have to wear blinders," stated the Court, "not to see that the mere efforts of Pacific Northwest to get into the California market, though unsuccessful, had a powerful influence on El Paso's business attitudes within the state."[20] Pacific Northwest was therefore found to be a potential competitor of El Paso at the time of the acquisition.

The following passage reflects the interest of the Supreme Court in the outlying area of potential competition occupied by Pacific Northwest:

> Pacific Northwest had proximity to the California market — 550 miles distant in Wyoming, even nearer in Idaho, only 250 miles away in Oregon. Moreover, it had enormous reserves in the San Juan Basin, the Rocky Mountains, and western Canada. Had Pacific Northwest remained independent, there can be no doubt it would have sought to exploit its formidable geographic position vis-a-vis California. No one knows what success it would have had. We do know, however, that two interstate pipelines in addition to El Paso now serve California — one of the newcomers being Pacific Gas Transmission Co., bringing down Canadian gas. So we know the opportunities would have existed for Pacific Northwest had it remained independent.[21]

The Penn-Olin Case (1964). In *United States* v. *Penn-Olin Chemical Co.*[22] the Supreme Court held that the formation of a joint venture by two chemical companies to produce sodium chlorate in the southeastern quadrant of the United States would be unlawful under Sec. 7 of of the Clayton Act if either of the parent companies would have entered this market individually, with the other remaining at the edge of the market as a potential competitor. Prior to the formation of Penn-Olin, one of the parents of the joint venture, Pennsalt Chemicals, produced sodium chlorate at its plant in Portland, Oregon. Under the terms of a sales arrangement, the other parent, Olin Mathieson, sold a third of the plant's output on the southeastern part of the United States. This sales arrangement was entered into on a temporary basis for the purpose of testing the southeastern market with a view toward the formation of a joint venture located at Calvert City, Kentucky.

The District Court found that, at the time of the formation of the joint venture, Pennsalt was not an effective competitor in the southeast because it labored under a freight handicap in shipping from Oregon. Pennsalt's competitors, American Potash and Hooker Chemical, each had a sodium chlorate plant located in Mississippi, and together accounted for over 90 per cent of the sodium chlorate sales in the southeast. After Penn-Olin was formed, Pittsburgh Plate Glass announced that it would build a sodium chlorate plant in Louisiana. The District Court found that Pennsalt and Olin Mathieson each possessed the resources and general capability needed to build its own plant in the southeast. However, this factor was not controlling, in the opinion of the District Court, except as a factor in determining whether *both* companies would have probably entered the market as individual competitors if the Penn-Olin joint venture had not been formed. "Only in this event would potential competition between the two companies have been foreclosed by the joint venture."[23].

The Supreme Court held that the District Court had used the wrong test. In the words of the Court,

> . . . Certainly the sole test would not be the probability that *both* companies would have entered the market. Nor would the consideration be limited to the probability that one entered alone. There still remained for consideration the fact that Penn-Olin eliminated the potential competition of the corporation that might have remained at the edge of the market, continually threatening to enter. Just as a merger eliminates actual competition, this joint venture may well foreclose any prospect of competition between Olin and Pennsalt in the relevant sodium chlorate market . . .[24]

The case was remanded to the District Court, which found that the evidence did not show that, but for the joint venture, Pennsalt as a matter of reasonable probability would have individually entered the southeastern sodium chlorate market.[25]

The Falstaff Beer Case (1973)

In the *United States* v. *Falstaff Brewing Corp.*,[26] the Supreme Court did not question the finding of the lower court that Falstaff, the only major beer manufacturer not selling in New England and which had acquired Narrangansett, the largest selling beer brand in New England, would not have entered that market independently without a merger. Nevertheless, the Supreme Court held that the District Court should have examined whether Falstaff was perceived by others as a potential entrant. Thus, Falstaff had to prove not only what was in its mind, namely that it was not an *actual* potential entrant into New England, but also had to prove what was in the minds of other companies. On remand, the District Court found that Falstaff was not perceived by other beer manufacturers in New England as an influence on the fringe of the market.[27]

The central hypothesis of the potential competition theory is that a company not even in a market can, by standing in the wings, affect the price behavior of those in a concentrated market. Since the time span to build a plant is several years, it must be assumed that the existing oligopolists are constrained in pricing today because of a fear that several years in the future someone may enter their market. It was hard to believe, and on remand the District Court was unwilling to find, that a leader in the New York area, such as Anheuser-Busch, would price its beer a little lower because it *erroneously* believed Falstaff might enter a market *de novo* in a few years. Indeed, it can be argued that the existing oligopolists should know their market better than the outsider or potential entrant. Consequently, the existing oligopolists will not be easily fooled into *perceiving* an outsider as a potential entrant to the point of limiting their competitive behavior when in fact that outsider has no intention of actually entering the market. It is not surprising that in recent years the government has not tried to argue the "perceived potential entry theory" of the *Falstaff* case.

ENDNOTES

1. 370 U.S. 294 (1962).
2. *Ibid.*, p. 326.
3. *Ibid.*, pp. 327-28.
4. 378 U.S. 441 (1964).
5. *Ibid.*, p. 455.
6. *Ibid.*, pp. 469-70.
7. Government Brief, p. 22, See 378 U.S. 441, 470.
8. *Ibid.*, p. 461; and 374 U.S. 321 (1963).
9. *Ibid.*, p. 475.
10. *United States* v. *Aluminum Company of America, 377 U.S. 271 (1964)*.
11. *Ibid.*, p. 286.
12. *Ibid.*, p. 281.
13. 370 U.S. 294 (1962).
14. Bock, *Mergers and Markets*, 5th ed., p. 80.
15. 370 U.S. 294, 339 (1962).
16. 374 U.S. 321 (1963).
17. *Ibid.*, p. 357.
18. *Ibid.*, p. 360, fn. 37.
19. 376 U.S. 651 (1964). Also see *Cascade Natural Gas Corp.* v. *El Paso Natural Gas Co.*, 386 U.S. 129 (1967).
20. *Ibid.*, p. 659.
21. *Ibid.*, p. 661.
22. 378 U.S. 158 (1964).
23. 217 F. Supp. 110, 130 (1963).
24. 378 U.S. 158, 173 (1964).
25. 246 F. Supp. 917 (1965).
26. 410 U.S. 526 (1973).
27. 383 F. Supp. 1020 (D.R.I., 1974).
28. *The Pillsbury Company*, Dkt. 9091, Initial Decision (Dufresne, A.L.J., May 15, 1978).
29. Opinion of the Federal Trade Commission *in the matter of British Oxygen Company, Ltd.*, Dkt. 8955 (1975).

THOUGHT QUESTIONS

1. In the *Brown Shoe* case the Supreme Court refused to recognize price as a basis for separating medium-priced shoes into a distinct market from lower-priced shoes. Should the product market have included baby shoes, sneakers, slippers, work boots, rubbers, sandals, mocassins, and all other types of men's, women's and children's type shoes? Compare the government's argument in the *Cellophane* monopoly case that moisture-proof cellophane was the applicable product market rather than all flexible wrapping material with the broad *Brown Shoe* market definition sought in a merger case.

2. In analyzing the market shares and product market involving the merger of two frozen pizza manufacturers, a Federal Trade Commission Administrative Law Judge had to determine whether local pizza parlors competed with the frozen pizza pies purchased in food stores. Should the judge have accepted an invitation by the manufacturer to taste, in a blind test, both a frozen and a fresh pizza? Discuss his possible findings (other than heartburn).[28]

3. In the *Continental Can-Hazel Atlas* case the Supreme Court noted that glass containers and metal containers were in separate industries. Discuss whether the Supreme Court was attempting to construct market shares for a non-existent market.
   a) Could any other product market definition have allowed the Supreme Court to find the merger illegal?

4. In the *Alcoa-Rome Cable* case Alcoa had 27.8% of the aluminum conductor field. Do you believe a 1.3 increment to 29.1% would have changed Alcoa's market power to any significant extent?
   a) What is the importance of the downward market share trend of Alcoa for aluminum conductor?
   b) Do you believe that the only purpose of the Supreme Court in treating aluminum conductor as a separate market was to achieve higher market shares which could enable the Court to find the merger illegal?

5. Discuss the finding reached by the Federal Trade Commission in its case against the proposed merger between British Oxygen Company (BOC) and Airco:

   > Although most industrial gases are sold and distributed in regional markets of a few hundred miles distance from the point of manufacture, it is appropriate to use the nation as a whole as the section of the country affected by the merger. . . . The interest evinced by BOC in some regional firms was whether they would constitute feasible footholds for subsequent building of a national company.[30]

   a) Can a series of regional markets add up to a national market?
   b) How far would a service station operator on the East coast travel for a tank of acetylene gas for welding?
   c) Is the FTC in the *British Oxygen* case suggesting a "potential geographic market" theory?

6. Assume that a memorandum is written which states that it is unwise for the company to enter a given market *de novo* at the present time. The company then attempts to merge with an existing company in the market and introduces this memorandum in court to prove that it was not a potential entrant. Discuss whether the court should be able to second guess the company and consider whether the company might have changed its mind in five years when market conditions could be different?

7. Should the "actual potential entrant" doctrine be confined to cases where "subjective" proof (like a written memorandum) exists showing that the acquiring firm would have entered a market but for the acquisition?

    a)   Or, should "objective" proof be allowed where a court can reach a conclusion which may in some cases be opposite to that reached by the management of a company?

8. Discuss whether it is realistic from a business viewpoint to assume that a large company in a related industry would be discouraged or "fooled" from entering a market because a single firm was charging a "limit price" by currently keeping the price down.

    a)   Is it likely that a major corporation would be discouraged from entering a market because of a low price being set by the existing company?

    b)   In an oligopoly market, how would you distinguish (1) a tacit understanding by the oligopolists to keep out future entrants by discouraging them with a low price, from (2) healthy competitive rivalry among firms resulting in a low price?

9. Assume you are a marketing director of Budweiser beer for the New York area. Would you price your beer lower because Falstaff might enter your market in a few years? Would Schlitz and Pabst necessarily agree with your thinking? Are possible new entrants the least of your worries in an oligopolistic market with existing strong price competition?

10. Do you agree with the Supreme Court's finding that suburban shoe stores compete with shoe stores in the center of a city? Where did you buy your last three pairs of shoes and sneakers?

11. In a preliminary injunction to stop a merger of two drug store chains, the FTC argued that a three mile circle should be drawn around the stores to analyze the existence of a geographic competitive overlap.

    a)   Is one store a market?

    b)   Should it make a difference in geographic market analysis that some items, such as food and drugs, are purchased by older people who do not drive, and must walk to neighborhood stores?

12. Discuss the competitive significance of small city stores with floor space less than 10,000 square feet and a limited product line in types and sizes competing with major tenants in suburban shopping centers with parking and floor space over 100,000 square feet and an enormous product line.

    a)   Should ten little city stores equal one large suburban store for the purpose of market analysis?

13. Most major cities in the United States have areas with urban blight and other areas with luxury apartments and expensive neighborhoods. Should these two geographic areas be combined for appraising the competition in a retail store merger case?

    a)   Do customers from Park Avenue in Manhattan, realistically, shop in the South Bronx stores which are less than a mile away?

    b)   How wide should a geographic market be for retail stores?

14. Assume there are 20 Mobil gasoline stations, 10 Exxon gasoline stations, as well as a large number of other chain and independent gasoline stations, in a standard metropolitan statistical area covering several counties around a city and taking more than an hour, with traffic, to travel from one end to the other. What significance would a market share have which grouped all the gas stations together in a city, a county or the multiple county SMSA (Standard Metropolitan Statistical Area)?

B. RELATIVE CONCENTRATION IN MERGER CASES

Absolute measures of concentration refer to the percentages of assets, employees, or value of shipments accounted for by a given number of leading firms in an industry. Relative measures of concentration, which are less frequently employed, consider the size of competitors in relation to each other. An industry with sales fairly evenly divided among a few firms may simultaneously possess a high degree of absolute concentration but a low degree of relative concentration. For example, an industry including four firms each with 25 percent of total sales has a high degree of absolute concentration since the top three firms account for 75 percent of sales, but the relative concentration in this industry is nil since each competitor is equal in size as measured by their respective sales. As an analytical tool, relative concentration measures can be applied as usefully as the more conventional measures of absolute concentration.

THE MANUFACTURERS HANOVER CASE (1965)

The District Court decision in *United States* v. *Manufacturers Hanover Trust Co.*[1] applied the concept of relative concentration. The case involved the merger of two New York City banks, Manufacturers Trust and the Hanover Bank, into the Manufacturers Hanover Trust Company. Before the merger, Hanover was primarily a wholesale bank, generating most of its business from the deposits and loans of large corporate customers. Manufacturers, on the other hand, had a tradition of retail banking, emphasizing service to smaller individual customers. At the time of the merger, eight of the New York City banks held over $1 billion in assets, five others over a half billion, and eleven others over $100 million.

Measured by deposits before the merger, Manufacturers was fourth largest among 72 commercial banks in the metropolitan area and Hanover ranked eighth. (See Table 10-1B.) The Government claimed this merger eliminated substantial competition between the parties and constituted an unreasonable restraint of trade, in violation of Sec. 1 of the Sherman Act, as well as Sec. 7 of the Clayton Act.

TABLE 10-1B
Market Structure in the Manufacturers Hanover Bank Case

Pre-merger Rank	Name of Bank	Percent N.Y. Deposits	Pre-Merger Absolute Concentration	Pre-Merger Relative Size*	Post-Merger Relative Size*
1	Chase Manhattan	20.0	20.0%	100	100
2	First National City	17.6	37.6%	88	88
	(Manufacturers Hanover)	(13.8)	—	—	70
3	Chemical Bank	10.2	47.8%	51	51
4	Manufacturers Trust	9.2	57.0%	46	—
5	Morgan Guaranty	9.1	66.1%	46	46
6	Bankers Trust	7.8	73.9%	39	39
7	Irving Trust	5.3	79.2%	27	27
8	Hanover	4.6	83.8%	23	—
9	Franklin National	1.9	85.7%	10	10
10-12	Other banks	14.3			
	Total	100.0			

*Chase Manhattan's 20.0 percent of deposits in the New York metropolitan area in 1960 is equal to 100.

The relative concentration in the metropolitan New York market is shown in the last two columns of Table 10-1B. Before the merger, Chase, the largest New York bank, was more than twice the size of Manufacturers, the fourth ranking bank. After the merger, Chase was only one and a half times as large as Manufacturers Hanover, which now ranked third. The 9 percent of Manufacturers combined with the 5 percent of Hanover gave the new bank 14 percent of the deposits in the New York metropolitan area, and placed it in the size category of the top two banks, Chase and First National City. In terms of relative concentration, the market structure for the three leading firms changed from (100-88-51) before the merger to (100-88-70) after the merger.

In comparing the relative concentration existing in the metropolitan area before and after the merger, the District Court found that "there can be no question that the merger created a firm with an increased share, but the increment resulted in a bank over one-third to one-half smaller than its two larger local competitors, and only slightly larger than the next three."[2] Therefore, the District Court concluded, the gap previously existing in the market structure between the second and third largest bank was narrowed, and the "merger thereby improved the competitive structure and intensified competition for the three leaders."[3] Nevertheless, the District Court found the merger to be a violation of Section 7 of the Clayton Act. A year later, Congress passed the 1966 Bank Merger Act, which included a provision terminating the legal proceedings against the merger.[4] The decision of the District Court was thereby nullified.

THE PHILADELPHIA BANK CASE (1963)

The most immediate comparison with the *Manufacturers Hanover* case is the Supreme Court decision in *United States* v. *Philadelphia National Bank*,[5] which involved the proposed merger of Philadelphia National Bank, hereafter abbreviated PNB, with Girard Trust. As shown in Table 10-2B, the proposed merger would have combined PNB with 21 percent of the market and Girard with 15 percent into a single bank, which would have created a bank of a greater size than even First Pennsylvania, the largest bank in the market before the merger. The new bank, PNB-Girard, would enjoy "better than a 50 percent advantage in market share over its nearest rival. Moreover, if the merger was consummated significant disparities would separate each bank except two from its closer smaller competitor thereby upsetting the competitive balance of the market structure."[6] In terms of relative concentration, as shown in Table 10-2B, the market structure in the Phidelphia case would change for the three leading firms from (100-96-66) before the merger to (100-62-25) after the merger.

TABLE 10-2B
Market Structure in the Philadelphia Bank Case

Pre-merger Rank	Name of Bank	Percent Phila. Deposits	Pre-Merger Absolute Concentration	Pre-Merger Relative Size*	Post-Merger Relative Size†
	(PNB-Girrard)	(35.8)	—	—	100
1	First Pa.	22.1	22.1%	100	62
2	PNB	21.3	43.4%	96	—
3	Girard	14.5	57.9%	66	—
4	Provident	9.9	67.8%	45	28
5	Fidelity	9.3	77.1%	42	26
6-42	37 other banks	22.9			
	Total	100.0			

*   First Pa.'s 22.1 percent of deposits in metropolitan Philadelphia area in 1959 is equal to 100.
†   PNB-Girard's combined share of 35.8 percent is equal to 100.

In the *Manufacturers Hanover* case the defendant could have argued that the proposed merger of the fourth and eighth largest ranking banks would intensify competition against the disproportionately larger top two banks, namely, Chase Manhattan and First National City. However, in the *Philadelphia Bank* case the proposed merger would place the newly formed bank not only first in its market but also in a position one and a half times larger than the next bank, First Pennsylvania. Before the merger, the top two banks in Philadelphia were approximately equal in size, but after the merger the top two banks became substantially unequal in size. Thus the proposed merger could offer no favorable attributes to the competitive balance existing in the Philadelphia area. However, the defense argued that competition would be intensified with the larger New York City banks. The argument was rejected by the Supreme Court:

> . . . it is suggested that the increased lending limit of the resulting bank will enable it to compete with the large out-of-state bank, particularly, the New York banks, for very large loans. We reject this application of the concept of 'countervailing power.'[7]

A related argument was made that Philadelphia needed a larger bank in order to bring business into the city and stimulate its economic development. The court rejected this argument:

> We are clear, however, that a merger the effect of which "may be substantially to lessen competition" is not saved because, on some ultimate reckoning of social or economic debts and credits, it may be deemed beneficial. A value choice of such magnitude is beyond the ordinary limits of judicial competence. . . .[8]

Finally, the Supreme Court was of the opinion that the merger between the two banks would trigger further mergers among the remaining smaller banks:

> If anticompetitive effects in one market could be justified by precompetitive consequences in another, the logical upshot would be that every firm in an industry could, without violating Sec. 7, embark on a series of mergers that would make it in the end as large as the industry leader.[9]

THE BETHLEHEM-YOUNGSTOWN CASE (1958)

A similar position was taken by the District Court in the earlier case of *United States* v. *Bethlehem Steel Corp.*[10] The District Court held that the proposed merger between Bethlehem (No. 2 in the steel industry) with Youngstown (No. 6 in the steel industry) "offers an incipient threat of setting into motion a chain reaction of further mergers by the other less powerful companies in the steel industry."[11] (See Table 10-3B.) If there were logic in the argument that the merger of Bethlehem and Youngstown was justified to offer challenging competition to U.S. Steel (No. 1 in the steel industry), then, concluded the District Court, "the remaining large producers in the 'Big 12' could with equal logic urge that they, too, be permitted to join forces and to concentrate their economic resources in order to give more effective competition to the enhanced 'Big 2'. . . ."[12] The court in this statement focused only on the upward potential competition resulting from the newly merged smaller companies. If the procompetitive effects among the larger companies with respect to the newly merged company were weighed against the potential anticompetitive effects of the large companies *vis-à-vis* the lesser-sized companies, all the remaining companies would not necessarily have as a matter of "equal logic" the right to merge.

TABLE 10-3B
Market Structure in the Bethlehem Youngstown Case

Pre-merger Rank	Name of Bank	Percent Ingot Capacity	Pre-Merger Absolute Concentration	Pre-Merger Relative Size*	Post-Merger Relative Size*
1	U.S. Steel	29.7	29.7%	100	100
2	Bethlehem	15.4	45.1%	52	—
	(Beth.-Youngstown)	(20.1)	—	—	68
3	Republic	8.3	53.4%	28	28
4	Jones & Laughlin	4.9	58.3%	17	17
5	Youngstown	4.7	63.0%	16	—
6	National	4.6	67.6%	15	15
7	Armco	4.5	72.1%	15	15
8	Inland	4.1	76.2%	14	14
9-24	16 other integrated producers	13.8			
	Total	90.0			

U.S. Steel's ingot capacity in 1957 of 29.7 percent of the steel industry equals 100.

As the structure of an industry moves away from one dominant industry leader with no competitors in its size category, the need for upward competition diminishes and the need for protecting the competitive balance between lesser-sized firms is correspondingly enhanced. For example, in the *Bethlehem-Youngstown* case there was a leader with 30 percent of the market and its largest competitor was half its size. In the *Manufacturers Hanover* case there were two large leaders on top, approximately equal in size; consequently, the need for upward competition was not as great.

The contrast between the polar market conditions of pure competition and pure monopoly has given rise to the proposition, or at least an inference, that as the number of independent firms in a market is reduced competition is lessened. The use of numbers of firms as an index of competition cannot be justified by the fact that as the number of independent sellers reach unity, the market obviously reaches monopoly. Within the spectrum of market structures existing between monopoly and pure competition, the intensity of competition is not always lessened as the number of firms is reduced. A market with six firms may not necessarily be less competitive than a market with five firms.

In considering the proposed merger between Bethlehem and Youngstown, the District Court had to accept as an unalterable, pre-existing power structure the presence of U.S. Steel as the acknowledged price leader and holder of 30 percent of the steel industry's ingot capacity. Since U.S. Steel was not a party to the case, the District Court could not directly affect the position of this company. The court was limited in its choice between the following two market structures: (1) a market in which the largest company was twice the size of the second largest company, and (2) a market in which the largest company was one and a half times the size of the next company. In either of these market structures the two leading firms would account for over 45 percent of the industry capacity.

The choice the District Court faced in the *Bethlehem-Youngstown* case was therefore not between unconcentrated or concentrated market structures, nor oligopoly or pure competition, but between two highly concentrated market structures with differences primarily in the relative size of the leading firms.

MERGER VERSUS INTERNAL GROWTH

The proposed merger in the *Bethlehem-Youngstown* case involved two large companies, as evidenced by the fact that Bethlehem at the end of 1957 had total assets of $2.2 billion and Youngstown had total assets of $636 million. Bethlehem, which was located primarily in the East, argued that it needed the ingot facilities of the Youngstown Chicago plant as a prerequisite to building a new plate mill and new structural shape mill in the Chicago area. The District Court recognized that "it is undoubtedly easier and cheaper to acquire and develop existing plant capacity than to build entirely anew." However, each defendant, in urging the merger, took a "dim view of its ability to undertake, on its own, a program to meet the existing and anticipated demand for heavy structural shapes and plates in the Chicago area." The District Court was not convinced that without the merger the companies would not enter the Chicago plate and structural shape market. The following quotation by the District Court showed remarkable foresight: "The defendants' apprehensions, which, of course, involve matters of business judgment and, in a sense, matters of preference, are not persuasive in the light of their prior activities and history, their financial resources, their growth and demonstrated capacity through the years to meet the challenge of a constantly growing economy."[13] Six years after this decision, in 1964, Bethlehem's first of three ingot mills in the Chicago area began operations. On its Burns Harbor site along the Indiana shore of Lake Michigan, Bethlehem undertook at the time one of the largest private construction projects in the nation.

The competitive implications of Burns Harbor are noteworthy. Bethlehem, by not being able to buy the older and partially outmoded Chicago facilities of Youngstown, built in the 1960's one of the most efficient steel mills in the country. Bethlehem may have accomplished, even more effectively than by merger, both the potential for vigorous upward competition against U.S. Steel, as well as the ability for strong downward competition against the smaller, less efficient steel producers. The District Court, by finding illegal the proposed merger between Bethlehem and Youngstown, encouraged the independent entry of new capacity in the Chicago area by Bethlehem.

In 1978, twenty years after the Bethlehem-Youngstown decision, Youngstown laid off 5,000 steel workers and closed most of its Youngstown, Ohio plant. The Antitrust Division of the Department of Justice allowed Youngstown and its parent, The Lykes Corporation, to merge with LTV Corporation, which owned Jones & Laughlin. The resulting combination formed the fourth largest steel company in the United States. The basis of the approval was that Youngstown was a "failing company" and was losing close to five million dollars a month. The Antitrust Division gave no indication whether they placed any weight on the argument advanced by Lykes and LTV that the formation of the larger and stronger steel company would increase upward competition in the steel industry.

THE CONCEPT OF COUNTERVAILING POWER

The logical development of relative concentration, which considers inequality of firm size in an industry, is a concept of balance of power, which takes the further step of translating disparity in firm size into disparity in market power. By allowing some weaker firms to merge, a closer balance in the market structure is achieved and competition with the formerly larger rival firms may be intensified. Professor John Kenneth Galbraith, in *American Capitalism*, maintained that in markets of few sellers, the active restraint in terms of price levels is provided not by competitors, but from the other side of the market by strong buyers exercising "countervailing power." In situations where the bargaining power between buyers and sellers is substantially unequal, the government should allow countervailing power to develop even though absolute economic concentration may increase. Although Professor Galbraith limited his analysis to the power relationship between buyers and sellers, his observation that the economic power of a group in a market should not be viewed in isolation but in terms of its effect on other related power structures has a much broader application. The following passage by Galbraith is noteworthy in this respect:

> . . . the mere possession and exercise of market power is not a useful criterion for antitrust action. The further and very practical question must be asked: Against whom and for what purposes is the power being exercised? Unless this question is asked and the answer makes clear that the public is the victim, the antitrust laws . . . can as well enhance as reduce monopoly power.[14]

The seeming paradox of the enforcement of the antitrust laws sometimes increasing, or at least preserving, monopoly power instead of reducing it can be readily understood when market groups are analyzed in terms of interwoven market structures whose balance can be either favorably or unfavorably upset. Leading firms in an industry may have achieved their present positions largely as a result of mergers and a weakly enforced set of antitrust laws. The market positions of these companies are often perpetuated and insulated by an active set of antitrust laws which prevent lesser-sized companies from merging on the grounds that undue concentration already exists. The antitrust laws can therefore be used to reach the anomalous result that protection is afforded to the larger, leading companies, which need it the least, and their market power is preserved, whereas stronger competition from the merger of smaller companies is correspondingly stifled.

ENDNOTES

1. 240 F. Supp. 867 (S.D.N.Y., 1965).
2. 240 f. supp. 867, 932.
3. *Ibid.*, p. 933.
4. The Bank Merger Act of 1966, enacted as Public Law 88-356, 80 Stat. 7, was an amendment to Sec. 18(c) of the Federal Deposit Insurance Act, 12 U.S.C.A., Sec. 1828(c). Section 2(c) of the Amendment terminated pending antitrust actions involving bank mergers consummated after June 16, 1963. The *Manufacturers Hanover* case was covered by this section.

5. 374 U.S. 321 (1963).
6. 240 F. Supp. 867, 931 (S.D.N.Y., 1965).
7. 374 U.S. 321, 370 (1963).
8. *Ibid.*, p. 371. In contrast, the 1966 Bank Merger Act, Sec. 5(B), provides that the responsible agency shall not approve any proposed merger transactions which shall violate the specified antitrust standards "unless it finds that the anticompetitive effects of the proposed transaction are clearly outweighed in the public interest by the probable effect of the transaction in meeting the convenience and needs of the community to be served."
9. In December, 1965 the Central-Penn National Bank of Philadelphia and the Provident National Bank of Philadelphia applied to the Comptroller of the Currency for permission to merge. In April, 1966 the Department of Justice filed an action to enjoin the proposed merger. The injunction was upheld by the Supreme Court, 386 U.S. 361 (1967).
10. 168 F. Supp. 576 (S.D.N.Y., 1958).
11. *Ibid.*, p. 618.
12. *Ibid.*,
13. 168 F. Supp. 576, 616 (S.D.N.Y., 1958).
14. *American Capitalism*, (Boston: Houghton Mifflin Company, 1952), p. 149.

THOUGHT QUESTIONS

1. In 1980 the First Pennsylvania Bank was still the largest bank in Philadelphia, but experienced serious financial difficulties. Many of its loans were made to high risk national companies, such as Chrysler, which were unable to repay its loans. Discuss whether the bank's larger market share reflected greater assumption of risk and correspondingly greater weakness and vulnerability. Compare your analysis to that of the Supreme Court in the 1963 *Philadelphia Bank* case.

2. Since most banks charge the prime rate to credit worthy customers, and the prime rate is related to other non-bank credit sources such as commercial paper, what competitive difference does it make that one bank has more deposits and a larger market share than another?
   a) Should commercial and consumer deposits be grouped together for computing market shares?
   b) Should automobile loans, credit card loans, first and second mortgages also be included?
   c) Should the consumer loans outstanding, made by consumer finance companies, credit unions, and savings banks have been included?

3. Does the fact that one bank has more local offices for the convenience of its customers imply it has more market power than a competing bank with less offices?
   a) How many offices of your local bank do you personally use?
   b) Did you select your present bank primarily because of its size of assets, the number of offices, the current prime rate it was charging, the fact that it gave you a mortgage, or because it had a nearby local office which was convenient for making deposits and cashing checks?

4. Do you think the prime rate charged by PNB-Girard to leading customers would be different if the merger between them was allowed?

5. In the *Bethlehem-Youngstown* case, the District Court used percent ingot capacity to measure market shares. Do you think all the steel companies operated at the same level of capacity in 1957?
   a) Would dollar shipments of ingot have been a better basis for computing market shares? How would you value the captive steel ingot used within the same plant to make fabricated steel products?
   b) Should steel exports, which had little effect on domestic steel pricing, have been included?
   c) Should steel imports have been excluded by defining "domestic capacity" as the measure of market share?

C. CONGLOMERATE MERGERS

In the 1960's the Antitrust Division of the Department of Justice challenged several conglomerate mergers as possible violations of Section 7 of the Clayton Act. Three large conglomerate companies were singled out as principal targets: LTV (Ling-Temco-Vought), Northwest Industries, and ITT (International Telephone & Telegraph Co.).[1] LTV was challenged in its acquisition of Okonite Cable and Jones & Laughlin Steel. Northwest Industries was challenged in its acquisition of Goodrich Tire Company, and ITT was challenged for its acquisition in the insurance industry of Hartford Fire Insurance and also Grinnell, which manufactures automatic sprinklers for fire protection systems.

LTV is an example of a "conglomerate" which grew primarily by acquisition. Starting in 1961 the Justice Department tried, without success, to stop the merger of Ling-Temco, an electronics company, with Chance Vought, a military aircraft manufacturer. The resulting company was LTV. In 1965 the government challenged LTV on their acquisition of Okonite, a manufacturer of electric cable, and in 1969 it challenged the partial acquisition of the Jones & Laughlin Steel Corporation. The government did not challenge the acquisition by LTV of Braniff Airways, a major commercial airline, National Car Rental, or Wilson, a meat packing company which also had a pharmaceutical division and a sporting goods division.

In its complaint challenging the acquisition by LTV of Jones & Laughlin, the government raised the issue of potential reciprocity between various divisions of the large conglomerate. For example, potential reciprocity was alleged to be possible between Braniff, which purchases substantial amounts of jet fuel from oil producers and refiners, who in turn are actual or potential users of steel products manufactured by Jones & Laughlin. But the amount of commerce that could be affected by potential reciprocity of this kind was remote and minimal. The real argument by the government in the conglomerate merger cases was that Section 7 of the Clayton Act is violated by the consolidation of any two of the country's largest corporations without the need to show any lessening of competition in a specific product or geographic market. The argument of the Government in the *ITT, Northwest,* and *LTV* cases was summarized by the District Court in the *Northwest (Goodrich)* case:

> The issue of concentration raises a special question, for the Government is here urging that given a trend to economic concentration, the consolidation of two of the country's one hundred largest corporations constitutes a violation of Section 7 without any specific demonstration of a substantial lessening of competition in any section of the country. We do not so read Section 7.[2]

The conglomerate issues in these cases never reached the Supreme Court since Northwest Industries, LTV, and ITT settled each of their cases with the Government by giving up certain companies. For example, LTV divested itself of Okonite and Braniff, and was allowed to keep Jones & Laughlin. Ironically, the Government in the late 1960's challenged LTV for acquiring Jones & Laughlin, as a conglomerate merger. But in the late 1970's the Government permitted a financially weak LTV to merge horizontally with the failing Youngstown Tube & Steel Company, and form the fourth largest steel company in the United States. The classification of a company as a "conglomerate" was no longer viewed as a guarantee of profits, market power, or even viability. Some conglomerates had risen, and some had fallen, with no predictable outcome in terms of competition or performance.[3]

CONGLOMERATE POWER AND SUBSIDIZATION

The advantages of "conglomerate power" accrue to any company which is able to take funds from one geographic or product market, or from one stage of production, and use these funds to subsidize other areas under its operation. Subsidization can be shown to encompass not only rational conduct for the multiple-product firm, but also for the single-product firm. What constitutes an actual stage of production can often be a matter of cost accounting rather than the actual ability of a producer to resell a partially finished product. Similarly, geographic markets can be split up into various accounting units and treated as separate markets. A firm will operate one of its stages of production, or sell in one of its geographic markets, at a lower profit margin than other stages or markets. The more profitable markets are subsidizing or partially carrying the less profitable ones. Whatever the justification — maintaining an efficient level of production, broadening a sales base for protection against seasonal fluctuations, anticipating future company growth — the practices of every firm reflect instances of subsidization in almost every facet of its business behavior.

There are many forms of subsidization. In some cases the subsidization appears as an attempt by management to equalize its profits in various markets or stages of production. Every accounting transfer of profit between different products of a firm, or any manipulation of a rate of return between different stages of production can be interpreted as subsidization. A product does not have to be sold at a loss in order for subsidization to occur.

In *United States* v. *New York Great Atlantic and Pacific Tea Company*[4] the District Court interpreted subsidization as an equalization of profit rates. In analyzing the pricing of A&P in various geographic markets, the court stated:

> When the gross profit rate is reduced in Area X, it is an almost irresistible conclusion that A&P had the power to compensate for any possible decline in net profits by raising the gross profit rate and retail prices in Area Y, where it was in a competitive position to do so. The record is replete with instances of deliberate reductions of gross profit rates in selected areas. . . . There must inevitably be a compensation somewhere in the system for a loss somewhere else, as the overall policy of the company is to earn $7 per share per annum on its stock.[5]

A second meaning of subsidization requires a company to use profits from its operations in one market to support *actual losses* in a second market. Whether one of the products of a company is sold at a loss may depend upon the accounting method selected.[6] Similarly, as the firm increases in complexity either through vertical integration or diversification, the determination of precisely which departments, stages of production, or products are responsible for the over-all profit level of the firm can be ambiguous as a result of the problem of complementarity. Different products, or stages of production, share in the use of capital equipment, management, and selling expenses. Therefore, profits which are attributable to the complementary interactions of elements within the aggregate structure of a firm are often rather arbitrarily allocated by cost accounting methods to specific stages of production or distribution.

A third interpretation of subsidization is related to the act of "price squeezing" by a vertically integrated firm. Some of the profits derived from the sale of products from one stage of production may be used to carry another stage operated at or below cost, with the result that competing non-integrated, independent firms are injured. Accompanying this type of subsidization is usually a restriction of supply, or an overcharging on price, by the vertically integrated firm to its customers. The customers are generally independent processors or fabricators, who depend upon the vertically integrated firm for raw materials, and must also face the vertically integrated firm in the market for the final product.

The previous discussion of the *Alcoa* case pointed out that the offense committed by Alcoa was the forward subsidization of the sheet manufacturing operation, which was performed at a near loss, by the "profits" made at the earlier stage of ingot production. The court segregated the various technological levels of the integrated firm and treated each as an independent operation. Alcoa was found guilty of squeezing fabricators that purchased ingot from it at allegedly enhanced prices, and then had to meet Alcoa's unduly low prices for fabricated sheet.

In the *A&P* case, the company was alleged to have followed a business strategy of cutting prices in a particular geographic area in order to increase volume, which in turn would lower expenses, and permit a higher over-all rate of return. If A&P was successful in achieving a larger volume in a particular area, it would earn a higher return relative to its initial position. If A&P was unsuccessful in its price reduction campaign, it would sustain a loss or lower return on an unchanged volume.[7] In many instances the losses were so great that A&P had to close its stores. In the 1970's A&P closed hundreds of unprofitable stores and came upon financially hard times.

FIG. 10-1. Subsidization Between Vertical Stages of Production

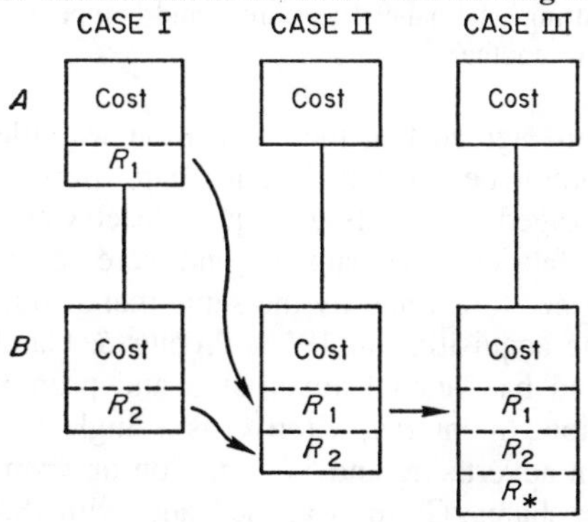

The problem of subsidization in relation to predatory pricing can be analyzed in terms of Fig. 10-1, which depicts three cases involving rates of return at different vertical stages of production. Case I illustrates vertical integration, where the firm earns the same rate of return of a "normal profit" from both the A and B stages of production. Case II shows a situation where the integrated firm decides to take all its return in the lower B stage by using the higher A stage as a source of subsidy. The firm earns the same rate of return on its investment in the B stage of production ($R1 + R2$) as it formerly earned on a combined basis from the A stage ($R1$) and the

B stage (*R2*). Case III shows a firm earning an additional "monopoly profit" (*R**) as a result of predatory pricing practices.

A fallacy often found in the discussion of subsidization is that the return on capital for some of the vertically integrated stages of production can be neglected by a firm. When a firm sells a product at cost from any of its various stages of production, and receives no return on the corresponding capital involved in the production process, it is working, to a certain extent, for nothing. The vertically integrated firm is in no different position from the non-integrated firm when it consumes its own capital through the selling of products at or below cost. Therefore, the advantage possessed by the integrated firm for price cutting is not its multiple stages of production, but the probable existence of larger financial resources that can be drawn upon in the consumption of internal capital.

THE PROCTER & GAMBLE (CLOROX) CASE

In *Federal Trade Commission* v. *The Procter & Gamble Co.* (1967)[8] an acquisition by Procter & Gamble, the leading manufacturer of soap and detergent with sales of household products over $1 billion, of the smaller Clorox Company, the leading manufacturer of household liquid bleach with sales of $40 million and assets of only $12 million, was found to be illegal. In the earliest stages of this case, a Federal Trade Commission Hearing Examiner rested his initial decision on the "conglomerate power" of Procter & Gamble,

> . . . the deciding factor is the ability of Procter & Gamble's conglomerate organization to shift financial resources and competitive strength through a broad front of different products and markets and its ability to strategically alter the selected point of greatest impact as time, place and market conditions require. . . . The test of conglomerate power is whether a corporation is able to concentrate its competitive efforts at one point by shifting its financial resources and competitive strength from one industry or market to another.[9]

The Supreme Court agreed that the acquisition was illegal, but viewed the merger as one of "product extension," rather than "purely conglomerate." The Court found that packaged detergents and liquid bleach were used complementarily in the washing of fabrics by consumers, and were generally sold to the same customers, at the same stores, and by the same merchandising methods.

At the time of the acquisition in 1957, Procter & Gamble was the nation's largest advertiser and had annual advertising and promotion expenditures in excess of $125 million. In contrast, Clorox, as a single product company, spent only $3.7 million on advertising and $1.7 million on promotion.

In terms of market shares, Clorox was the leader with 48.8 percent. Purex was second with 15.7 percent and Roman Cleaner was third with 5.9 percent of the market. The remaining 30 percent of the household liquid bleach market was accounted for by approximately 200 small firms.

The Federal Trade Commission and the Circuit Court found that there was no reasonable probability that Procter & Gamble would have entered the household liquid bleach market on its own. The Supreme Court disagreed and held that Procter & Gamble was the most likely entrant into this field: "It is clear that the existence of Procter at the edge of the industry exerted considerable influence on the market.'' Furthermore, the number of potential entrants into the household liquid bleach field was "not so large that the elimination of one would be insignificant.''

Justice Harlan, in a concurring opinion, objected to the majority opinion written by Justice Douglas, which "set its judgment on the facts against the concurrent findings below" of the Circuit Court of Appeals and the Federal Trade Commission which held that Procter & Gamble would not have entered the liquid bleach market on its own. A Procter & Gamble internal memorandum introduced in evidence specifically showed that the company had decided against entering the liquid household bleach market "because we feel it would require a very heavy investment to achieve a major volume in the field, and . . . the payout period would be very unattractive.''

Procter & Gamble, as a multi-product producer, was found by the Court to enjoy substantial advantages in advertising and sales promotions. For example, Procter & Gamble, by obtaining discounts on radio and television commercials, could advertise at a lower unit cost than a firm with only one product. The Supreme Court was concerned that,

> . . . the substitution of the powerful acquiring firm for the smaller, but already dominant, firm may substantially reduce the competitive structure of the industry by raising entry barriers and by dissuading the smaller firms from aggressively competing.

Justice Harlan, in his concurring opinion, observed that it could equally be assumed that smaller firms would become more aggressive in competing because of their fear that otherwise Procter & Gamble might ultimately absorb their markets.

Before the acquisition, Clorox had greater economic power than most of its rivals. Clorox was three times larger than the Number 2 firm in its industry, and eight times larger than the Number 3 firm. The finances of Clorox, although not comparable with Procter & Gamble's, appeared more than adequate in view of its relative size and success in its industry. As a result of the popularity of its product, Clorox was able to obtain ample shelf space in most supermarkets. Since Clorox was the leader in its industry and three times larger than its next largest competitor, it already had the power, in terms of relative size, which Procter & Gamble was supposed to give it. It is therefore questionable whether the merger with Procter & Gamble changed any of the competitive options Clorox possessed as the leading firm in its industry.

THE REYNOLDS METAL (ARROW BRANDS) FLORIST FOIL CASE

The acquired firm in *Reynolds Metals Co. v. Federal Trade Commission*[10] did not already possess a relatively greater size than its competitors before the acquisition took place. Reynolds Metals, the largest producer of aluminum foil in the world, with assets in 1957 over $730 million, acquired one of its customers, Arrow Brands, one of the "eight or ten" small producers of decorative aluminum florist foil with assets under $1 million. Arrow accounted for approximately 33 per cent of the sales in this industry. From the initial facts one might easily conclude that the antitrust offense was the foreclosure of suppliers by vertical integration.

That is, Reynolds, by acquiring one of its customers, Arrow Brands, could now foreclose other competing foil suppliers, such as Alcoa, from selling to Arrow Brands. But the Federal Trade Commission expressly stated that even if Reynolds did not supply aluminum foil to Arrow Brands, the acquisition would still be considered illegal. In an opinion written by Chief Justice Burger, as a Circuit Court judge, the vertical supply relationship between Reynolds and Arrow Brands was minimized:

> When Arrow was vertically integrated through the Reynolds' acquisition, one minor anti-competitive effect foreseeable was the exclusion of other manufacturers of raw foil (Reynolds' competitors) from selling to approximately 33% of the florist foil converting industry. However, neither the examiner nor the Commission rested their conclusions that Sec. 7 had been violated on this basis, nor should we.

The Circuit Court characterized the acquisition by Reynolds as "the intrusion of 'bigness' into a competitive economic community otherwise populated by commercial 'pygmies'." In holding the acquisition illegal, the Circuit Court stated,

> Arrow's assimilation into Reynolds' enormous capital structure and resources gave Arrow an immediate advantage over its competitors who were contending for a share of the market for florist foil. The power of the "deep pocket" or "rich parent" for one of the florist foil suppliers in a competitive group where previously no company was very large and all were relatively small opened the possibility and power to sell at prices approximating cost or below and thus to undercut and ravage the less affluent competition.[11]

Reynolds purchased Arrow Brands in 1956 at a time when the company did not even own its own plant, but carried on business from leased space. Reynolds constructed a plant for Arrow in Torrance, California, for $500,000. After this decision in 1962, Reynolds argued that the Federal Trade Commission had no authority to require it to divest assets not obtained by the acquisition. The Circuit Court agreed and the net result of the litigation was that Reynolds disrupted a new facility, had to sell off a few hundred thousand dollars of equipment, and left an industry which had such low barriers to entry that anyone could enter with almost no capital. More perplexing than the case, is why did Reynolds Metals want to enter such a limited fabricating operation as a business strategy? And why did the Federal Trade Commission want to challenge a merger where the value of the assets of the company approached the cost of legal fees to litigate the matter?

THE BRUNSWICK BOWLING ALLEY CASE

The Supreme Court in 1977 rejected the "deep pocket" theory of conglomerate power in *Brunswick Corp.* v. *Pueblo Bowl-O-Mat, Inc.*[12] Brunswick acquired a number of bowling alleys after the former proprietors could not pay for equipment on which Brunswick had given them loans. In a private treble damage case, an owner of several bowling alleys which competed with the bowling alleys taken over by Brunswick alleged that Brunswick's "deep pocket" and ability to finance the bowling alleys constituted a substantial lessening of competition. The Court of Appeals found that a jury could reasonably conclude that Brunswick was a "giant" whose entry into a "market of pygmies" might lessen horizontal competition because it "has greater ease of entry into the market, can accomplish cost savings by investing in new equipment, can resort to low or below cost sales to sustain itself against competition for a longer period, and can obtain more favorable credit terms."[13]

The Supreme Court held that the competitors would have faced the same competition if some other company had taken over the financially troubled bowling alleys. In the words of the Court:

> . . . respondents' injury — the loss of income that would have accrued had the acquired centers gone bankrupt — bears no relationship to the size of either the acquiring company or its competitors. Respondents would have suffered the identical "loss" — but no compensable injury — had the acquired centers instead obtained refinancing or been purchased by "shallow pocket" parents . . .

The plaintiffs basically sought to force Brunswick to close its bowling alleys so that they would not face any competition. The entire proof of damages by plaintiffs was based on their claim to profits that they would have earned had the bowling centers acquired by Brunswick been closed. The Supreme Court held that "Brunswick's entry into the picture did not increase concentration, but only acted as a substitution of competitors." The plaintiffs were therefore not entitled to damages. The fable of "giants and pygmies" as a theory of conglomerate power was thereby quietly put to rest by a new Supreme Court seeking the stronger force of competition over the weaker shield of protectionism.

CONCLUSION

When the subsidization constitutes a potential resort to a "deep pocket," the concept of conglomerate power reduces to an attack on relative size or bigness. A second product or geographic market, or several stages of production, is no longer required for the exercise of conglomerate power. There is no reason why a single product company cannot also dip into its cash reserves and simulate the same system of subsidization alleged to exist in most conglomerate merger cases.

When a firm starts a research and development department, it is financing one department with the profits earned at another stage of production. A new product that a firm is attempting to introduce to the public is almost invariably an initial losing proposition because of low volume and high advertising and distribution costs. The building of a new plant requires expenditures from internal reserves, from another geographic product market, from a vertical stage of production, or from the "deep pocket" of a bank. In other words, the term conglomerate power reduces in the end to some form of subsidization, and subsidization is not necessarily bad. All investment, either in new plant expansion, new product innovation or new market development requires some temporary amount of subsidization.

At the core of the concept of conglomerate power is a belief that a substantial disparity in the size of firms in the same market may be incompatible with the forms of competition which our antitrust laws are expected to preserve. A market structure of a large number of firms, no one of which has significant market power, does meet some of the requirements for the classical definition of "pure" competition. But in a market structure already concentrated with a *limited* number of firms, equality in size may *not* be more desirable than some degree of inequality of size. Inequality of size may be a vital stimulus for firms to improve their product, to compete more vigorously, and, as an over-all policy, to refuse to settle for a smaller share of the market. There exists no ready answer to the question whether an industry composed of firms approximately the same size can be expected to be more or less competitive than an industry whose firms are equal in size.

ENDNOTES

1. *United States* v. *ITT (Grinnell-Hartford Fire)*, 1969 *Trade Cases*, Para. 72,943 (D.C. Conn., 1969); *United States* v. *Northwest Industries (Goodrich)*, 1969 *Trade Cases*, Para. 72,853 (D.C. N. Illinois, 1969); and *United States* v. *Ling-Temco-Vought* 1970 *Trade Cases*, Para. 73,105 and 73,227 (W.D. Pa., 1970).
2. 1969 *Trade Cases*, Para. 72,853 (D.C. N. Illinois, 1969).
3. See generally, J. W. Markham, *Conglomerate Enterprise and Public Policy* (Harvard Business School, 1973); Federal Trade Commission, *Economic Report on Corporate Mergers*, Staff Report (U.S. Government Printing Office, 1969); C. W. Edwards, "Conglomerate Bigness as a Source of Power," in *Business Concentration and Price Policy*, p. 336.; D. Turner, "Conglomerate Mergers and Section 7 of the Clayton Act," *Harvard Law Review*, Vol. LXXVIII (May, 1965), pp. 1313-95; M. Gort, *Diversification and Integration in American Industry*, National Bureau of Economic Research (Princeton, N.J.: Princeton University Press, 1962); J. C. Narver, *Conglomerate Mergers and Market Competition* (Berkeley, Calif.: University of California Press, 1967).
4. 67 F. Supp. 626 (E.D. Ill., 1946), *affirmed* 173 F. 2nd 79 (7th Cir., 1949).
5. *Ibid.*, p. 87.
6. See J. A. Menge, "The Backward Art of Interdivisional Transfer Pricing," *Journal of Industrial Economics*, Vol. IX (July, 1961), 215-32.
7. M. A. Adelman, "The A&P Case: A Study in Applied Economics," *Quarterly Journal of Economics*, Vol. XLIII (May, 1949), p. 238-57.
8. 386 U.S. 568 (1967).
9. Docket No. 6901, Second Initial Decision (February 28, 1962), p. 62 of the mimeographed text.
10. 309 F. 2nd 223 (1962).
11. *Ibid.*, pp. 229-30.
12. 429 U.S. 477 (1977).
13. *NBO Industries Treadway Cos.* v. *Brunswick Corp.*, 523 F. 2d 262, at p. 268 (Third Circuit Court of Appeals, 1975). NBO Industries was acquired by Pueblo Bowl-A-Matic.

THOUGHT QUESTIONS

1. Discuss the statement by the Supreme Court in the Clorox case that substitution of P&G for Clorox would lessen competition by "dissuading the smaller firms from aggressively competing." Would a smaller liquid bleach company be likely to fight less for its life against P&G than against Clorox?
2. Discuss the reasons why P & G should move bleach prices higher, lower or the same as those prices previously being charged by Clorox?
3. Assume that a smaller liquid bleach manufacturer, such as Rose-X, does not own a

corporate jet, does not advertise, maintains inexpensive offices, but has similar plant production costs as Clorox.

    a)   Is it likely that the marginal and average cost of the smaller Rose-X would be lower than those of P&G-Clorox?

4.   In the Kodak-Berkey case, discussed in Chapter 5, the District Court stated,

> "It is at least a little demure for defendant to describe itself as a mere company with a "large market position." Kodak is . . . a "giant," with a nearly unique agglomeration of enormous powers over adjoining markets in a huge industry."

Discuss whether market share, rather than absolute size, should have been the relevant consideration.

5.   Discuss the behavior of Borden, as described in the *ReaLemon* case in Chapter 5, which was to "increase the size of the allowances to as much as $1.20 per case, or 10 cents per bottle . . ." in those markets "where competition has been making inroads."

    a)   Should Borden meet the prices of its competitors in these regional areas or lose market share?

    b)   Discuss why Borden chose to meet their competition with promotional discounts rather than heavy spot or national TV advertising?

    c)   Would your reasoning also apply to liquid bleach?

6.   Would the court have reached the same decision in the *Reynolds Metals-Arrow Brands* case if a giant conglomerate which did not manufacture aluminum sheet purchased the smaller Arrow Brands?

    a)   Assume Arrow Brands was already owned by a large conglomerate not engaged in the aluminum industry. This conglomerate then sold its Arrow Brands subsidiary to Reynolds Metal. Would these facts have changed the decision of the court?

D. PRODUCT EXTENSION MERGERS

THE BLACK & DECKER (MCCULLOCH CHAIN SAW) CASE (1976)

In *United States* v. *The Black and Decker Mfg. Co.* (1976), the District Court in Maryland found that the acquisition of McCulloch, a leading manufacturer of gasoline powered chain saws, by Black & Decker, the leading manufacturer of portable electric tools, did not eliminate any actual or potential competition between the companies, and did not violate Section 7 of the Clayton Act. The merger allowed Black & Decker to broaden and extend its product line of electric small tools to include gasoline powered chain saws.

The relevant product market in the *Black & Decker* case was defined by the District Court as encompassing the manufacture and sale of *gasoline* powered chain saws. In addition, the District Court found a "home-owner" submarket existed for lightweight, inexpensive (under $200 suggested retail price) units sold to occasional users, primarily the "do it yourself" homeowner. These occasional user saws were sold predominantly in retail hardware stores, chain stores and garden centers. They were advertised typically through popular media, such as television, while saws for professional users were primarily advertised in specialty trade publications.

The top four companies in the gasoline powered chain saw market accounted for 82% of the total units sold in 1974. This concentration ratio was deemed by the court to be sufficiently high to establish a *prima facie* case for the government that the market was concentrated and lacked competitive vigor:

> The burden thus shifts to the defendants to demonstrate with evidence of actual competitive market performance that these concentration ratios do not accurately reflect the competitive nature of the gasoline powered chain saw markets.

Black & Decker introduced evidence that a substantial number of new manufacturing companies recently entered the industry with the result that the top two manufacturers, including McCulloch, lost market share. Despite this evidence, the court found:

> The number of new entrants also does not belie the substantial entry barriers characteristic of the gasoline powered chain saw market. . . .

The court noted that firms which entered this market tended to be foreign chain saw manufacturers or companies with prior gasoline engine experience. It is difficult to reconcile these contradictory findings of "substantial entry by foreigners" and "substantial barriers to entry."

On the finding of price competition, the court again had paradoxical findings. The court reasoned that since the manufacturers were developing new products at the cheaper end of their product line, the price competitiveness of all their products could not be readily compared. There was a downward bias on the average of all gasoline powered chain saws caused by the expansion of the "occasional user," cheaper segment. In the words of the court:

> Price competitiveness is one of the most reliable indicators of desirable market behavior. Without doubt, the average prices paid for gasoline powered chain saws have decreased markedly in the last years. . . .
>
> The impact of this average price decline is clouded, however, since it results primarily from the expansion of the gasoline powered chain saw market into the occasional user segment where smaller, lower priced products are offered. . . .
>
> Thus, while gasoline powered chain saw manufacturers were adapting their product line by introducing smaller, lower priced models in order to capture a share of the occasional user submarket, no overall market pricing competitiveness clearly emerges.

Price competitiveness is demonstrated precisely by the product development of the less expensive line of saws. The smaller, lighter weight saws gave consumers a cheaper alternative to more expensive, heavier units. This type of product innovation at the lower end of the spectrum of prices of a line of products would only be forthcoming in an industry with high sensitivity to price competitiveness.

In its analysis of the gasoline powered chain saw market, the court did not mention that McCulloch, despite its status as a leader in a concentrated market, earned a profit in only one year in the past decade before the merger with Black & Decker. In this period, McCulloch sustained losses of over $32 million. Its stock fell in value from $72 million to $9 million. The company was in default with its bank, which agreed to waive temporarily the default on the express condition that the company pursue its merger negotiations with Black & Decker. Despite these facts, the government refused to concede that McCulloch was a failing company, and argued that it could have rehabilitated itself by terminating its unprofitable lines. The District Court disagreed:

> Even had McCulloch pruned its operations to its marginally profitable chain saw division, the company's debts were so large, its cash shortage so acute, its paucity of unpledged assets so pronounced, and its possibilities for obtaining new capital so slight that business failure would probably still have resulted.

Nevertheless, the court stated that "McCulloch was not a failing company." A better choice of words by the court would have been that McCulloch had not established the failing company defense to Section 7 of the Clayton Act. The failing company defense requires both a high probability of busines failure, which was found, and a finding that there was no available purchaser of the company which would be less competitive. The court found that "McCulloch single-mindedly explored the possibility of acquisition by Black & Decker without consideration of other companies." McCulloch argued that the bank, which by the terms of their loan agreement with McCulloch had to approve any merger, believed that any attempt to secure an alternative merger partner to Black & Decker could be disruptive to the negotiations and delay the merger. The court noted in only a footnote that McCulloch's debt with the bank doubled from $9.1 million in 1971 to $18.2 million in September, 1973, at which time its working capital amounted to only $1.2 million dollars. Indeed, the court noted that the company's financial position was such that, but for the proposed merger with Black & Decker, McCulloch's independent auditors would not have valued the company as a going concern.

The government alleged in the *Black & Decker* case a "perceived potential entrant" theory. The government argued that Black & Decker was perceived by existing manufacturers as the "most likely entrant" into the gasoline powered chain saw market by either internal expansion (*de novo*), or by a toehold acquisition of a small competitor in the industry. The court disagreed, and found that all of Black & Decker's new products were restricted to applications of *electric* motors since it lacked any technical expertise in *gasoline* motors.

Industry witnesses testified that it would take three to five years for a company without prior experience to develop a *gasoline* powered chain saw. By that time, technological innovations would probably render the product obsolete. Major competitors testified in court that they did not perceive Black & Decker as a potential entrant. The court also found that no electric tool company had ever entered the gasoline powered chain saw market by internal expansion. The more likely potential entrants were found to be foreign companies with gasoline, small-motor knowledge, such as manufacturers of gasoline powered lawn mowers or motorcycles.

Finally, the government argued an "entrenchment theory" which asserted that "the combination of a major portable electric tool manufacturer, Black & Decker, with one of the largest gasoline chain saw manufacturers, McCulloch, will entrench and dominate an already oligopolistic gasoline powered chain saw market." The court rejected this argument and found that many of the companies in the market equaled or surpassed Black & Decker in financial ability. For example, one of the larger manufacturers of gasoline powered chain saws was Homelite, a division of Textron, a company with multi-billion dollar sales. The marketing, engineering and manufacturing expertise of Black & Decker was found to be not complementary to McCulloch's. In distinguishing the *Proctor & Gamble* case the court noted:

> Unlike liquid bleaches which were chemically indistinguishable and therefore relied exclusively on advertising for product differentiation, gas powered chain saws offer a variety of different features tailored to heterogeneous types of purchasers and requirements . . . product design and engineering can play a critical role in consumer acceptance; Black & Decker could assist McCulloch in neither of these areas.

In retrospect one might ask what the government sought to accomplish by the years of litigation. All the arguments of potential entry were devoid of any substantial evidence since Black & Decker had no experience in gasoline engines. All the evidence of economic concentration and oligopoly had little merit in the face of the acquired company being at the brink of bankruptcy.

The Antitrust Division of the Department of Justice decided against taking an appeal from this lower District Court ruling. It is questionable whether the Antitrust Division should have brought this case originally. Such a decision by the Government could have been predicated on a legal conclusion that all the theories of oligopoly power, high concentration, and perceived potential entry and entrenchment have little competitive significance when the company being acquired is both the leader and, more importantly, just short of bankruptcy.

THOUGHT QUESTIONS

1. Are you convinced that Black & Decker could not have developed independently or purchased from the outside, a small gasoline powered engine which it could have used in many different types of garden tools?
2. Is it likely that the knowledge of small gasoline motors, which Black & Decker gained from its acquisition of McCulloch, would make it a likely potential entrant into many other product markets such as lawnmowers? Should these types of pro-competitive factors in markets outside chain saws be considered by the court?
3. Assume the following facts: Black & Decker just patented a new battery powered fuel cell capable of powering, without gasoline, a chain saw and a broad line of garden tools. Black & Decker announces to the press that it has no interest in manufacturing gasoline powered chain saws, but intends to use the McCulloch name and reputation for introducing a new line of chain saws with battery powered fuel cells. Assume that it is highly likely that the new chain saw will be successful, that McCulloch will become a strong, dominant firm and that McCulloch could not possibly develop this fuel cell independently or purchase it from an outside source. Would these facts change the reasoning or the conclusion of the Court with regard to potential competition?

E. HORIZONTAL MERGERS BETWEEN A LEADING COMPANY AND A WEAK COMPETITOR

A substantial amount of the explanation for the declining rates of productivity in the United States can be attributed to the failure or reluctance of industry to replace its older, obsolete capital equipment. As a practical business policy, many companies have found it wiser to allow some plants to terminate their lives rather than attempt to modernize a basically outmoded facility. Mergers involving the purchase of outmoded and weak, but not yet failing companies are often temporary measures for allowing a plant to continue for a few more years before being closed.

THE BEER MERGERS IN THE 1970'S

The small breweries built over a hundred years ago are examples of plants where it did not pay to modernize. In the New York area the breweries for Schlitz, Schaefer, Piels, Ruppert and Rheingold were all closed in the 1970's. Most of these breweries had cobblestones near their loading platforms for horse drawn wagons which used to deliver draft beer in barrels to local bars and restaurants. The large trucks and tractor trailers could not fit easily into the narrow loading dock areas. Most of the ceilings of the warehouses were low since they were designed for barrels of beer and not for fork-lift trucks which could hoist six feet of cases filled with aluminum cans or bottles of beer.

In 1965, Ruppert closed its brewery in Manhattan and sold its trademarks to Rheingold. The Ruppert brewery was demolished and replaced by apartment houses. Rheingold moved the Ruppert production to its Brooklyn plant. In 1978 the Rheingold plant was also closed after being in operation for 122 years. The Rheingold and Ruppert production was shifted to Schmidt's in Pennsylvania which purchased the Rheingold and Ruppert trademarks.

As the number of small breweries in the United States which had formerly served regional markets declined, the larger national brewers, such as Anheuser-Busch, moved into the regional territories with packaged beer (cans and bottles) made in modern, highly automated breweries. The Justice Department, Antitrust Division, challenged a number of these mergers among weaker companies, such as the Rheingold acquisition of the Ruppert trademarks and the acquisition of the Blatz trademarks by Pabst, on the grounds that concentration was rising in metropolitan, regional markets and would further increase if these mergers among regional brewers were allowed.[1]

From the beginning, these mergers between the weak regional brewers were doomed since their economies were limited to increasing production temporarily by closing the plant and shifting production and warehousing to another similarly outmoded facility. There were also substantial labor problems in these older facilities since sales, production and profit margins were declining sharply. The large national brewers engaged in substantial promotions and discounts to increase their market shares with beer produced at a lower cost in newer production facilities. The rigid antitrust policy of the Antitrust Division of the Department of Justice in stopping the mergers of weak competitors did not result in stemming the tide of concentration, nor in permitting the possibility for eventual deconcentration. It simply resulted in these plants closing prematurely and in people losing their jobs sooner than if the companies could have merged while they were in "poor health" rather than having to wait until they were "terminally ill" and became "failing companies."

In the next two cases, *General Dynamics* and *National Tea-Applebaums*, the mergers involved weak competitors with little likelihood of their becoming strong competitive factors in the future with their existing inadequate physical facilities.

The cases are noteworthy in the willingness of the courts to look into the future and consider a wide number of economic factors in reaching their decision.

THE GENERAL DYNAMICS CASE (1974)

In *U.S.* v. *General Dynamics Corp.*,[2] a deep-mining coal producer (Freeman) acquired United Electric, a strip-mining coal producer. Freeman was owned by Material Service Corporation which was acquired by General Dynamics after this horizontal merger occurred. As a result of this acquisition, General Dynamics became the fifth largest coal producer in the United States. The Government challenged the acquisition and showed that concentration was rising and was already very high with the top two coal producers in the State of Illinois having over 50% of the production of coal and the top four companies 75%. Furthermore, the number of coal producing firms in Illinois decreased almost 73% in the period 1957-1967 from 144 to 39. Therefore, the Government argued the acquisition was inherently illegal and further economic analysis was unnecessary under the precedent of *U.S.* v. *Philadelphia National Bank*[3]. In 1963, the Supreme Court stated in the *Philadelphia National Bank* case that, "if concentration is already great, the importance of preventing even slight increases in concentration and so preserving the possibility of eventual deconcentration is correspondingly great." The *Philadelphia National Bank* case also stated,

"This intense congressional concern with the trend toward concentration warrants dispensing, in certain cases, with elaborate proof of market structure, market behavior or probable anticompetitive effects. Specifically, we think that a merger which produces a firm controlling an undue percentage share of the relevant market, and results in a significant increase in the concentration of firms in that market, is so inherently likely to lessen competition substantially that it must be enjoined in the absence of evidence clearly showing that the merger is not likely to have such anticompetitive effects."

The Supreme Court in 1974 under Chief Justice Burger, which heard the *General Dynamics* case, was a quite different Court than the Court in 1963 under Chief Justice Warren which decided *Philadelphia National Bank*. In their *General Dynamics* decision, the Supreme Court noted that the effect of adopting the *Philadelphia National Bank* approach which was advocated by the Government would be "to allow the Government to rest its case on a showing of even small increases of market share or market concentration in those industries or markets where concentration is already great or has recently been increasing." This the Supreme Court was unwilling to do.

The Supreme Court heard evidence in the *General Dynamics* case that the acquired firm, United Electric, had low coal reserves and therefore its potential to compete with other producers in the future was weaker than the past production figures and market shares would otherwise have indicated. Almost all of United Electric's proved reserves were depleted or committed by long-term contracts with large customers. Therefore, the company's market power was limited and diminishing. The Court emphasized that the appropriate standard for evaluating economic data is the future, not the past:

"Evidence of past production does not, as a matter of logic, necessarily give a proper picture of a company's future ability to compete. In most situations, of course, the unstated assumption is that a company that has maintained a certain share of a market in the recent past will be in a position to do so in the immediate future. Thus, companies that have controlled sufficiently large shares of a concentrated market are barred from merger by Section 7 not because of their past acts, but because their past performances imply an ability to continue to dominate with at least equal vigor.''

The Court concluded that the *General Dynamics* acquisition was legal and would not substantially lessen competition since the acquired company lacked sufficient coal reserves to be a significant competitive factor by itself in the future.

THE NATIONAL TEA — APPLEBAUMS CASE (1979)

In *FTC* v. *National Tea-Applebaums*,[4] the Circuit Court of Appeals for the Eighth Circuit relied primarily on the *General Dynamics* decision in affirming the lower District Court's denial to the Federal Trade Commission for a preliminary injunction that would bar the acquisition by National Tea of 26 grocery stores operated by Applebaums in the Minneapolis-St. Paul metropolitan area. National Tea was a national food chain which operated, at the time of the acquisition, 19 stores in the Minneapolis-St. Paul area. As a result of the merger, National Tea would become the number one firm in the Minneapolis-St. Paul area and the top four concentration ratio would increase from 44.5% to 49%.

Both the District Court and the Court of Appeals were not content to rely only on market shares. Both of the courts read a transcript of five days of testimony by various witnesses before a magistrate in Minneapolis which showed that National Tea was losing money and, but for this acquisition, was likely to leave the Minneapolis-St. Paul market. National Tea had losses in 1978 in 15 out of its 19 stores and more than half of its stores had not operated at a profit at any time during the past five years. National's stores were tiny and outmoded — having been built in the late 1950's and 1960's when the selection of various shelf items numbered approximately 6,000. There are now over 12,000 items which a supermarket must consider stocking to offer a wide selection of products to customers. Since 1967, National Tea tried to revitalize and modernize its store and, in the process, closed 36 stores in the Minneapolis-St. Paul area.

The Court of Appeals found that a basic problem facing National Tea was its inability to gain access to prime sites for new stores. Because National Tea was known to have the lowest sales per store of the sixteen major food retailers in its area and was also known to be experiencing losses, real estate developers would not offer it prime real estate sites on which they could build new and modern stores. In following the *General Dynamics* decision, the Court of Appeals noted that, ''while market share is an important indicator of a firm's future competitive strength, other factors may discount its significance.''

The Court of Appeals noted the District Court's finding that National Tea would leave the Minneapolis-St. Paul market if the merger was enjoined and cited this finding as evidence that the present market share of National Tea was not economically significant in terms of its future performance:

> Obviously, if National had experienced such serious marketing problems in the Minneapolis-St. Paul area that it was leaving the area, its present market share was an inaccurate reflecting of its future competitive strength.

In other words, a food chain's market share obtained by extensive losses over a protracted period of time is not an economically meaningful number. Higher market shares can always be achieved by "giving groceries away" or selling products at a loss. This is hardly a reflection of market power.

The Court of Appeals further considered, "what may happen if the merger occurs with what may happen if the merger does not occur." The prospective loss of National Tea from the Minneapolis-St. Paul market if the merger is enjoined was deemed a relevant factor of analysis. In other words, if National Tea were to leave the market, its share would more likely be picked up by some of the leading companies rather than by the smaller retailers. In the event of National Tea leaving the market, the Court of Appeals found that,

> the market share of the top four firms could rise at least from 44.5% to 47.5%. This compared to the four firm concentration increase expected with the merger from 44.5% to 49%.

There were two other competitors, Red Owl and Country Club, which had approximately the same market share as the proposed National Tea-Applebaums entity. Red Owl stores had 13.9% and Country Club stores had 13.8% as compared to National Tea-Applebaums with 14.2%. In the words of the Court of Appeals,

> Thus, even if National is able to maintain its statistical position after the merger, it will still be faced with vigorous competition from the two other leading firms as well as from the strong and growing second-tier firms.

There was considerable testimony in the *National Tea-Applebaums* case by economists concerning whether a relationship existed in food retailing between increased concentration and competition. The Federal Trade Commission argued a positive relationship existed and, therefore, the merger should be denied. To substantiate its claim, the Federal Trade Commission introduced in evidence the Joint Economic Committee of Congress Study of Food Retailing (1977) and called as a witness one of its principal authors, Dr. Williard F. Mueller of the University of Wisconsin, who previously had been the chief economist at the Federal Trade Commission. Dr. Mueller's testimony was challenged by an economic expert called on behalf of *National Tea*, Dr. Morris Adelman of Massachusetts Institute of Technology. Dr. Adelman testified that the Joint Economic Committee Study failed to demonstrate *any* positive relationship between concentration, prices and profits. In denying the motion by the Federal Trade Commission for a temporary restraining order, the Court of Appeals held,

> There was considerable conflict in the evidence as to whether increases in the top four firms' market concentrations in the interval from 40% to 50% of the total market, implied more than marginal increases in price, that is, decreases in competition.

A consent order in 1980 was signed between the parties whereby the FTC permitted the merger and National Tea agreed to divest itself of several stores and not to acquire any other stores for ten years within a radius of 500 miles of their warehouse outside Chicago.

CONCLUSION

There have been few, if any, propositions established in industrial organization which would allow a rapid disposition of an antitrust case because a concentration ratio or a market share was deemed high. Nevertheless, there will always be individuals who are convinced that critical levels of concentration exist and adversely affect competition, society and economic progress. These advocates urge passage of legislation which would make it *per se* illegal, and therefore not subject to debate or challenge by extensive economic evidence in the courts, for companies to possess a market share or a rate of return above a fixed percentage. A company could be subject to being broken up under a ''no fault monopolization'' law presently being discussed by some antitrust experts if the company had a critically large market share.[5] The fact that the market share was obtained by honest and competitive conduct, excellence in product performance and astuteness in management would be irrelevant. Rigid numerical standards in antitrust would allow all to know where we stood at a given point of time, but the sacrifice would be in where we were going.

A more flexible approach to antitrust policy is an appreciation of the rule of reason and the traditional deductive analysis of the judicial process. A fundamental humility is required when one leaves the security of absolutes. It is a far more difficult task for a judge to weigh the alternative economic and legal factors in a case then to follow blindly *per se* mechanical rules. In both *General Dynamics* and *National Tea-Applebaums*, the finding of economic concentration was not deemed by the courts to be the controlling factor. There was no abstract, national fear of a ''rising tide of economic concentration'' because a weak strip mining coal company with depleted reserves wanted to merge with another coal company or a food chain with old, small stores wanted to combine with a stronger competitor. Rather, the courts looked beyond the present level of market shares and, with reason as their guide, considered the future competitive environment. In reviewing a wide spectrum of present and probable future facts, the courts demonstrated in the words of Justice Oliver Wendall Holmes that, ''The life of the law has not been logic; it has been experience.''

ENDNOTES

1. *United States* v. *Pabst Brewing Co.*, 384 U.S. 546 (1966); also see *United States* v. *Falstaff Brewing Corp.*, 410 U.S. 526 (1973), on remand, 383 F. Supp. 1020 (D.R.I., 1974); *United States* v. *G. Heileman Brewing Co.*, 345 F. Supp. 117 (E.D. Mich., 1972); and *United States* v. *Jos. Schlitz Brewing Co.*, 253 F. Supp. 129 (N.D. Calif.), *affirmed per curiam* 385 U.S. 37 (1966), *United States* v. *Rheingold Corp.*, *et. al*, Civil Action No. 65 Civil 3372 (S.D.N.Y.). The Justice Department ultimately decided to withdraw its complaint against the Rheingold acquisition of the Ruppert trademarks and asked the Court to dismiss its action.
2. 415 U.S. 486 (1974).
3. 374 U.S. 321 (1963).
4. 603 F. 2d 694 (1979).

5. See, "No Fault Monopolization Proposal Debated by Presidential Commission on Antitrust Reform" BNA, Antitrust Trade Regulation Reporter, September 14, 1978; and "No Fault Monopoly: A Debate Within a Debate," *Across the Board* (The Conference Board Magazine), Vol. XVI (November, 1979), p. 54; and U.S., *Report to the President and the Attorney General of the National Commission for the Review of Antitrust Laws and Procedures*, (January 22, 1979), Vol. I, Chapter 8.

THOUGHT QUESTIONS

1. In 1951, the leading brewers in the U.S. were ranked as follows: Schlitz, Anheuser-Busch, Pabst, Ballantine, Liebmann (Rheingold), and Miller.
   a) With the benefit of hindsight, discuss whether the merger of Ballantine and Rheingold should have been permitted in 1951 under the existing antitrust laws.
   b) Discuss the meaning of the phrase from the Supreme Court's *Philadelphia National Bank* case concerning the "preserving the possibility of eventual deconcentration" in markets where concentration is already great.
   c) Is "eventual deconcentration" in terms of a return to small regional brewers a realistic possibility in the 1980's?
   d) Would you support a legislative bill to restrict the territorial marketing of beer by wholesalers in the same manner as franchised bottlers of soft beverages are presently protected?
2. Assume an almost reverse set of facts in the *General Dynamics* case. General Dynamics is assumed to have already owned the weak coal company, United Electric, which had very low coal reserves. General Dynamics aerospace division is assumed to have recently developed a new type of metal used in a revolutionary type of coal mining machine. General Dynamics seeks to acquire coal reserves to utilize their new machine which will allow them to achieve the lowest coal production costs in the nation, probably become the number one producer, and possibly solve some of our energy crisis. Should the fact that General Dynamics presently owns a coal company without reserves be critical to a decision of the Supreme Court with regard to this hypothetical merger?
3. In the *National Tea-Applebaum* case, should the relevant market have included only "food chain stores," as the FTC argued, or "*all* food stores," as the defendants maintained? Note: "All food stores" includes independent grocery and convenience stores, bakeries, butcher shops and delicatessens.
4. In recent years, leading food chains, such as A&P, Food Fair and National Tea, have experienced enormous losses. Does this fact negate a possible relationship between prices, profits and concentration?
5. Assume large new food stores provide greater food item selection, carry higher quality produce and provide ample parking. Customers prefer these new stores and are willing to pay higher prices with the result that the stores earn high profits and the market share of the chain and concentration increases. Do the higher average prices of these larger, new stores, and their higher profits, necessarily suggest a lessening of competition because market shares and concentration are both high and increasing?

APPENDICES

APPENDIX A:

ANTITRUST LAWS OF THE UNITED STATES

There are three antitrust principal statutes in the United States: the Sherman Act, enacted in 1890; the Federal Trade Commission Act, enacted in 1914; and the Clayton Act, also enacted in 1914; A brief explanation of these statutes and the text of the basic substantive provisions are given below.

THE SHERMAN ACT

Section 1 of the Sherman Act provides in part that:

> Every contract, combination in the form of trust or otherwise, or conspiracy, in restraint of trade or commerce among the several States, or with foreign nations, is hereby declared to be illegal.

This section requires the existence of two or more persons, since a contract, combination, or conspiracy must be formed as a prerequisite to a finding of illegality. Agreements between competitors to fix prices, allocate geographic markets, or boycott third parties are practices condemned by this section of the Sherman Act. Conviction under this statute is a felony punishable by a fine of up to one million dollars for a company and up to $100,000 for an individual. An individual could be imprisoned for a period of up to three years.

Section 2 of the Sherman Act is directed toward actual or attempted monopolization and provides in part that:

> Every person who shall monopolize, or attempt to monopolize, or combine or conspire with any other person or persons, to monopolize any part of the trade or commerce among the several States, or with foreign nations, shall be deemed guilty of a felony, . . .

The punishment for conviction is the same as for Section 1 of the Sherman Act.

THE FEDERAL TRADE COMMISSION ACT

Section 5 of the Federal Trade Commission Act, as amended, provides in part that:

Unfair methods of competition in or affecting commerce, and unfair or deceptive acts or practices in or affecting commerce, are hereby declared illegal.

Typical proceedings brought by the Federal Trade Commission under Section 5 include false or misleading advertising claims concerning the quality, physical ingredients, or performance of a product, or the "regular price" of a product from which a discount is offered. There is considerable overlap of Section 5 of the Federal Trade Commission Act with the major provisions of the Sherman and Clayton Acts.

THE CLAYTON ACT

Section 2: The Robinson-Patman Act.

Section 2 of the Clayton Act was amended in 1936 by the Robinson-Patman Act. The Act was passed in response to the complaints of independent wholesalers, that chain stores were obtaining from their suppliers unwarranted advantage in the form of lower prices, greater advertising allowance, and discounts. Those concessions that could not be justified by lower costs as a result of the large volume purchases by chain stores were to be curbed by the passage of the Robinson-Patman Act.

Section 2(a) of the Robinson-Patman Act condemns illegal price discrimination by providing in part that:

It shall be unlawful for any person engaged in commerce, in the course of such commerce, either directly or indirectly, to discriminate in price between different purchasers of commodities of like grade and quality, where either or any of the purchasers involved in such discriminations are in commerce, where such commodities are sold for use, consumption, or resale within the United States . . . (or any place under its jurisdiction) and where the effect of such discrimination may be substantially to lessen competition or tend to create a monopoly in any line of commerce, or to injure, destroy, or prevent competition with any person who either grants or knowingly receives the benefit of such discrimination, or with customers of either of them. . . .

Section 2(a) also includes the following "cost justification" defense to a charge of price discrimination:

. . . That nothing herein contained shall prevent differentials which make only due allowance for differences in the cost of manufacture, sale or delivery resulting from the differing methods or quantities in which such commodities are to such purchasers sold or delivered. . . .

Section 2(b) of the Robinson-Patman Act covers the "meeting competition" defense to a charge of price discrimination covered in Section 2(a). This section permits price discrimination if it is justified by the necessity of a seller to meet in good faith the equally low price of a competitor.

Section 2(b) of the Robinson-Patman Act provides in part:

> That nothing herein contained shall prevent a seller rebutting the prima facie case thus made by showing that his lower price or the furnishing of services or facilities to any purchaser or purchasers was made in good faith to meet an equally low price of a competitor, or the services or facilities furnished by a competitor.

Section 2(c) of the Robinson-Patman Act is directed against arrangements whereby buyers exact price discriminations disguised as brokerage commissions. It provides in part:

> That it shall be unlawful for any person engaged in commerce in the course of such commerce, to pay or grant, or to receive or accept, anything of value as a commission, brokerage, or any other compensation, or any allowance or discount in lieu thereof, except for services rendered in connection with the sale or purchase of goods, wares, or merchandise, either to the other party to such transaction or to an agent, representative, or other intermediary therein where such intermediary is acting in fact for or in behalf, or is subject to the direct or indirect control, of any party to such transaction other than the person by whom such compensation is so granted or paid.

Sections 2(d) and 2(e) cover discriminations in promotional allowances and services made available to purchasers who buy for resale. Promotional allowances and services include cooperative payments by manufacturers to retailers for advertising, special featuring of a product in a store sale, or having a representative of a supplier give a demonstration in a store of the advantages of a particular product. Section 2(d) applies where the supplier gives a payment to the buyer for the buyer to perform the services. Section 2(e) applies where the supplier furnishes the service itself to the buyer. Both sections require the supplier to treat his competing customers on proportionally equal terms.

Section 2(d) of the Robinson-Patman Act provides:

> That it shall be unlawful for any person engaged in commerce to pay or contract for the payment of anything of value to or for the benefit of a customer of such person in the course of such commerce as compensation or in consideration for any services or facilities furnished by or through such customer in connection with the processing, handling, sale or offering for sale of any products or commodities manufactured, sold, or offered for sale by such person, unless such payment or consideration is available on proportionally equal terms to all other customers competing in the distribution of such products or commodities.

Section 2(e) of the Robinson-Patman Act provides:

> That it shall be unlawful for any person to discriminate in favor of one purchaser against another purchaser or purchasers of a commodity bought for resale, with or without processing, by contracting to furnish or furnishing, or by contributing to the furnishing of, any services or facilities connected with the processing, handling, sale, or offering for sale of such commodity so purchased upon terms not accorded to all purchasers on proportionally equal terms.

Section 2(f) was directed against large buyers who use their buying power to exact more favorable treatment from their suppliers. Section 2(f) of the Robinson-Patman Act provides:

> That it shall be unlawful for any person engaged in commerce, in the course of such commerce, knowingly to induce or receive a discrimination in price which is prohibited by this section.

Section 3: Tying Arrangements and Exclusive Dealing.

Section 3 covers tying sales where the purchase of one good is conditioned upon the purchase of another good; exclusive dealing, where the purchaser cannot handle competing lines; and requirements contracts, where the purchaser fulfills all or most of his needs from a single supplier. These restraints are condemned where their effect may substantially lessen competition or tend to create a monopoly.

Section 3 of the Clayton Act provides in part:

> It shall be unlawful for any person in commerce, in the course of such commerce, to lease or make a sale or contract for sale of goods, wares, merchandise, machinery, supplies, or other commodities . . . on the condition, agreement, or understanding that the lessee or purchaser thereof shall not use or deal in the goods, wares, merchandise, machinery, supplies, or other commodities of a competitor or competitors of the lessor or seller, where the effect of such lease, sale, or contract for sale or such condition, agreement, or understanding may be to substantially lessen competition or tend to create a monopoly in any line of commerce.

Section 4: Private Suits for Treble Damages.

Section 4 of the Clayton Act gives a private party the right to sue for treble damages for an injury to his property or business received as a result of violations of the antitrust laws by an individual or corporation. The section has been resorted to in price-fixing cases, where customers purchased goods at prices higher than would have prevailed in the absence of a conspiracy to fix prices by suppliers, in boycott cases, where a buyer was unable to find suppliers or a seller was unable to find customers, and in price discrimination cases, where a customer paid more than his competitors, or a competitor was intentionally harmed by price cutting.

Section 4 of the Clayton Act provides:

> That any person who shall be injured in his business or property by reason of anything forbidden in the antitrust laws may sue therefor in any district court of the United States in the district in which the defendant resides or is found or has an agent, without respect to the amount in controversy, and shall recover threefold the damages by him sustained, and the cost of the suit, including a reasonable attorney's fee.

Section 4(a) of the Clayton Act allows suits to be brought and damages to be collected by the United States where the Government sustained actual injury from a violation of the antitrust laws. Section 4(b) provides a statute of limitation restricting actions which can be brought under this statute to four years after the cause of action accrued. Section 4(c) allows a state attorney general to bring suit on behalf of the residents of the state. These actions are referred to as "parens patriae" suits.

SECTION 4(d): Measurement of Treble Damages in Price Fixing Cases.

Section 4(d) of the Clayton Act is limited to price fixing cases and provides that a class action can prove aggregate damages for a group, such as all customers, without the necessity of proving injury for each and every customer. The section provides in part:

> In any action . . . in which there has been a determination that a defendant agreed to fix prices in violation of the Sherman Act, damages may be proved and assessed in the aggregate by statistical or sampling methods, by the computation of illegal overcharges, or by such other reasonable system of estimating aggregate damages as the court in its discretion may permit without the necessity of separately proving the individual claim of, or amount of damage to, persons on whose behalf the suit was brought.

SECTION 7: Mergers and Acquisitions.

Section 7 of the Clayton Act covers corporate acquisitions and mergers. It condemns those mergers or acquisitions, between corporations engaged in interstate commerce, where the effect of the transaction may be substantially to lessen competition or to tend to create a monopoly.

Section 7 of the Clayton Act provides in part that:

> No corporation engaged in commerce shall acquire, directly or indirectly, the whole or any part of the stock or other share capital and no corporation subject to the jurisdiction of the Federal Trade Commission shall acquire the whole or any part of the assets of another corporation engaged also in commerce, where in any line of commerce in any section of the country, the effect of such acquisition may be substantially to lessen competition, or to tend to create a monopoly.

SECTION 7(a): Notification of Pending Mergers.

In 1976 Congress passed the Hart-Scott-Rodino Antitrust Improvements Act which required notice for certain pending mergers to be given to the Federal Trade Commission and the Antitrust Division of the Department of Justice. A waiting period of 30 days is required before the consummation of a merger between companies affected by this section of the Clayton Act. The statute applies to those companies to be acquired which have annual net sales or total assets of $10,000,000 or more and an acquiring or purchasing company which has annual net sales or assets of $100,000,000 or more. The purchase must involve at least 15 percent of the stock or assets of the acquired company or be valued at over $15,000,000. The notice requires filling out a detailed form which asks for dollar revenues for manufactured products in terms of the Standard Industrial

Classification Codes. In particular, 7-digit product code shipment data are required by the form for all manufactured products. In addition, the form requests copies of the most recent annual reports and "all studies, surveys, analyses and reports which were prepared by or for any officer(s) or director(s) . . . for the purpose of evaluating or analyzing the acquisition with respect to market shares, competition, competitors, markets, potential for sales growth or expansion into product or geographic markets . . ."

APPENDIX B:

THEORETICAL COMPARISON OF THE MODELS OF PURE COMPETITION AND PURE MONOPOLY

THE MODEL OF PURE COMPETITION

The economic model of pure competition is a market structure with the following features: (1) a large number of buyers and sellers, (2) a standardized product, (3) freedom of entry and exit, (4) inability of any individual buyer or seller to influence price, and (5) absence of any collusion. The adjective "pure" indicates an absence of all monopoly elements. In contrast, the term "perfect competition" implies an absence of monopoly elements, and in addition, instantaneous mobility of factors of production, and complete knowledge as to prevailing prices and future events.

FIG. B-1 The Firm in Pure Competition (P = MC = MR)

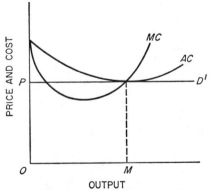

In pure competition a firm can sell at the going market price as many units as it produces. Its demand curve is a horizontal line at a height corresponding to the going market price. In Fig. B-1 the equilibrium output for the competitive firm is at OM, where the marginal cost curve MC is rising and intersects the horizontal demand curve D' at the going market price P. The demand curve (or average revenue curve) coincides with the marginal revenue curve and, in equilibrium, the following conditions exist: $P = MC = MR$. The competitive firm will continue to increase its output and sell it at the going market price until the total cost of producing an additional unit (MC) is equal to the revenue (MR = P) derived from its sale. In the long run, as a result of freedom of entry into and exit out of an industry, the average cost curve will be tangent at its minimum point to the demand curve and the competitive firm will achieve a normal return, which is the minimum remuneration necessary to keep the firm in business.

THE MODEL OF PURE MONOPOLY

The economic model of pure monopoly is a market structure of one firm which faces neither the threat of entry of other firms into its industry nor the competition of close substitute products. The pure monopolist controls a complete industry. It competes only in the restricted sense of vying with all other firms in the economy for the limited incomes of consumers.

The monopolist, unlike the purely competitive firm, cannot sell all its output at a going market price. As a monopolist increases output, the market price for its product can be expected to decline. Thus, the monopolist faces a downward sloping demand curve. In Fig. B-2 the monopolist will maximize its profits by increasing its output to Q_m, where its marginal revenue curve MR intersects its marginal cost curve MC. Note that as a consequence of the downward sloping demand curve DD', the price charged by the monopolist OP_m will be greater than marginal revenue OP_c at the profit maximizing output Q_m.

FIG. B-2 Pure Monopoly (P > MR = MC)

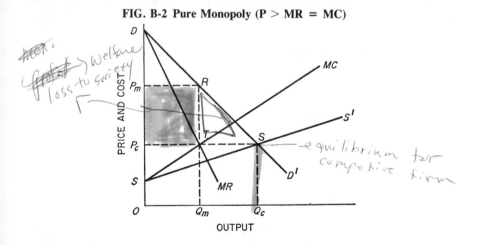

COMPARISON OF THE THEORETICAL RESULTS OF THE MODELS

The output of a monopolist, which represents the total industry output, can be compared with the output of the same industry under pure competition. Assume that DD' in Fig. B-2 represents the demand curve for the monopolist as well as the demand curve for the competitive industry. SS′ represents the long run competitive supply curve and is equal to the average cost curve.[1] The competitive industry will be in equilibrium at output Q_c, where the industry demand curve DD′ intersects the industry supply curve SS′.

If the monopolist takes over this competitive industry, and no changes in cost or demand occur, the industry output will be contracted to Q_m. At Q_m the monopolist's marginal cost MC, which is marginal to the average cost curve SS′, intersects the marginal revenue curve MR, and the profits of the monopolist are maximized. Thus, the monopolist by restricting output to maximize profits initially appears to produce a lower level of output than that achieved by a purely competitive industry.   *ans. to q 1*

The monopolist earns "monopoly profits" equal to P_cTRP_m in Fig. B-2 which represents a transfer of funds from consumers to the monopolist. The triangle TRS disappears when output is reduced to Q_m and the price is raised by the monopolist to P_m. This triangle is referred to as the "deadweight welfare loss" resulting from the inefficient allocation of resources.[2] At the restricted output level, Q_m, and higher price, P_m, some consumers will have to settle for a different mix of products which will be less satisfying to them.

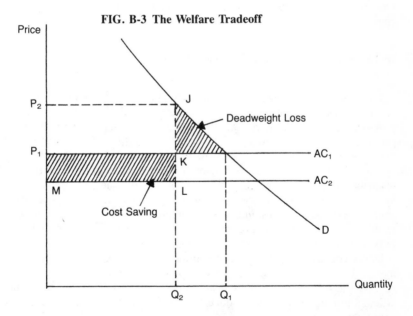

FIG. B-3 The Welfare Tradeoff

The monopoly profits may transfer wealth from some underprivileged or less fortunate consumers to middle and upper class owners or stockholders of the monopoly. This redistribution of income can affect the ultimate allocation of resources in determining the types of consumer goods which the economy will produce. For example, welfare choices may be primarily in terms of the alternative demands for luxury goods for the benefit of those with greater wealth rather than basic or subsistence type goods for the less fortunate. However, to the extent that labor unions and pension funds invest in stocks, the "monopoly profits" may not necessarily result in a redistribution of income. The static analysis of monopoly and welfare does not consider the effects on costs from past conduct or the impact on future technological change. In the past periods, there may have been substantial costs such as from excessive advertising which were associated with a company attempting to monopolize an industry. These costs, some economists would argue, should be added to the lost "deadweight welfare" costs.[3] It could also be argued that these are the competitive battle costs associated with each firm trying, more frequently than not without success, to obtain the position of leadership in an industry.

Future periods can be affected by lower costs resulting from technological or product innovation by the monopolist. In Fig. B-3, a firm is shown to achieve economies of scale, either through a merger or internal expansion, with the result that the "deadweight welfare loss" from higher prices is more than offset by the "welfare gains" from cost savings.[4]

A similar analysis can be applied to the welfare trade-off between oligopoly and technology. If concentration and large firm size is necessary to innovation, then the alleged higher prices and profits from oligopoly may be more than offset by the increase in the productivity resulting from technological progress.[5] Thus, the static welfare model with a "loss welfare triangle" resulting from monopolistic elements does not portray the future welfare of the economy in terms of redistribution of income, new and improved goods and services, or technological change.

WELFARE IMPLICATION OF THE MODELS

The classical economist Pareto maintained that the welfare of society would be optimized and an ideal allocation of resources would be achieved provided no person could be made more satisfied without at the same time making another person less satisfied.[6] A number of economic conditions must be fulfilled before the consumer sector and producer sector of an economy can reach a Pareto optimum. In the consumer sector, an optimum allocation of goods will be realized when there exist no further situations in which a mutual advantage can be obtained by any two consumers in further exchanging goods. In the producer sector, an optimum allocation of resources will be realized when inputs cannot be further reallocated among firms in order to increase the output of one firm without at the same time decreasing the output of another firm.

Under conditions of perfect competition, the firm expands its output until its marginal cost is equal to the product price. The final step in achieving the necessary conditions for a Pareto optimum allocation of resources requires the efficient product mix of the producer sector to conform to the preferences of the consumer sector.

Critics of the "classic welfare economics" have contended that, in a mixed economy with a number of regulated and unregulated industries not operating under conditions of pure competition, it may be undesirable in terms of economic welfare to attempt to restructure some but not all of these monopolistic industries. The "theory of second best" states,

. . . it is not true that a situation in which more, but not all, of the optimum conditions are fulfilled is necessarily, or is even likely to be, superior to a situation in which fewer are fulfilled.[7]

If the condition that marginal cost equal marginal revenue is not established for one firm in the economy, the "second best optimum" requires that this equality be departed from in other firms. The second best position can therefore be one in which some firms have marginal revenues greatly in excess of their marginal costs, and others have only a slight departure, with the remaining firms having their marginal revenues falling short of their marginal costs.

The theory of second best presents a profound lesson to the antitrust policy maker:

> To apply to only a small part of an economy welfare rules which would lead to a Paretian optimum if they were applied everywhere, may move the economy away from, not toward, a second best optimum position.[8]

There may exist, of course, political advantages far outweighing the allocation of resource considerations of economic welfare. But the interdependence of the network of industries, economic efficiencies and income redistribution effects must be carefully considered in effecting any structural changes in the economic system.

MATHEMATICAL NOTE ON THE PARETIAN OPTIMUM EQUATIONS

A Paretian allocation of goods in the consumer sector requires that the ratio of marginal utilities for any two goods should be the same for any pair of individuals consuming both of them.[9] Any two consumers, denoted by superscripts i and j, must face the same prices under conditions of perfect competition. A consumer maximizes his satisfaction when the ratio of his marginal utilities for any two goods, denoted by subscripts x and y, equals the ratio of their respective prices. Only in this position will the consumer be unable to increase his total utility by reallocating his limited funds in order to obtain more of a good X and less of good Y, or vice versa. Since both consumers face the same fixed prices, the ratios of their marginal utilities for any two goods are equal. The consumers' rate of substitution (CRS) represents the rate at which consumers can substitute one good, such as X, for another good, such as Y, given a limited budget. The following chain equation summarizes these relationships:

$$\text{CRS} = \frac{P_x}{P_y} = \frac{MU^i_x}{MU^i_y} = \frac{MU^j_x}{MU^j_y}$$

An optimum allocation of resources in the producer sector requires that the ratio of marginal products for any two inputs should be the same for any pair of products using both of these inputs. The marginal product of input A is defined as the extra output of good X resulting from an additional unit of input A. An optimum allocation of resources for producing good X requires the ratio of the marginal product of input A over the marginal product of input B should be equal for both goods X and Y. Inputs A and B will be combined efficiently in terms of an optimum allocation of resources when the ratios of their marginal products equal the ratio of their respective prices. Denoting the inputs A and B as superscripts, and the final goods X and Y as subscripts, the condition for an optimum allocation of the inputs is as follows:

$$\frac{P_a}{P_b} = \frac{MP^a_x}{MP^b_x} = \frac{MP^a_y}{MP^b_y}$$

The above marginal productivity analysis can be translated into the more familiar marginal cost analysis. By definition, the cost of an input such as A, which contributes to an increase in one unit of product X, is the same as the marginal cost of product X. Hence, for inputs A and B, which are used in the production of good X, the following relationships exist when the inputs are optimally allocated:

$$\frac{P_a}{MP^a_x} = \frac{P_b}{MP^b_x} = MC_x$$

$$\frac{P_a}{MP^a_y} = \frac{P_b}{MP^b_y} = MC_y$$

The above equations state the proper proportions in which a firm should combine optimally inputs A and B. The absolute amount of these resources which the firm should employ in terms of its optimum output level is determined by the profit maximizing condition equating marginal cost to marginal revenue. Under conditions of perfect competition, the firm expands its output until its marginal cost is equal to the product price (its marginal revenue). Hence,

$$P_x = MC_x$$

$$P_y = MC_y$$

The producers' rate of transformation (PRT) is the rate at which producers can substitute the output of product X for product Y given a fixed level of inputs. The producers' rate of transformation between goods X and Y is equal to the ratio of their marginal costs under conditions of perfect competition. Therefore, for an optimum allocation of resources the ratio of market prices for a pair of goods must be equal to their respective marginal costs:

$$\frac{P_x}{P_y} = \frac{MC_x}{MC_y} = PRT$$

Alternatively stated, and generalized for Z products, the condition for efficient allocation of resources between the consumer and producer sectors becomes:

$$\frac{P_x}{MC_x} = \frac{P_y}{MC_y} = \ldots = \frac{P_z}{MC_z}$$

The final necessary condition for a Pareto optimum requires efficient product mix of the producer sector to conform to the preferences of the consumer sector.

This is accomplished by having the producers' rate of transformation (PRT) between any two products equal to the consumers' rate of substitution (CRS) for the same two products:

$$PRT = CRS$$

MONOPOLY INDEXES

The Measurement of Monopoly Power

The basic heterogeneity of competition in the United States makes the identification of monopoly power by a select number of salient characteristics difficult. If nonquantitative factors are deemed essential for measuring monopoly power, one will not be able to construct a suitable scale of monopoly power or a "competitive thermometer." The forces of monopoly may be so complex and nonquantifiable that they cannot be characterized by a single number for an industrial sector.[10]

This basic problem in developing an index for measuring monopoly power is finding a set of variables that will describe uniquely different degrees of monopoly power. Control of price or supply, and conditions of entry are important factors which, directly or indirectly, must be considered. Thus, monopoly indexes have taken into account slopes and the elasticity of demand curves, rates of profits, degree of product substitution, marginal costs, and related conditions of supply.

Professor Lerner defines a monopolist as a firm with a downward sloping demand curve. In contrast, Professor Chamberlin observes that a firm with a declining demand curve may face competition from other firms with similar, although not identical, products. All products have some type of substitutes, either close or imperfect. The continuum of substitute products results in all industries shading into each other; therefore, the case of pure monopoly, in which by definition all substitutes are excluded, is impossible. Professor Chamberlin concludes that unless a firm controlled all products in an economy, it could not be a pure monopolist. Other economists, however, have not abandoned the concept of an industry: close, competitive substitute products, which serve as practical alternative sources of supply for customers, are classified in the same industry.[11]

The Lerner Index

Professor Lerner proposed as a measure of monopoly power the following index.[12]

$$\text{Lerner index} = \frac{\text{Price} - \text{Marginal cost}}{\text{Price}}$$

The degree of monopoly power in the Lerner index depends upon the divergence between price and marginal cost. In pure and perfect competition, price is equal to marginal cost for each product in the economy, and the Lerner index is equal to zero. For a costless output, with zero marginal cost, the index equals unity, indicating the ability of a seller to charge a price for a free good.[13] In the case of overproduction, marginal cost may exceed price and the index will have a negative value. The index defines monopoly in terms of the slope of a demand curve. This is seen clearly where the profit maximizing firm is in equilibrium: marginal revenue is equal to marginal cost, and the Lerner index is equal to the inverse of the elasticity of demand,

$$\frac{\text{Price}}{\text{Price} - \text{Marginal revenue}}$$

Professor Lerner was primarily interested in obtaining an index of monopoly which would reflect not the measure of tribute individuals could obtain from others by virtue of being in a monopolistic position, but rather the divergence of the economy from the "social optimum that is reached in perfect competition." Since the Lerner index is essentially static, it does not indicate whether the present deviation of marginal cost from price and the present alteration in the allocation of resources are worthwhile costs to pay for future advances which may leave society on an even higher level of economic development in the longer run.[14] Furthermore, the theory of second best questioned the validity of viewing in isolation the equality of price and marginal cost in one industry as evidence of an optimum allocation of resources.

The Lerner index does not reveal whether the level of marginal costs is a reflection of superior efficiency, which takes advantage of the existing body of knowledge and fosters further technical development, or, in contrast, a reflection of anachronistic methods of production in plants of uneconomic size and purchasing practices which exploit suppliers.[15] Application of the Lerner index is also affected by changes over time in the ratio of capital to labor in an industry.[16] Despite these shortcomings, as well as the difficult problem of obtaining even an approximation of marginal cost over the applicable range of output, there have been several attempts toward the application of this index.[17]

The Bain Index

Professor Bain uses the divergence between price and *average* cost to measure monopoly power rather than the difference in the Lerner index between price and marginal cost. Professor Bain justifies his index on the grounds that it is possible to view the divergence between price and average cost as evidence, on a probability basis, of the existence of a discrepancy between price and marginal cost: "Although excess profits (a price-average cost discrepancy) are not a sure indication of monopoly, they are *if persistent*, a probable indication."[18]

In Fig. B-4 the firm produces output OQ and charges a price OP. Assume the firm has a demand curve D and an average cost curve in position AC'. In this case a discrepancy will exist both between price and average cost (line segment AE) and between price and marginal cost (line segment AB). Professor Bain maintains that the existence of a line segment such as AE is evidence that a line segment such as AB probably exists.

FIG. B-4 Monopolistic Competition and the Bain Index

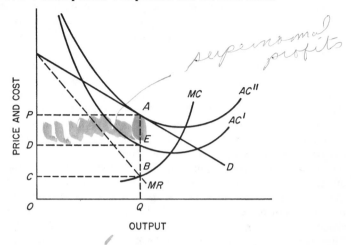

The firm will earn excess profits in Fig. B-4, where the applicable average cost curve is AC', equal to $DEAP$ at output OQ. In other words, where a firm's price exceeds its average cost, excess profits exist. Since the Bain index depends upon the discrepancy between price and average cost, it is utilizing a profit rate as a measure of monopoly power. The rate of profit is defined by Professor Bain as "that rate which, when used in discounting the future rents of the enterprise, equates their capital value to the cost of those assets which would be held by the firm if it produced its present output in competitive equilibrium. If this rate is greater than the rate of interest (or 'normal rate of return'), the difference may be defined as a rate of excess profit."[19]

The calculation of excess profits is performed as follows. Let R be the total annual sales revenue, and let C be the currently incurred costs for materials, wages, and salaries. Let D represent the past incurred costs allocable to the above current revenue, depreciation charges for the plant and machinery bought in previous years, and amortization expenses for stock and materials bought in prior years but used in the current year. Finally, let V be the owners' investment and i be the current interest rate for capital funds requiring the same degree of risk.[20] By definition,

$$\text{Economic excess profit} = R - C - D - i{\cdot}V$$

That is, excess profits are equal to total revenue less current costs, depreciation and amortization, and imputed interest on owners' investment.

"Accounting profit," on the other hand, which is generally published in the annual reports of corporations, does not deduct the imputed interest on owners' investment. Hence,

$$\text{Accounting profit} = R - C - D$$

If accounting profit just equals interest on owners' investment ($R - C - D = i{\cdot}V$), there will be no economic excess profits, and the price the firm charges for its product will be equal to its average cost.

Although the existence of a discrepancy between price and average cost may be grounds for inferring a probable divergence between price and marginal cost, the validity of the converse proposition is questionable. A divergence between price and marginal cost does not imply a probable difference between price and average cost. For example, in Fig. B-4 assume that the applicable average cost curve for the firm is AC''. In this case a price-marginal cost discrepancy exists, but there is no discrepancy between price and average cost at output OQ. Hence, when the firm's average cost curve is tangent to its demand curve at its given level of output, the firm will earn no excess profits even though it may possess monopoly power in the Lerner sense that it has a downward sloping demand curve.

Professor Chamberlin has described a market structure, entitled "monopolistic competition," in which firms are relatively small, and, since little capital is required, can enter and manufacture a product very similar to products already on the market.[21] The existence of product differentiation implies that the firms in a given market do not manufacture precisely the same product, and that any monopoly power of these firms is limited by the overhanging of substitute products which can enter the market if the firm raises its price substantially. In Chamberlinian fully adjusted equilibrium, the average cost curve is at position AC'' in Fig. B-4; price exceeds marginal cost; and price is equal to average cost.[22] Thus, there can exist a downward sloping demand curve, as well as a divergence between price and marginal cost, without a firm necessarily earning excess profits.

There are a number of other problems encountered in using the accounting rate of profit as an indicator of the degree to which monopoly power is exercised. The calculation of profit rates on the basis of book values of assets may cause profit rates to rise because of the time lag, which generally is a number of years, for book values to be adjusted to the increased demand and earnings of the firm.[23] In contrast, low rates of profit can conceal elements of monopoly if the assets of the firm are overvalued or are carried on the corporate books even though they are no longer productive. Profits may also be kept low by excessive selling costs and advertising which serve to raise barriers to entry around a strong market position of a firm. Finally, a monopoly index based on profits leaves unclear whether the profits accruing to the firm are a result of monopolistic selling practices, monopsonistic buying practices,[24] or, in contrast, superior efficiency resulting from specialized factors of production, newer manufacturing techniques, and expertise in management.[25]

The Rothschild Index

The curve dd' in Fig. B-5 describes the conventional demand curve for a firm, whereas DD' describes the industry demand curve. The former is sometimes referred to as the "species" demand curve, and the latter as the "genus" demand curve.[26] The dd' demand curve, which assumes that competitors hold their prices constant at the level OP, is less steep and more elastic than the demand curve DD', since a greater quantity of the product of a firm will be demanded if its competitors do not match its price reductions.

The Rothschild index measures the degree of monopoly by taking the ratio of the slope of dd' to the slope of DD'.[27] In pure competition the Rothschild index equals zero, since the demand curve for a firm will be horizontal. In pure monopoly the firm and the industry are identical, dd' coincides with DD', and the Rothschild index is equal to unity. Between zero (pure competition) and unity (pure monopoly) exist various degrees of monopoly in terms of the Rothschild index.

$$\text{Rothschild index} = \frac{\text{Slope of } dd'}{\text{Slope of } DD'} = \frac{\dfrac{ab}{aK}}{\dfrac{ac}{aK}} = \frac{ab}{ac}$$

The practicality of using slopes of different types of demand curves for the empirical evaluation of the degree of monopoly is questionable. Only if the firm has experimented in its price policy under comparable circumstances can the shape of the demand curve of the firm be estimated. Where the demand curve of the firm has shifted during the period of time considered, an econometric problem arises in identifying the demand curve.[28] Even with the benefit of econometric tools, the identification of demand curves is seldom satisfactory enough to determine the slope of a demand curve for the relevant output range.

FIG. B-5 The Rothschild Index

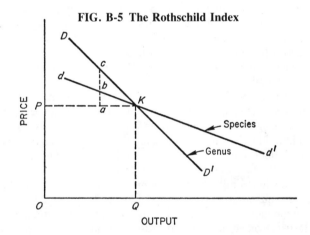

It is doubtful that a seller will take the extreme positions of either believing that all competitors will hold their prices constant, or that all their prices will readjust to remain identical with his own. Yet these calculations are necessary for the computation of the Rothschild index. Finally, the Rothschild index of the degree of monopoly is based solely upon demand factors, to the exclusion of supply and cost conditions.

The Papandreou Index

Indexes of monopoly which employ the concept of cross-elasticity of demand for defining market structures suffer from a logical difficulty: Pure competition cannot be defined in terms of cross-elasticity of demand in a manner which keeps it distinct from its antithesis, pure monopoly.[29] Under conditions of pure monopoly no firm can affect the monopolist's sales, since by definition there are no competitors in existence. However, under conditions of pure competition the sales of a given firm will also be immune from the actions of a competitor since by definition there are numerous firms — no one of which is of sufficient size to affect appreciably the sales volume of another firm in the market.

One measure of monopoly proposed by Papandreou is entitled the *coefficient of penetration*.[30] This index measures the capacity of a firm, in terms of its available supply, to penetrate the markets of its competitors by lowering its price. For example, if a firm alone lowers its price it may attract so many new customers that it will be unable to fill their demand requirements. The limitation of plant facilities may not only prevent the firm from benefiting through higher profits from an increase in demand, but may be a deterrent against the firm's penetrating the markets of many of its competitors.

Papandreou maintained that supply factors, as well as conditions of demand, must be evaluated for the determination of the degree of monopoly. Furthermore, not only must the ability of the firm to penetrate the markets of its competitors be considered, but also its ability to withstand the attacks, such as price cuts, made by its competitors. Changes in market forces must be examined in both directions: forces generated by the firm against its rivals, and forces aimed toward the firm by its rivals. The latter direction of market forces is accounted for by a *coefficient of insulation,* which measures the degree of nonresponsiveness of the sales of a firm to price reductions initiated by its competitors.

Logically, one might conclude that if enough variables could be included in an index, and all statistical difficulties for measuring cross-elasticity could be overcome, an ideal monopoly index would exist. On the other hand, Professor Chamberlin argues that the relative strength of monopoly cannot be measured. The problem of measuring monopoly is akin, in Chamberlin's words, to ascertaining the state of an individual's health. "Some aspects of health can be measured and others cannot. Among the former we have body temperature, blood pressure, metabolism, weight, etc. But these do not lend themselves to the construction of a single index of health. Similarly, in economics it does not follow that because certain indices are quantitative themselves, they can be averaged or in some way reduced to a single index,. . ."[31] Finally, the lack of strict formulas for defining markets, industries, or competition affords the courts an important degree of jurisprudential flexibility.

APPENDIX B FOOTNOTES

1. See J. Robinson, *Economics of Imperfect Competition* (London: Macmillan & Co. Ltd., 1961; 1st ed., 1933) Chap. 9.
2. V. Goldberg, "Reflections on the Welfare Loss Rectangle," 4 Industrial Org. Rev. p. 151 (1976); Tullock, "The Welfare Costs of Tariffs, Monopolies and Theft," 5 Western Econ. J. 224 (1967); A. Harberger, "Monopoly and Resource Allocation," 44 Amer. Econ. Rev. 77 (1954); D. Schwartzman, "The Effect of Monopoly on Price," *Journal of Political Economy,* Vol. 67 (August, 1959), pp. 352-362 and "The Burden of Monopoly," *Journal of Political Economy,* Vol. 68 (December, 1960), pp. 627-630; A. Bergson, "On Monopoly Welfare Losses," *American Economic Review,* Vol. 63 (December, 1973), pp. 853-870; and S. Peltzman, "The Gains and Losses From Industrial Concentration," *Journal of Law and Economics,* Vol. 22 (1978), p. 229.

3. R. A. Posner, *Antitrust Law: An Economic Perspective* (Univ. of Chicago Press, 1976).
4. O. Williamson, "Economics as an Antitrust Defense Revised," 125 Univ. of Penn. Law Review, pp. 699-736 (1977).
5. J. Schumpeter, *Capitalism, Socialism and Democracy* (Harper and Bros., 1942); E. S. Mason, "Schumpeter on Monopoly and the Large Firm," *Review of Economics and Statistics*, Vol. 33 (May, 1951), pp. 139-144; J. W. Markham, "Concentration: A Stimulant or Retardant to Innovation," in *Industrial Concentration: The New Learning, op. cit.*, pp. 247-272; D. Hamberg, "Size of Firm, Oligopoly, and Research: The Evidence," *Canadian Journal of Economics and Political Science*, Vol. 30 (February, 1964), pp. 62-75; and J. Halverson, "The Relationship of Antitrust Policy and Technological Progress," *Washington University Law Quarterly*, pp. 409-420 (1975).
6. See J. M. Henderson and R. E. Quandt, *Microeconomic Theory* (New York: McGraw-Hill Book Company, 1958), pp. 202-8; see T. Scitovsky, *Welfare and Competition: The Economics of a Fully Employed Economy* (Homewood, Ill.: Richard D. Irwin, Inc., 1951); R. H. Leftwich, *The Price System and Resource Allocation* (New York: Holt, Rinehart & Winston, Inc., 1956); and A. Lerner, *The Economics of Control: Principles of Welfare Economics* (New York: The Macmillan Company, 1944).
7. R. G. Lipsey and K. Lancaster, "The General Theory of Second Best," *Review of Economic Studies*, Vol. XXIV (1956-57), p. 11; also see C. Morrison, "The Nature of Second Best," *Southern Journal of Economics*, Vol. XXXII (July, 1965), pp. 49-52; E. J. Mishan, "Second Thoughts on Second Best," *Oxford Economic Papers*, Vol. XIV (October, 1962), pp. 205-17; M. McManus, "Comments on the General Theory of Second Best," *Review of Economic Studies*, Vol. XXVI (June, 1959), 209-24; and L. W. McKenzie, "Ideal Output and the Interdependence of Firms," *Economic Journal*, Vol. LVI (December, 1951), 785-803.
8. Lipsey and Lancaster, "The General Theory of Second Best," p. 17.
9. See J. M. Henderson and R. E. Quandt, *Microeconomic Theory* (New York: McGraw-Hill Book Company, 1958), pp. 202-8. Also see T. Scitovsky, *Welfare and Competition: The Economics of a Fully Employed Economy* (Homewood, Ill.: Richard D. Irwin, Inc., 1951); R.H. Leftwich, *The Price System and Resource Allocation* (New York: Holt, Rinehart & Winston, Inc., 1956); A. Lerner, *The Economics of Control: Principles of Welfare Economics* (New York: The Macmillan Company, 1944); and J. W. Markham, "Goals for Industrial Organization: A Theoretical Analysis," *The American Economy*, J. W. Markham, ed. (New York: George Braziller, Inc., 1963), pp. 28-42. Only the necessary marginal conditions will be discussed; these first-order conditions are necessary but not sufficient for an optimum. For a discussion of second-order conditions, which must be satisfied for a welfare optimum, see J. de V. Graff, *Theoretical Welfare Economics* (London: Cambridge University Press, 1957), pp. 66-70; and W. J. Baumol, "External Economics and Second-Order Optimality Conditions," *American Economic Review*, Vol. LIV (June, 1964), 358-71.
10. J. P. Miller, "Measures of Monopoly Power and Concentration: Their Economic Significance," *Business Concentration and Price Policy*, p. 119.
11. Compare A. P. Lerner, "The Concept of Monopoly and the Measurement of Monopoly Power," *Review of Economic Studies*, Vol. I (June, 1934), 157-75; E. H. Chamberlin, "Measuring the Degree of Monopoly and Competition," *Monopoly and Competition and Their Regulation*, Papers and Proceedings of A Conference Held by the International Economic Association, E. H. Chamberlin, ed. (London, 1954); reprinted in his *Towards A More General Theory of Value*, p. 83; and M. Olson and D. McFarland, "The Restoration of Pure Monopoly and the Concept of the Industry," *Quarterly Journal of Economics*, Vol. LXXVI (November, 1962), 623.
12. Lerner, "The Concept of Monopoly."
13. S. Weintraub, *Price Theory* (New York: Pitman Publishing Corporation, 1949), p. 146.
14. Schumpeter, *Capitalism, Socialism and Democracy*, Chap. 8.
15. Miller, "Measures of Monopoly Power and Concentration," p. 124.
16. See R. H. Whitman, "A Note on the Concept of 'Degree on Monopoly'," *Economic Journal*, Vol. LI (June-September, 1941), 261-70. Reply by M. Kalecki, "'Degree of Monopoly' — A Comment," *The Economic Journal*, Vol. LII (April, 1942), 121-27; and P. T. Bauer, "A Note on Monopoly," *Economica*, Vol. VIII, New Series (May, 1941), 194-203.
17. Professor Dunlop applied the Lerner index to selected industries to ascertain the changes in the degree of monopoly over the course of the business cycle. J. T. Dunlop, "Price Flexibility and the Degree of Monopoly," *Quarterly Journal of Economics*, Vol. LIII (August, 1939), 522-33. Professor Kalecki attempted to evaluate statistically the degree of monopoly for the whole economy. M. Kalecki, "The Determinants of the Distribution of the National Income," *Econometrica*, Vol. VI (April, 1938), 97-112. For a criticism of the latter article, see F. Machlup, *The Political Economy of Monopoly* (Baltimore: Johns Hopkins University Press, 1952), p. 517.

188

18. J. S. Bain, "The Profit Rate as a Measure of Monopoly Power," *Quarterly Journal of Economics*, Vol. LV (February, 1941), 271-93.
19. *Ibid.*, pp. 276-77.
20. This discussion is taken from J. S. Bain, *Industrial Organization* (New York: John Wiley & Sons, Inc. 1959), pp. 364-65.
21. E. H. Chamberlin, *The Theory of Monopolistic Competition*, 7th ed. (Cambrdige, Mass.: Harvard University Press, 1958).
22. Bain, *Industrial Organization*, p. 273.
23. F. Machlup, *The Political Economy of Monopoly*, p. 493.
24. K. W. Rothschild, "A Further Note on the Degree of Monopoly," *Economica*, N. S., Vol. X (February, 1943), 69-71; and J. S. Bain, "Measurement of the Degree of Monopoly: A Note," *ibid.*, pp. 66-68.
25. Professor Milton Friedman has suggested that economic rents from specialized resources or factors of production, which give rise to profits, should be capitalized into the average cost curve for the firm. An inequality between price and average cost may reflect the imperfection of the capital markets in taking into account the value of specialized resources of a firm, such as its favorable plant location. See M. Friedman, Comment on Caleb A. Smith's article, "Survey of the Empirical Evidence on Economies of Scale," in *Business Concentration and Price Policy, op cit.*, p. 235.
26. The origins of these terms is attributed to M. A. Copeland, "The Theory of Monopolistic Competition," *Journal of Political Economy*, Vol. XLII (August, 1934), 531.
27. K. W. Rothschild, "The Degree of Monopoly," *Economica*, Vol. IX, N.S., (February 1942), 24-40.
28. T. C. Koopsmans, "Identification Problems in Economic Model Construction," in W. C. Hood and T. C. Koopsmans, *Studies in Econometric Method* (New York: John Siley & Sons, Inc., 1953), and L. Klein, *A Textbook of Econometrics* (New York: Harper & Row, Publishers, 1953) Chap. 3.
29. The use of cross-elasticities of both supply and demand in classifying market structures has been discussed in detail in the economic literature. See F. Machlup, "Monopoly and Competition: A Classification of Market Positions," *American Economic Review*, Vol. XXVII (September, 1937), 445-51, and "Competition, Pliopoly and Profit: Part I," *Economica*, N.S., Vol. IX (February, 1942), 1-24; Part II, *ibid.*, (May, 1942), pp. 153-74; R. Triffin, *Monopolistic Competition and General Equilibrium Theory* (Cambridge, Mass.: Harvard University Press, 1940); S. Weintraub, "The Classification of Market Positions: Comment," *Quarterly Journal of Economics*, Vol. LVI (August, 1942), 666-73 and E. F. Beach, "Triffin's Classification of Market Positions," *Canadian Journal of Economics and Political Science*, Vol. IX (February, 1943), 69-74; J. S. Bain, "Market Classification in Modern Price Theory," *Quarterly Journal of Economics*, Vol. LVI (August, 1942), 560-74; A. G. Papandreou, "Market Structure and Monopoly Power," *American Economic Review*, Vol. XXXIX (September, 1949), 883-97; C. M. Birch, "Papandreou's Coefficient of Penetration and Insulation," *ibid.*, Vol. LX (June, 1950), 407-10; R. L. Bishop, "Elasticities, Cross-Elasticities, and Market Relationships," *ibid.*, Vol. XLII (December, 1952), 779-803; Comments by W. Fellner and E. H. Chamberlin, *ibid.*, Vol. XLIII (December, 1953), 898-915; Reply by Bishop, *ibid.*, pp. 916-24; Comment by Hieser, *ibid.*, Vol. XLV (June, 1955), 373-82; Reply by Bishop, *ibid.*, pp. 283-86; E. H. Chamberlin, *Towards a More General Theory of Value*, pp. 84-91; R. W. Pfouts and C. E. Ferguson, "Market Classification Systems in Theory and Policy," *Southern Economic Journal*, Vol. XXVI (October, 1959), 111-18, "Conjectural Behavior and Classficiation of Oligopoly Situations," *ibid.*, Vol. XXVII (October, 1960), 139-41, and "Theory, Operationalism, and Policy: A Further Note on Market Classification," *ibid.*, Vol. XXVIII (July, 1961), 90-95; R. L. Bishop, "Market Classification Again," *ibid.*, pp. 83-90; A. Heertje, "Market Classification Systems in Theory," *ibid.*, Vol. XXVII (October, 1960), 138-39; and Olson and McFarland, "The Restoration of Pure Monopoly and the Concept of the Industry."
30. Papandreou, "Market Structure and Monopoly Power," pp. 883-97.
31. Chamberlin, "Measuring the Degree of Monopoly and Concentration," p. 83.

APPENDIX C:

OLIGOPOLY MODELS

Writers have argued through the past decades that the concept of pure monopoly is an abstraction that does not describe the market position of any actual firm. It is difficult to conceive of a firm which possesses such economic power that it can totally exclude all potential entrants from its field, and faces virtually no substitutes for its product. The concept of pure competition, where a large number of buyers and sellers exist and any firm can sell as many units as it produces at the going market price, is also largely an abstraction. Neither of these theoretical models is particularly useful in explaining the *process of competing* whereby firms meet or undercut prices, expand or contract sales, and fight to preserve or extend a share of a market.

The duopoly and oligopoly models offer a theoretical framework for studying the strategic maneuvers of firms in changing their prices and levels of production. These models offer no single solution or strategy for a firm to follow. Prices and production levels cannot be predicted without assumptions being made as to the reaction of firms to various output and price changes initiated by its opponent. In the Cournot model each seller assumes that the output of its rival will remain constant regardless of any change it may make in its own output level. In the Bertrand model each seller assumes that the price of its rival will remain constant regardless of any change it may make in its own price. Thus, the interdependence of competitive actions on the conduct of a rival firm is ignored in both the Cournot and Bertrand models.

These two models are useful as an introduction to more complex oligopoly models where each firm within a market structure recognizes the interdependence between its own actions and the actions of its rivals, and anticipates a number of possible countermoves by an opponent for each competitive move of its own.

THE COURNOT DUOPOLY OUTPUT MODEL

In 1838 Augustin Cournot considered the duopoly problem arising between the producers of mineral water from two neighboring springs. The two firms, or duopolists, each hold their price fixed, but compete with each other by offering for sale various amounts of the same quality of mineral water. Each of the duopolists in the Cournot model acts independently under the naïve belief that regardless of what changes in output it makes, the level of output of its opponent will remain constant.[1] However, every time one of the firms sets an output level, the second firm is induced to change its output level in order to maximize profits, which in turn causes the first firm to readjust its output level. The process continues until an equilibrium position is reached and the expectation that the other will not change its output is finally correct.

The seeming obliviousness of each firm in the Cournot model to the repercussions its movements may have on the other firm has brought forth considerable criticism. The expectation that an opponent will offer no retaliation is difficult to reconcile with the rationality of profit maximization in the Cournot model. But despite its shortcomings, the Cournot model is almost indispensable as a starting point to the theory of duopoly. In the words of Professor Fellner,

> A realistic approach to oligopoly problems cannot be based on Cournot's theory. Yet now, after more than a century, it is still difficult to see what is involved in an oligopoly theory without showing how the theory is related to Cournot's basic construction.[2]

The Cournot model begins with a demand curve which shows the dependence of the market price of mineral water on the total quantity offered by the duopolists, firm A and firm B. Therefore, for a given price, an increase in either firm's output will cause a reduction in the optimum level of the other firm's output. For any level of output offered by firm A, there exists an output for firm B which will maximize firm B's profits. In Fig. C-1 the locus of these points gives the output reaction curve R_bR_b for firm B. Similarly, for any level of output offered by firm B, there exists an output for firm A which will maximize firm A's profits. The locus of these points gives the output reaction curve R_aR_a in Fig. C-1.

FIG. C-1 The Cournot Model

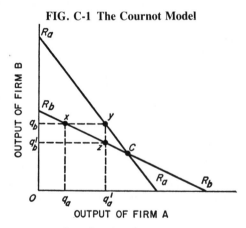

If firm A produces output Oq_a, firm B will move to point x on its output reaction curve where it produces output Oq_b. The output level Oq_b will maximize firm B's profits for the existing level of firm A's output. However, the change in firm B's output will leave firm A unsatisfied with its previous output level Oq_a, since its profits are no longer being maximized. The profits of firm A were reduced by the increased output of firm B. To maximize profits firm A must move on its output reaction curve to point y, or output level Oq'_a. At this new level firm A will be doing the best it can so long as firm B continues to produce output Oq_b.

After firm A changes its output to Oq'_a, firm B finds that it is advantageous once again to change its output, this time to Oq'_b. The process continues with the duopolists staying on their reaction curves and stubbornly adhering to the belief that each time they move their opponent will not retaliate by also changing its output. Finally, the two firms will reach point C, where their output reaction curves intersect, their strategies coincide, and an equilibrium is achieved. Point C in Fig. C-1, which is often referred to as the "Cournot point," gives the solution to this duopoly model.

An understanding of the derivation of output reaction curves is necessary before we proceed to more advanced duopoly models. The dashed curves in Fig. C-2, which are concave to the horizontal axis, are profit indifference curves for firm A. Each curve represents various combinations of outputs of firm A and firm B which leave firm A with the same amount of profit. Initially, firm A believes erroneously that firm B has a horizontal reaction curve such as $q_bR'_b$ in Fig. C-2, and will maintain a constant output at a level Oq_b. Firm A will produce output Oq_a, which is determined by the point of tangency of firm A's profit indifference curve Π^1_a and $q_bR'_b$. This point of tangency marks the greatest profit which can be earned by firm A when firm B produces output Oq_b.

In the next period, firm B changes its output from Oq_b to Oq'_b. Firm A once again takes the output level of its opponent as fixed and attempts to maximize its own profits. Firm A will select output Oq'_a, which is determined by the tangency of its profit indifference curve Π^2_a and $q'_bR''_b$. The connection of these points of tangency forms the actual output reaction curve of firm A, designated R_aR_a. Firm A's output reaction curve shows the most profitable output level for firm A for each level of output produced by firm B.

Note that the profit indifference curves of firm A represent higher levels of profit for firm A as they approach the horizontal axis. For a given output of firm A, a lower profit indifference curve for firm A implies a lower output level for the competitor firm B, and hence, a higher profit for firm A. Thus, Π^2_a represents a higher level of profit for firm A than Π^1_a. As firm B produces less output, the profit indifference curves that are closer to the horizontal axis become available to firm A, and firm A can earn a higher total profit.

FIG. C-2 Construction of the Output Reaction Curve for Firm A

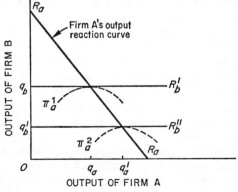

Output reaction curves for firm B can be similarly constructed. In Fig. C-3, firm B erroneously believes in the first period that firm A has a vertical output reaction curve such as $q'_a R'_a$, and that firm A will maintain a constant output at a level Oq'_a. Firm B will produce that level of output which, taken in conjunction with firm A's given output Oq'_a, will maximize firm B's profits. The point of tangency of the profit indifference curve Π'_b with $q'_a R'_a$ represents the greatest profit that can be earned by firm B when firm A produces output Oq'_a. In the next period, firm A changes its output level to Oq_a, and firm B selects output Oq_b, where its profit indifference curve Π^2_b is tangent to $q_a R''_a$.

FIG. C-3 Construction of the Output Reaction Curve for Firm B

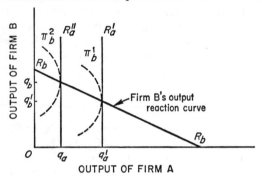

The connection of these vertical points of tangency gives the output reaction curve of firm B, designated $R_b R_b$. Note that firm B's profit indifference curves are concave to the vertical axis, and represent higher fixed levels of profit for firm B the closer they are to the vertical axis.

THE BERTRAND DUOPOLY PRICE MODEL

Each of the duopolists in the Bertrand model acts independently under the naïve belief that regardless of what price changes it makes, the price charged by its opponent will remain fixed.[3] The behavior of each duopolist is described by a price reaction curve which is analogous to the output reaction curves in the Cournot model. In Fig. C-4 firm A has a price reaction curve, $R_a R_a$, which shows the prices which maximize its profits at various price levels maintained by firm B. Similarly, firm B has a price reaction curve, $R_b R_b$, which shows the prices which maximize its profits at various price levels maintained by firm A.

The duopolists arrive at the equilibrium point C in Fig. C-4 through successive movements along their price reaction curves. The behavior pattern followed by the duopolists in the Bertrand model is similar to that of the duopolists in the Cournot model with the modification that the competitive moves are in terms of price changes rather than output changes.

If the duopolists produce an identical product, a divergence of prices between each firm can last only temporarily. Therefore, for an equilibrium to be obtained, both firms must have the same price, and their price reaction curves must intersect on a 45-degree line from the origin. However, if some extent of product differentiation is introduced, the price reaction curves need not intersect on the 45-degree line in order for an equilibrium to occur. Bertrand argued that if a competitor assumes that his rival's price will not change, the competitor will charge a slightly lower price and thereby dispose of his entire output. His rival, making the same assumption, will also continue to undercut price until finally they both eliminate all profit and reach the competitive equilibrium.

FIG. C-4 The Bertrand Model

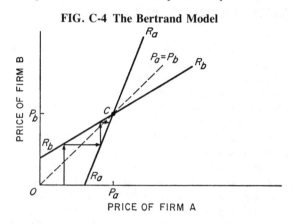

A price reaction curve for firm A is constructed in Fig. C-5. The axes have price rather than output, and the profit indifference curves are convex rather than concave to their respective axes. If firm B is selling its product at price OP_b, firm A will sell its product at OP'_a in order to get to the higher profit indifference curve II^4_a, which is tangent to $P_bR'_b$. Similarly, when firm B is selling its product at price OP'_b, firm A will sell its product at price OP_a in order to reach indifference curve II^3_a. The connection of the respective points of tangency of firm A's profit indifference curves and the horizontal lines in Fig. C-5, which represent given output levels for firm B, describes firm A's price reaction curve.

FIG. C-5 Construction of the Price Reaction Curve for Firm A

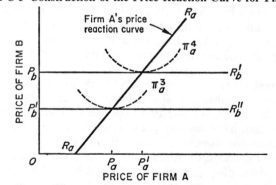

Note that in the duopoly price models higher profit indifference curves represent greater amounts of profit for a given firm. In Fig. C-5, II^4_a represents a greater profit for firm A than II^3_a. Firm A's price becomes relatively lower as firm B charges higher prices. Thus, for a given output P'_a, firm A can reach higher profit indifference curves such as II^a_a only if firm B raises its price to OP_b. In this connection the convexity of the profit indifference curves can, in part, be explained. The positively sloped segments of these profit indifference curves indicate that a rise in firm A's price will reduce its profits unless firm B also increases its price.

THE EDGEWORTH DUOPOLY MODEL

Edgeworth extended the analysis of Bertrand by considering a market divided evenly between two sellers, in which the sellers undercut each other's price until both approach the point of competitive equilibrium where price equals marginal cost.[4] At this price, one firm puts the rest of its supply on the market and thereby leaves the other firm in a position where it can raise its price to almost the monopoly level in serving the remaining customers.

Unlike the Bertrand and Cournot models, where each firm has practically an unlimited capacity to produce, the Edgeworth model limits the output of the duopolists so that neither can supply the whole market demand at a low price.[5] "In order for the price to descend, their individual markets are completely merged into one, each drawing customers freely from the other by a slight reduction in price. But in order for it to rise again, their markets are completely separated," with the result that each seller becomes a monopolist dealing with a portion of the buyers in isolation.[6] Thus, the Edgeworth duopoly solution consists of a fluctuating price in the approximate range of the monopoly price and the competitive equilibrium price.

AN OUTPUT LEADERSHIP MODEL

In the more complex duopoly models the duopolists recognize the interdependence of their prices and output levels. For example, the output of firm A (q_a) could be positively related to the output of firm B (q_b) in such a manner that firm A always produces some multiple k of the output produced by firm B. In mathematical notation, $q_a = kq_b$. Firm A might be prepared to match the output from firm B ($k = 1$) in order to maintain a constant market share of 50 percent. Similarly, each firm might react to a definite rule which keeps its prices, its profits, or its advertising expenditures as a fixed proportion of the amount maintained by its rival duopolist.

A duopoly model which has one firm react according to some given multiple k times a variable of another firm almost forces a solution. In the more general duopoly case the firm is not sure of its opponent's future course of conduct. Alternatively stated, the firms may not react according to some single function once they observe that alternative courses of conduct may yield higher profits. Under these circumstances, the reaction curves are discarded and the moves and countermoves of the duopolists involve a high degree of market strategy. The following two duopoly output models illustrate the results that can be obtained when one or both of the duopolists abandon their reaction curves.[7]

Suppose firm A finally learns the actual behavior pattern of firm B. In a Cournot model firm A would observe that its opponent is a follower, i.e., firm B always follows the moves initiated by firm A. Firm A has the opportunity to become a leader and ignore its own "follower" reaction curve which it abided by in the Cournot model. The optimum strategy for firm A, now that this firm alone knows about its rival's reaction curve, is to select that output which will evoke an output reaction from firm B such that the profits for firm A will be maximized.

Assume that firm A selects output Oq'_a in Fig. C-6. Firm B will follow with a change in output to Oq'_b, which allows firm A to attain the profit indifference curve Π^2_a. By ignoring its output reaction curve, firm A has moved the equilibrium point from point C (the Cournot point) to point T, where firm B has a lower output and firm A has a higher profit and output. The analysis suggests that firm A obtains an advantage of higher profits when it becomes an output leader rather than an output follower.

FIG. C-6 Output Leadership

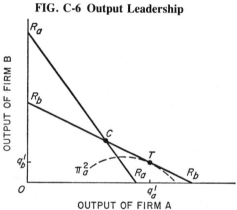

Suppose firm A and firm B both seek to be leaders and dispense with their output reaction curves. In Fig. C-7 firm A selects output Oq'_a, expecting firm B to stay on reaction curve R_bR_b and produce output Oq'_b. This output combination would place the firms at point T, an advantageous profit position for firm A. Firm B, however, has other plans: it also wants to be an output leader. Firm B produces output Oq''_b, expecting firm A to stay on reaction curve R_aR_a and produce output Oq''_a. This output combination would place the firms at point S, an advantageous profit position for firm B. However, firm A and firm B will be surprised to find that their opponent has not behaved as expected, with the result that the two firms end up neither at point S (firm B's expected equilibrium point) nor at point T (firm A's expected equilibrium point). Rather, the firms end up at point M, which is off both their reaction curves.

Both firms may be worse off when each attempts to be an output leader than when one consents to be a follower. In Fig. C-7 the profit indifference curves of firm A represent higher profits as they approach the horizontal axis, and the profit indifference curves of firm B represent higher profits as they approach the vertical axis. Consequently, firm A earns a higher profit at point T than at point M, and firm B earns a higher profit at point S than at point M. It is, therefore, possible that the output combinations represented by points S or T may yield a greater aggregate profit to the duopolists than the output combination represented by point M. In this event one solution to the model might be for firm B to consent to be a passive follower, provided that firm A gives it a side payment or some other form of compensation.

FIG. C-7 Contesting Output Leadership

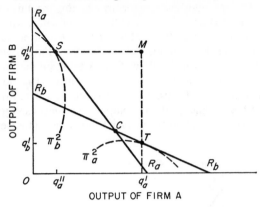

The determination of which firm will become the follower and which one the leader becomes of paramount importance once the duopolists recognize that neither their individual nor aggregate profits are maximized when both attempt to be output leaders. The German economist von Stackelberg maintained that contending output leadership results in economic warfare.[8] Both duopolists are in a worse position as contending output leaders than they would be if one were to give up and retire as a follower.[9]

Only in special cases, Stackelberg argued, will a duopolist come to the conclusion that his follower position will secure him higher profits than his leadership position. Therefore, he argued, duopoly market structures are almost always unstable. The next section on price leadership finds that the *prices* of duopolists, in contrast to their *outputs*, tend to find stable positions.

ENDNOTES*

1. A. Cournot, *Researches into Mathematical Principles of the Theory of Wealth* (1838), translated by N. T. Bacon, 2nd ed. (New York: The Macmillan Company, 1927), Chap. 7; F. Machlup, *The Economics of Sellers Competition* (Baltimore: Johns Hopkins University Press, 1952), pp. 372-77; W. J. Fellner, *Competition Among the Few* (New York: Alfred A. Knopf, Inc., 1949), Chap. 2; Chamberlin, *The Theory of Monopolistic Competition*, 7th ed., Chap. 3; M. Shubik, *Strategy and Market Structure* (New York: John Wiley & Sons, Inc., 1959), p. 92; R. D. Theocharis, "On the Stability of the Cournot Solution on the Oligopoly Problem," *Review of Economic Studies*, Vol. XXVII (February, 1960), 133-34; M. McManus and R. E. Quandt, "Comments on the Stability of the Cournot Oligopoly Model," *ibid.*, Vol. XXVIII (February, 1961), 136-39; F. H. Hahn, "The Stability of the Cournot Oligopoly Solution," *ibid.*, Vol. XXIX (October, 1962) 329-31; M. McManus, "Dynamic Cournot-type Oligopoly Models: A Correction," *ibid.*, pp. 337-39; R. L. Bishop, "The Stability of the Cournot Oligopoly Solution," further comment, *ibid.*, pp. 332-36; and C. R. Frank, Jr. and R. E. Quandt, "On the Existence of Cournot Equilibrium," *International Economic Review*, Vol. IV (January, 1963), 92-96.
2. Fellner, *Competition Among the Few*, p. 57.
3. J. Bertrand, Review of Cournot and Walras in *Journal des Savants* (Paris: September, 1883), pp. 499-508. Also see W. J. Baumol, *Business Behavior, Value and Growth* (New York: The Macmillan Company, 1959), pp. 18-20; H. G. Lewis, "Some Observations on Duopoly Theory," *American Economic Review*, Vol. XXVIII (Proceedings, 1948), 1-9; and Machlup, *The Economics of Sellers Competition*, pp. 377-80.

4. F. Y. Edgeworth, *Papers Relating to Political Economy*, Vol. I (London: Macmillan & Co., Ltd., 1925), 111-42, and *Mathematical Physics* (London: Routledge & Kegan Paul, Ltd., 1881); A. J. Nichol, "Edgeworth's Theory of Duopoly Price," *Economic Journal*, Vol. XLV (March, 1935), 51-66; and G. W. Nutter, "Duopoly, Oligopoly, and Emerging Competition," *Southern Economic Journal*, Vol. XXX (April, 1964), 342.
5. F. Machlup, *The Economics of Sellers Competition*, pp. 380-87.
6. Chamberlin, *The Theory of Monopolistic Competition*, 7th ed., pp. 40-41.
7. A discussion of these two models can be found in Weintraub, *Price Theory*, pp. 160-68. A learning curve duopoly model is given in P. Suppes and J. Carlsmith, "Experimental Learning Theory," *International Economic Review*, Vol. III (January, 1962), 60-78.
8. H. Von Stackelberg, *Marktform und Gleichgewicht* (Berlin: Julius Springer, 1934); W. Leontieff, "Stackelberg on Monopolistic Competition," *Journal of Poltical Economy*, Vol. XLIV (August, 1936), 554-59; E. J. R. Heyward, "H. von Stackelberg's Work on Duopoly," *Economic Record*, Vol. XVIII (June, 1941), 99-106; J. R. Hicks, "Review of Stackelberg, 'Marktform und Gleich-gewicht'," *Economic Journal*, Vol. XLV (June, 1935), 334-36; and Henderson and Quandt, *Microeconomics*, pp. 180-82.
9. H. von Stackelberg, *The Theory of the Market Economy* (1934), translated from the German by A. T. Peacock (New York: Oxford University Press, 1952), p. 194.

*This appendix is reprinted from my Antitrust Economics: Selected Legal Cases and Economic Models (Prentice-Hall, 1968), Chapters 9 and 10.

A PRICE LEADERSHIP MODEL

Price leadership constitutes a tacit or informal understanding among oligopolists that they will adhere to a price change initiated by a designated member. The varieties of price leadership models range from cases where the leader is acting as a market barometer for the rest of the industry, and sets a price which reflects the prevailing demand and supply conditions, to instances of outright collusion among member firms with the price leader directing a conspiracy in setting an unduly high price for the benefit of the industry.

Oligopolists selling a homogeneous or identical product cannot attain an equilibrium position so long as their respective prices diverge. The existence of a degree of product differentiation permits different prices to exist simultaneously in the same market, and allows a continuation of the leadership-followership analysis applied in the preceding chapter to output determination.

Von Stackelberg defined a price leader as a firm which does not observe its reaction curve. A follower is a dependent or passive firm which remains on its reaction curve and sets its price to maximize its own profits after its rival has made a price decision. Price leadership equilibrium implies an asymmetric duopoly market structure in which one firm is content to remain as a follower and allow the other firm to act as a leader. If both firms attempt to be followers, as in the Cournot case, or if both firms attempt to be leaders, the duopoly structure is said to be symmetric. In the words of Professor Fellner: "Thus, follower's policies on the part of both firms result in an equilibrium corresponding to the intersection point of the two reaction functions, while leadership policies of one firm coupled with followership policies of the other result in leadership equilibrium, and leadership policies on the part of both firms result in Stackelberg disequilibrium."[1]

A model of contesting price leadership is presented in Fig. C-8, which shows both firm A and firm B attempting to be price leaders, each assuming that the other will be a price follower.[2] The profit maximizing position for firm B, as a price leader, is point S, where its profit indifference curve Π^2_b is tangent to R_aR_a, the price reaction curve of firm A. Similarly, the profit maximizing position for firm A, as a price leader, is point T, where its profit indifference curve Π^2_a is tangent to R_bR_b, the price reaction curve of firm B. In the contesting price leadership model, each firm ignores its own price reaction curve, and forecasts erroneously that its rival will remain a follower. Consequently, the firms end up at point M, which is on neither firm's reaction curve.

FIG. C-8 Contesting Price Leadership

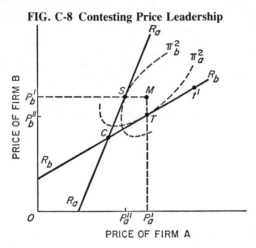

Unlike the *output* leadership case in Fig. C-7, where an error in forecasting that one's rival would be a follower rather than a leader proved to be costly, an error in the contesting price leadership model can be advantageous to both firms. Since a higher profit indifference curve in a price leadership model implies a higher profit, it can be shown that point M will leave each firm better off in Fig. C-8 than either of the price leadership positions (points S and T).

FIG. C-9 The Profit Indifference Curves for Firm A

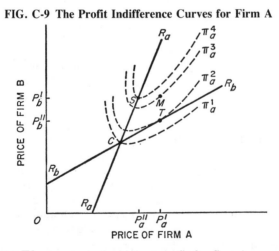

In Fig. C-9 Π^4_a represents the highest profit for firm A among the four profit indifference curves shown. When firm A acts as a price leader, it selects price P'_a in order to attain profit indifference curve Π^2_a, which is tangent to point T to firm B's price reaction curve. At point T firm A is at the highest possible point of tangency between its rival's reaction curve (R_bR_b) and its own profit indifference curve system. The decision of firm A to be a price leader has not placed it in the highest possible profit position. In terms of the model in Fig. C-9, firm A would earn a higher profit at point S (where firm A is a follower and firm B is a leader) or point M (where firms A and B are both leaders).

An examination of Fig. C-10, where $\Pi^4{}_b$ represents the highest profit for firm B among the profit indifference curves shown, will show why firm A is always in a better position when firm B is a price leader. If firm B acts as a price leader, it will raise its price from P''_b to P'_b in order to attain point S on its profit indifference curve $\text{II}^2{}_b$. This price increase by firm B will leave firm A's price relatively lower. Thus, once firm B acts as a price leader and raises its price, firm A will be in a relatively better position regardless of whether it continues as a price leader or changes to a price follower.

The same reasoning can lead firm B to induce its rival to be a leader. Firm B earns higher profits in Fig. C-10 when firm A is a leader. Firm B's highest level of profit, in terms of the indifference curves shown, is at $\Pi^4{}_b$ or point T, where it is a follower and firm A is a leader. A lower level of profits for firm B is at point M, where firm A is a leader and firm B is also a leader. However, both of these points (T and M), where firm A is a leader, place firm B in a better profit position than points S and C, where firm A becomes a follower.

FIG. C-10 The Profit Indifference Curves for Firm B

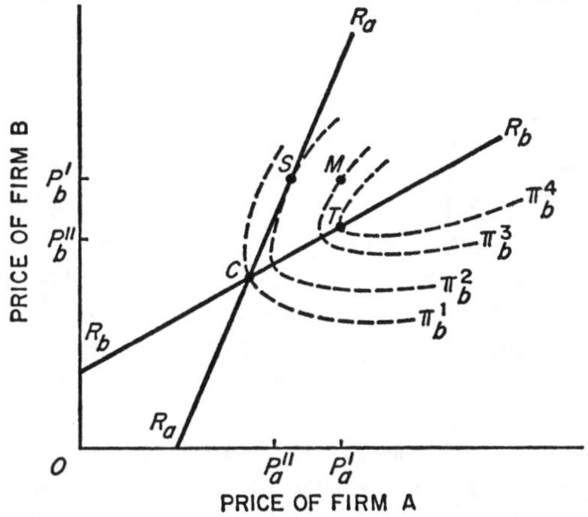

The foregoing model suggests that once a firm becomes a price leader, it is more profitable for the rival to be a follower than a leader.[3] Therefore, an incentive exists for each firm to be a follower once it expects its rival will act as a price leader. If the firm is wrong in its expectation, and its rival remains a follower, both firms will arrive at point C. The next section will explain in terms of game theory matrices why the firms will be reluctant to stay at the mutually disadvantageous point C.

A GAME THEORY MODEL

A game can be described within the previously described duopoly market structure by noting that there exist two strategies for firm A and two strategies for firm B. Firm A can attempt to be either a price leader (A_L), or a price follower (A_F); similarly, firm B can be either a price leader (B_L), or a price follower (B_F). A game matrix can be constructed which has the strategies of firm B in the columns, and the strategies of firm A in the rows. The matrix in Fig. C-11 describes the possible outcomes of the previously discussed Fig. C-8. For example, if firm A and firm B each attempts to be a price leader, they will end up at point M, which is given by row A_L and column B_L. If each firm attempts to be a follower (A_F, B_F), point C is reached in both the diagram and the matrix.

FIG. C-11 A Price Leadership Game Matrix   **FIG. C-12 Payoff Matrix for Firm A**

	B_L	B_F
A_L	M	T
A_F	S	C

	B_L	B_F
A_L	3	2
A_F	4	1

The profit indifference curves for firm A and firm B, which are given in Figs. C-9 and C-10 respectively, are numbered from 1 to 4. As the firm achieves higher levels of profits, its profit indifference curves increase in value from 1 to 4. These values can be substituted into the above matrix and will yield a *payoff matrix* for each firm. The payoff matrix describes the profit resulting to a particular firm for various outcomes within a game.

FIG. C-13 Payoff Matrix for Firm B   **FIG. C-14 Combined Payoff Matrix**

	B_L	B_F
A_L	3	4
A_F	2	1

	B_L	B_F
A_L	(3,3)	(2,4)
A_F	(4,2)	(1,1)

The payoff matrix for firm A is shown in Fig. C-12. At point M in Fig. C-9 firm A is on its profit indifference curve $\Pi^3{}_a$; its corresponding position in its payoff matrix (A_L, B_L) is therefore given the value 3. The values of the remaining profit indifference curves for firm A are placed in their appropriate matrix positions.

Firm B's payoff matrix can be constructed from Fig. C-10, which shows the values of its profit indifference curves for the various outcomes of the game. Firm B's payoff matrix is shown in Fig. C-13.

The two payoff matrices can be combined into one by placing in each parenthesis found in the matrix in Fig. C-14, first, firm A's profits, and second, firm B's profits. Hence, the pair of strategies (2, 4) shows that firm A would gain 2 and firm B would gain 4.

The Cournot point (A_F, B_F) was described previously as an equilibrium point, determined by the intersection of the reaction curves of each firm. But the equilibrium point in the output model ceases to be an equilibrium point in the context of the price leadership game in Fig. C-14. The pair of price strategies (A_F, B_F) gives the lowest possible profit to the two firms; any other pair of strategies leaves these firms better off, since either firm can gain more than one unit by choosing another strategy.

If firm B knew that firm A was going to pursue its follower strategy, firm B would select its leadership strategy. Conversely, if firm A knew that firm B was going to adhere to a leadership strategy, firm A would select its follower strategy. Thus, profit position (4, 2) is an equilibrium position under these circumstances.

However, the same argument will show that profit position (2, 4) is also an equilibrium position. Since each of these equilibrium points favors a different firm, the difficulty in the game involves whether a firm can enforce the strategy most beneficial for itself. If neither firm has such power, the outcome of the game can oscillate between different profit combinations, depending upon the behavior paths followed by the firms.

Suppose the firms have tacitly agreed to follow the joint leadership strategy in order to obtain an even division of profits (3, 3) but firm B double-crosses firm A by switching to his "follower" strategy in order to receive an additional unit of profit (2, 4).

Firm A has two alternatives: (1) to allow the wayward firm B to earn its extra unit of profit at the expense of firm A, or (2) to punish firm B by also employing its own "follower" strategy. The second alternative, which leaves the firms in the (1, 1) profit position, can be rationalized by firm A as the cost of teaching firm B not to deviate from the joint leadership strategy which divides profit evenly at (3, 3). It is doubtful whether the players would stay at (1, 1) for any protracted period of time since either firm, by employing a leadership strategy, can be guaranteed a minimum security above the 1 unit of profit regardless of the strategy selected by the other. For example, firm B by playing strategy B_L is guaranteed to receive 2 units of profit, but in playing strategy B_F is assured of receiving only 1 unit. Similarly, firm A can be confident of 2 units in playing strategy A_L, but can be confident of only 1 unit of profit in playing strategy A_F. If each firm selects the strategy which gives it the maximum value of its guaranteed profits, then each is following a *maximin* strategy (maximum of the minimum security levels of profits), and the firms will settle at position (A_L, B_L).[4]

THE DOMINANT FIRM MODEL

One type of price leadership consists of a dominant firm which sets a price, allows minor firms to sell what they wish, and supplies the remainder of the quantity demanded.[5] In this model the minor firms have no reason for charging a lower price, since they are able to sell as much as they wish at the leader's price. The leader knows that at any price he might set the followers will sell the quantity that equates their marginal costs to that price, leaving the remainder of the market to the leader. The dominant firm will therefore select the price which is most profitable for itself.

The additional assumptions implicit in the model of dominant firm price leadership are "(a) the large producer has almost complete control of market price; (b) other firms act like pure competitors (each regarding its own demand function as perfectly elastic at the leader's price); (c) all firms, excepting the dominant firm, ignore any effects they may have on market price and output; (d) the dominant firm can estimate the market demand curve for the product (presumably, his 'subjective' feeling concerning the 'objective' demand function, both as to position and shape); and (e) the dominant firm can predict with reasonable accuracy the supplies of other sellers at each price."[6] The dominant firm, as summarized by Professor Stigler, "supplies a substantial part of total sales (probably one-fourth at a minimum). It has small, independent rivals, but the situation can be viewed as one of duopoly because all these firms behave competitively (i.e., they operate at the output where marginal cost equals price). The dominant firm behaves passive-ly — it fixes the price and allows the minor firms to sell all they wish at this price."[7]

In Fig. C-15 the industry demand curve (D_i) for a product is composed of the demand curve for the dominant firm (D_d) and the demand curve for the remaining firms. The profit-maximizing output of the dominant firm is at OQ, the level at which its marginal revenue curve (MR_d) intersects its marginal cost curve (MC_d). Since the industry price is set by the dominant firm, the price for output OQ is determined by the dominant firm's demand curve rather than by the demand curve for the industry. The remaining firms, whose horizontal sum of their marginal cost curves is given by the supply curve MC_s, sell all their output, OR, at the price set by the dominant firm. The demand curve for the remaining firms is the horizontal line PS when the dominant firm sets the price at OP. Therefore, at any price OP there will be a total industry demand of PI, of which PS is supplied by the smaller firms and the remainder, $PI - PS = PD$, is demanded from the dominant firm. It follows from the geometry that $DI = PS$.

FIG. C-15 Dominant Firm Price Leadership

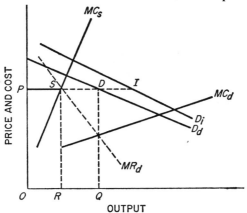

Professor Markham has observed that "the rationale of price making by the dominant or partial monopolist differs but little from that employed by the pure monopolist. They both, presumably, have complete control over prices, but the partial monopolist, unlike the pure monopolist must take account of the quantity that the competitive sector of the industry will offer at any price he may set."[8] Therefore, the dominant firm price leader may not necessarily charge the same price that a monopolist operating in the same market would charge. For example, a dominant firm may fear that setting a price which maximizes industry profit would "fatten" the smaller firms and encourage their output expansion.[9]

One of the real tests of a dominant firm price leader is the extent to which "followership" is maintained in soft markets.[10] A model of dominant firm price leadership may disintegrate once the remaining firms in an industry cease to be obedient followers. "The erratic behavior of the competitive fringe around the oligopoly core directly contradicts the implicit assumption of the models that fringe firms will accept the leader's prices in a manner similar to the pure competitor."[11] With dissimilar cost curves between different-sized firms, the same price may not maximize short-run profits for both large and small firms. "Under some market conditions large firms may be operating beyond the range of least-cost outputs; consequently, they may be anxious for increased sales. The fringe may not be at capacity output, however, and thus may not follow the leader's prices. In periods of slack demand, the fringe and others may attempt to stimulate sales by lowering prices.''[12]

Smaller firms, aware that price cutting or over-stepping market shares will probably result in retaliation by larger firms, may still take a chance on not being obedient followers. The smaller firms may believe that the larger firms will be reluctant to upset an entire market merely to punish violators of negligible size. However, as the number of fringe firms which refuse to be obedient followers increases, the pressure will mount on the dominant firm or oligopolistic core of firms to lower the existing price level.

The price leader in the above market setting will have at least two possible motives for lowering its price: (1) to protect its own market share from being nibbled away by the smaller firms that are cutting prices, and (2) to retaliate with the hope that the future will be marked by greater price discipline throughout the whole industry. If the smaller firms operate at higher costs than the larger firms, they may be vulnerable to a protracted decrease in their volume as a result of the larger firms' lowering of the oligopoly price level. Thus, the fringe firms must weigh carefully the short-term transitional profits gained by not following the leader's price changes against the repercussions which may ensue if they upset the entire market and the oligopolistic core or dominant firm lowers the industry price level.

THE CONSTRAINED SALES MAXIMIZATION MODEL

Professor Baumol has suggested that oligopolists may seek to maximize sales after a minimum level of profits has been achieved.[13] A model of a firm maximizing sales subject to a minimum profit constraint is shown in Fig. C-16. The firm's sales, or total revenue, are represented by curve TR, and its total costs by curve TC. Point S is the point of maximum sales, and is achieved when the firm sells quantity OQ_s. Point P marks the peak of the total profit curve, and is achieved when the firm sells quantity OQ_p.

FIG. C-16 Constrained Sales Maximization Model

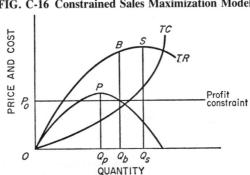

Professor Baumol argues that an oligopolist will generally select neither the sales-maximizing output level nor the profit-maximizing output level. Rather, the oligopolist will expand sales to an intermediate point, such as OQ_b, where any further expansion of sales will decrease profits below a minimum acceptable level. The latter profit constraint is determined by the need for oligopolists to provide its shareholders with "competitively acceptable earnings," and to retain a sufficient amount of funds for future plant expansion.

In the language of organizational theory, the firm in the Baumol model "satisfices" rather than maximizes its profits.[14] Satisficing consists of settling for a course of conduct that is "good enough," *i.e.*, satisfactory although not optimal. Thus, a firm may satisfice for a "fair price," or a "normal profit," or a "competitively acceptable level of earnings."[15]

The rejection of the profit-maximizing goal of the firm raises one of the most important questions in oligopoly theory: What is the goal, or complex of goals, which gives direction to oligopolistic behavior? If the firm is considered a bureaucratic organization with communication problems within its own framework, its actions may be as difficult to predict as the myriad of executive personalities affecting its administration. For example, fear of either a labor strike if men are laid off, or the loss of important distributors may place the expansion of sales over profits as the goal of the firm. On the other hand, the fear of a dissident stockholders' suit may encourage top management to improve its earnings per share through the elimination of unprofitable products.

Some firms may recognize a dependence of future profits on present sales and may seek to maximize long-term profits by extending present sales beyond the maximum level of short-term profits.[16] Other companies, sensitive to their market share positions, may seek to maximize short-term profit subject to the constraint to maintain a minimum percentage of industry sales.[17]

Another interesting question raised in the Baumol model concerns the degree of interdependence in an oligopoly market structure. In contrast to the previous von Stackelberg duopoly models, the oligopolist in the constrained sales maximization model does not fear retaliation by rivals; the firm is free to choose between lower sales at higher prices or higher sales at lower prices.[18] In other words, the oligopolist seeks to exploit his own market by extending his sales subject only to a profit constraint. The interdependence found in most of the earlier duopoly and oligopoly models is therefore rejected.

Professor Baumol maintains that the decision-making apparatus is too clumsy and slow-moving in most large departmentalized organizations for the effective interplay of strategy and counter-strategy among oligopolists.[19] However, where communication has been highly developed in companies and market structures, such as in a number of basic industries, the competitive reactions of firms to price changes may be swift — often a matter of one or two days. The important point is that the degree of interdependence as well as the extent of independent rivalry depends upon the organization within firms as well as among firms.[20]

THE KINKY DEMAND CURVE MODEL

The kinky demand curve model is not directly concerned with the determination of output and price under conditions of price leadership; rather, the model is utilized by those who seek to justify the apparent rigidity of oligopoly prices. In other words, the model may reveal why oligopoly prices remain where they are, but it does not explain how the prices got to their present level.

Professor Sweezy describes the kinky oligopoly demand curve model as follows:

> If producer A raises his price, his rival producer B will acquire new customers. If, on the other hand, A lowers his price, B will lose customers. Ordinarily the reaction to a gain in business is a pleasurable feeling calling for no particular action; the reaction to a loss in business, however, is likely to be some viewing with alarm accompanied by measures designed to recoup the loss. If the cause of the loss is obviously a rival's price cut, the natural retaliation is a similar cut. From the point of any particular producer this means simply that if he raises his price he must expect to lose business to his rivals (his demand curve tends to be elastic going up), while if he cuts his price he has no reason to believe he will succeed in taking business away from his rivals (his demand curve tends to be inelastic in going down). In other words, the imagined demand curve has a "corner" at the current price.[21]

Professor Sweezy concludes that there is little incentive for a firm in this market setting to change its price from the level at which the kink or "corner" in its demand curve exists. In Fig. C-17 an oligopolist has a demand curve dKD' with a kink at point K.

FIG. C-17 The Kinky Demand Curve

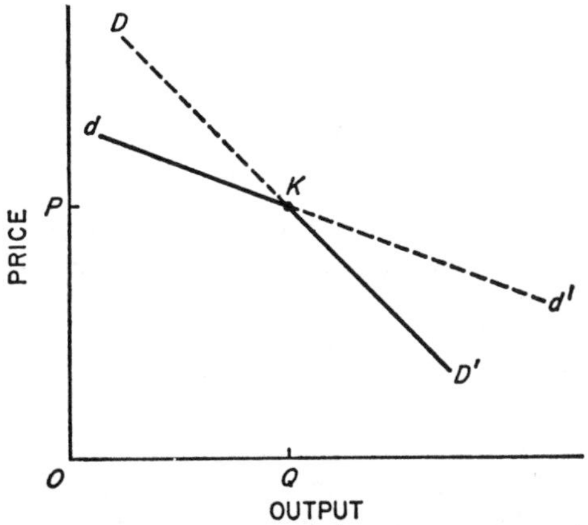

The derivation of the kinky demand curve is related to the construction of two types of demand curves. The first demand curve (DD'), describes the demand facing the firm if all other firms in an industry match its price changes. The second demand curve (dd'), describes the demand facing a firm under the assumption that its rivals hold their prices constant after the firm changes its price. In Fig. C-18 the "genus" demand curve (DD') is applicable to downward price changes from price OP, i.e., line segment KD'. But the "species" demand curve (dd'), where the prices of competitors are assumed to be constant, is applicable to price increases from price OP, i.e., line segment Kd. Under these assumptions, there is little incentive for the firm to change its price.

The marginal revenue curve has a discontinuity directly beneath the point where the demand curve in Fig. C-18 has a kink. If the marginal cost curve passes through this gap in the marginal revenue curve, several interesting theoretical results can occur. First of all, the conditions for short-run equilibrium become ambiguous. The condition that marginal revenue equal marginal cost cannot be applied, since marginal revenue is not determinate at output OQ. All one can know at this output level is that marginal cost is not greater than marginal revenue; it can be the same or less. Second, any change in the marginal cost curve, such as a shift from *MC'* to *MC''* in Fig. C-18, will have no effect on either the profit-maximizing price or output so long as this curve passes through the gap in the marginal revenue curve.

FIG. C-18 The Kinky Demand Curve and Changes in Marginal Costs

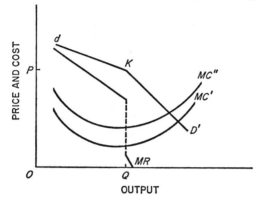

The Kinky Demand Curve and Inflation

It is possible that the Sweezy proposition, that rivals of an oligopolist will not follow a price rise but will follow a price reduction, is limited to periods of slack demand and excess capacity. A firm in this situation will have decreasing short-run average costs and will be eager for sales. Consequently, the firm can be expected to prefer increased volume to higher prices. "The belief that rivals are operating at less than optimum scale and are therefore so hungry for orders that they will not raise prices, even when costs rise or demand increases, is the very signum of depression."[22] Rivals operating at excess capacity also tend to be highly fearful of reduced sales from a competitor's price cut, and can reasonably be expected to follow any downward price cut by a fellow oligopolist.

In a period of inflationary demand, however, the cost position of the firm reverses itself. As the firm approaches its capacity point, each addition in the level of output increases the firm's short-run average costs. Therefore, a firm facing an abundance of orders, many of which it may be unable to fulfill, is likely to follow a price rise made by a rival firm, but will be reluctant to follow a price reduction which would simply induce further volume. In short, in periods of inflationary demand the firm prefers a higher price to increased volume, and can generally be expected to follow a price rise.

Professor Lange states: "An increase in the demand for the products of the firms as a rule strengthens the 'discipline' of the oligopolistic group and leads to higher markups. For, when the market is expanding, firms need have little fear that they will get out of step with the rest of the group by increasing their prices. Each such action is likely to be followed by similar actions of other members of the group."[23] Professor Cyert, in contrast, departs from the belief in greater price discipline during periods of prosperity and rising demand. In an empirical study of three oligopolistic industries (cigarettes, automobiles, and potash), Cyert concludes that oligopoly price behavior is independent of the business cycle; the behavior patterns of the oligopolists were found to be no different in the upswing than they were in the downswing.[24]

The geometric implications of the above inflationary kinky demand curve, where the oligopolists are willing to follow a price rise but are reluctant to go along with a price reduction, are unusual.[25] First, the wings or line segments of the kinky demand curve in Fig. C-18 change from an obtuse angle to a reflex angle, as shown in Fig. C-19. The dashed line segments from the two types of demand curves facing the oligopolist in Fig. C-17, which were ignored in the kinky demand curve, are now utilized to form the inflationary kinky demand curve. A marginal cost curve which passes through the gap in the marginal revenue curve intersects the marginal revenue curve both to the left and right of the discontinuity. Finally, the profit-maximizing output of the firm will not be directly below the kink in the demand curve. In Fig. C-19 area A represents the loss in total revenue involved in moving from output OQ' to OQ (a range in which MC exceeds MR). Area B represents the gain in total revenue in moving from output OQ to OQ'' (a range in which MR exceeds MC). The firm will not produce at output OQ, since it has assumed a loss equivalent to area A and has denied itself a much larger gain, as drawn in Fig. C-19, equivalent to area B.[26] If it is assumed that a condition of inflation exists, there will be an upward pressure on marginal costs. If this cost push is greater than the increase in demand for the firm's product, the marginal cost curve will tend to shift upwards more than the marginal revenue curve. Consequently, area B will become smaller than area A, and the profit-maximizing output of the firm will be reduced from OQ'' to OQ'.

FIG. C-19 The Inflationary Kinky Demand Curve

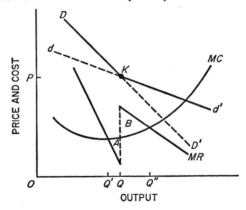

Empirical Verification of the Kink

Professor Stigler, after an analysis of seven oligopolies (cigarettes, automobiles, anthracite coal, steel, potash, dynamite, and gasoline) in the period 1929-37, concluded that "the empirical evidence reveals neither price experiences that would lead oligopolists to believe in the existence of a kink nor the pattern of changes of price quotations that the theory leads us to expect."[27] He finds for the seven oligopolies, "that price increases are more nearly simultaneous than price decreases — the opposite of the kinky demand curve assumption."[28]

The Stigler test was verifying empirically the kink in the oligopoly demand curve was criticized by Professor Efroymson: "Stigler here seems to imply that 'belief' in the kinked demand curve, and even its existence (as a basis of entrepreneurial decision) depend on continuing or repeated corroboration by (unhappy) experiences of the conjectures which it describes. . . . But the fact that in these cases, oligopolistic demand curves were proven, as it were by the events, to be unkinked does not mean that they are never or only infrequently kinked. It appears, merely, that the oligopolists raised prices when they had reason to believe that rivals would follow."[29]

During periods of prosperity or inflation the oligopolists in an industry may be eager to increase price. A price leader in such an industry may know with confidence that if it increases its price, the other firms will follow, if not simultaneously, at least promptly thereafter. The price leader is unlikely to encounter a kink in its demand curve where the prices of its competitors move together with its own. Under entirely different market conditions, such as a period of slack demand, the price leader is apt to encounter a kink in its demand curve if it initiates a price rise. Any upward price revision would leave the leader in the disadvantageous position of being the firm with the highest price in its field. Under these conditions the leader would be forced to retreat and return to the going market price being maintained by the remaining firms.

A leader which is forced to withdraw a recently attempted price increase has made an error in initiating a price move. The leader believed erroneously that its price increase would stick for the industry. If the leader correctly knew that there was a kink in its demand curve, and no one would follow, it would not have attempted a price rise. Only when the leader does *not* believe there is a kink in its demand curve, but is wrong, and must make a price retreat, will evidence of a kinky demand curve occur.

CONCLUSION

A price leader may not know the precise location of either his own or the industry's demand curve. Consequently, a price leader may have to grope and move in discrete steps in terms of price changes, over a period of years, searching for a profit-maximizing position which, in turn, is continually moving. Or the price leader may seek to develop a wider market for the industry's basic product: the less erratic the prices for the products of the industry, the easier it may be for potential customers to plan ahead and compute probable cost economies for new uses of the product. A price leader with these long-run objectives, lasting over periods of economic fluctuations, may also take into account the threat of potential entry, development of new capacity and the threat of foreign competition.

ENDNOTES*

1. Fellner, *Competition Among the Few*, p. 102.
2. For a discussion of this model see Weintraub, *Price Theory*, pp. 191-93; W. J. Baumol, *Economic Theory and Operations Analysis*, p. 228, and *Business Behavior, Value and Growth*, p. 20; and Fellner, *Competition Among the Few*, p. 109.
3. Different price leadership models can be constructed by changing the slopes of the reaction curves, the shapes of the indifference curves, and the various points of tangency. For example, in Fig. C-8 if the point of tangency of Π^2_a with R_bR_b was at t' instead of T, both firms acting as price leaders would no longer arrive at higher indifference curves than they had expected. Firm A will be worse off, since the final meeting place of the two leaders will be at a point (not shown) directly below t'.
4. See L. Hurwicz, "The Theory of Economic Behavior," *American Economic Review*, Vol. XXXV (1945), 909-25; reprinted in American Economic Association, *Readings in Price Theory* (Homewood, Ill.: Richard D. Irwin, Inc., 1952), pp. 505-26; and O. Morgenstern, "Oligopoly, Monopolistic Competition, and The Theory of Games," *American Economic Review*, Vol. XXXVIII (1948), 10-18.
5. See A. J. Nichol, *Partial Monopoly and Price Leadership* (Philadelphia, 1930); Fellner, *Competition Among the Few*, p. 138; and G. J. Stigler, "The Kinky Oligopoly Demand Curve and Rigid Prices," *Journal of Political Economy*, Vol. LV (October, 1947), 432-49; reprinted in American Economic Association, *Readings in Price Theory* (Homewood, Ill.: Richard D. Irwin, Inc., 1952), p. 433. Also see his "Notes on the Theory of Duopoly," *Journal of Political Economy*, Vol. XLVIII (August, 1940), 521-41.
6. Reprinted by permission of the publishers from R. F. Lanzillotti, "Competitive Price Leadership — A Critique of Price Leadership Models," *Review of Economics and Statistics*, Vol. XXXIX (February, 1957) (Cambridge, Mass.: Harvard University Press), copyright 1957 by the President and Fellows of Harvard College, pp. 55-56. Also see R. M. Cyert and R. G. March, "Organizational Factors in the Theory of Oligopoly," *Quarterly Journal of Economics*, Vol. LXX (February, 1956), 44-64.
7. G. J. Stigler, *The Theory of Price* (New York: The Macmillan Company, 1947), p. 227.
8. J. W. Markham, "The Nature and Significance of Price Leadership," *American Economic Review*, Vol. XLI (December, 1951), 891-905; reprinted in American Economic Association, *Readings in Industrial Organization and Public Policy* (Homewood, Ill.: Richard D. Irwin, Inc., 1958), p. 179.
9. J. S. Bain, "A Note on Pricing in Monopoly and Oligopoly," *American Economic Review*, Vol. XXXIX (March, 1949), 448-64; reprinted in American Economic Association, *Readings in Industrial Organization and Public Policy*, pp. 220-35.
10. Lanzillotti, "Competitive Price Leadership," p. 61.
11. *Ibid.*, p. 63.
12. *Ibid.*, p. 56.
13. W. J. Baumol, "On the Theory of Oligopoly," *Economica*, New Series, Vol. XXIV (August, 1958), 187-98, and *Business Behavior, Value and Growth*.
14. The concept of "satisficing" is discussed in H. A. Simon, *Models of Man* (New York: John Wiley & Sons, Inc., 1957) and *Administrative Behavior* 2nd ed. (New York: The Macmillan Company, 1957). Also see J. Margolis, "The Analysis of the Firm: Rationalism, Conventionalism, and Behaviorism," *Journal of Business*, Vol. XXXI (July, 1958), 187-99; N. W. Chamberlain, *A General Theory of Economic Progress* (New York: Harper & Row, Publishers, 1955); and F. Machlup, "Theories of the Firm: Marginalist, Behavioral, Managerial," *American Economic Review*, Vol. LVII (March, 1967), 1-33.
15. J. W. McGuire, *Theories of Business Behavior* (Englewood Cliffs, N.J.: Prentice-Hall, Inc., 1964), p. 182.
16. D. K. Osborne, "The Goals of the Firm," *Quarterly Journal of Economics*, Vol. LXXVIII (November, 1964), 592-603. Cf. F. M. Fisher, Comment on "The Goals of the Firm," *Quarterly Journal of Economics*, Vol. LXXIX (August, 1965), 500-503; and Reply by Osborne, *ibid.*, p. 504.

---

*This appendix is reprinted from Antitrust Economics: *Selected Legal Cases and Economic Models* by Eugene Singer (Prentice-Hall, 1968), Chapters 9 and 10.

17. This situation, labeled as one of "constrained profit maximization," should be contrasted to the model of "constrained sales maximization." See F. M. Fisher, "Review of Professor Baumol's *Business Behavior, Value and Growth,*" *Journal of Political Economy*, Vol. LXVIII (June, 1960), 314-15 and Comment on "The Goals of the Firm," as cited in the preceding footnote; and J. Williamson, "Profit Growth and Sales Maximization," *Economica*, Vol. XXXIII (February, 1966), 1-16.

18. P. W. S. Andrews, *On Competition in Economic Theory* (London: Macmillan & Co. Ltd., 1964), p. 50.

19. *Business Behavior, Value and Growth*, p. 28. For a discussion of managerial models of the firm, see R. Marris, "A Model of the 'Managerial' Enterprise," *Quarterly Journal of Economics*, Vol. LXXVII (May, 1963), 185-209; and O. E. Williamson, *The Economics of Discretionary Behavior* (Englewood Cliffs, N.J.: Prentice-Hall, Inc., 1964), Chap. 1-4.

20. See A. Phillips, *Market Structure, Organization and Performance* (Cambridge, Mass.: Harvard University Press, 1962); O. E. Williamson, "A Dynamic Theory of Interfirm Behavior," *Quarterly Journal of Economics*, Vol. LXXIX (November, 1965), 579-607; R. M. Cyert and R. G. March, *A Behavioral Theory of the Firm* (Englewood Cliffs, N.J.: Prentice-Hall, Inc., 1963); and G. J. Stigler, "A Theory of Oligopoly," *Journal of Political Economy*, Vol. LXXII (February, 1964), 44-61.

21. P. M. Sweezy, "Demand Under Conditions of Oligopoly," *Journal of Political Economy*, Vol. XLVII (August, 1939), 568-73; reprinted in American Economic Association, *Readings in Price Theory*, pp. 404-9. Also see R. L. Hall and C. J. Hitch, "Price Theory and Business Behavior," *Oxford Economic Papers*, No. 2 (May, 1939), pp. 12-46; J. J. Spengler, "Kinked Demand Curves: By Whom First Used?" *Southern Journal of Economics*, Vol. XXXII (July, 1965), 81-84; and F. Machlup, "Marginal Analysis and Empirical Research," *American Economic Review*, Vol. XXXVI (1946), 519-54.

22. C. W. Efroymson, "A Note on Kinked Demand Curves," *American Economic Review*, Vol. XXXIII (March, 1943), 103.

23. O. Lange, *Price Flexibility and Employment* (Bloomington, Ind.: Principia Press, 1944), p. 41.

24. R. M. Cyert, "Oligopoly Behavior and the Business Cycle," *Journal of Political Economy*, Vol. LXIII (1955), 41-51.

25. C. W. Efroymson, "The Kinked Demand Curve Reconsidered," *Quarterly Journal of Economics*, Vol. LXIX (February, 1955), 119-36. Also see M. Bronfenbrenner, "Applications of the Discontinuous Oligopoly Demand Curve," *Journal of Political Economy*, Vol. XLVIII (June, 1940), 420-27.

26. Efroymson, "A Note on Kinked Demand Curves," p. 106.

27. "A Theory of Oligopoly," p. 435.

28. *Ibid.*, p. 427.

29. "The Kinked Demand Curve Reconsidered," pp. 122-24. The subsequent two paragraphs summarize a number of points made in this article.

APPENDIX D:

ECONOMIC THEORY OF VERTICAL INTEGRATION

The degree of vertical integration of a firm depends upon the extent to which it carries on the productive process from the extraction of raw materials to the transformation of these materials into a final product. Until a firm can achieve a level of volume high enough to justify its own manufacture of an input, it must make purchases from outside firms. Even in cases where a firm can produce an input with the same cost advantages achieved by a supplier, the firm may decide against assuming the capital investment and management problems associated with the input industry.

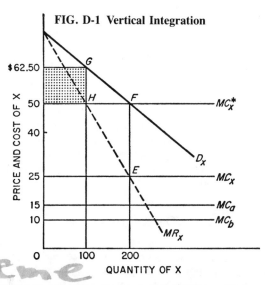

FIG. D-1 Vertical Integration

The economic rationale for a firm to integrate forward by acquiring its customers or by building facilities similar to those of its customers, or to integrate backward toward the suppliers of its inputs is analyzed in this appendix. A model of a firm which uses two inputs, A and B, in order to produce a final product, X, is

211

developed. Equilibrium positions of the firm are compared under various assumptions as to the market structure of the input and output industries. The focus of the analysis is on whether a firm with a monopoly over an input has an incentive, in economic theory, to integrate forward to a purely competitive final product industry; or whether a firm with a monopoly over a final product has an incentive to integrate backward to a purely competitive input industry.

Assume that inputs A and B are produced under conditions of pure competition and are available in perfectly elastic supply to the firms in industry X. A, B, and X are all produced under constant costs. The marginal cost curve for X, MCx, in Fig. D-1 is obtained by summing for each unit of output the marginal costs of input A, MC_a, and input B, MC_b. For simplicity, the inputs are assumed to be combined in fixed proportions to yield a unit of the final product X. Hence, one unit of input A plus one unit of input B yields one unit of final product X. Input B should be treated as including the costs of the producer in transforming inputs A and B into output X, as well as a normal return of profit. The demand curve is designated as D_z, and its corresponding marginal revenue curve as MR_x.[1]

COMPETITIVE INPUTS AND MONOPOLIZED OUTPUT

The profit maximizing output for a monopolist controlling industry X, with input industries A and B purely competitive, is given in Fig. 18-1 at point E, where the marginal cost and the marginal revenue curves for X intersect. The monopolist of X will maximize its profits by producing 200 units of product X and charging a price of $50. At this price and output level the monopolist of X will have a total revenue of $10,000, total costs of $5000, and a total profit of $5000.

COMBINED MONOPOLY OF INPUTS AND OUTPUT

The profit maximizing output for a monopolist controlling input industries A and B as well as the final product industry X is also given by the intersection of MC_x and MR_x at point E. If the integrated monopolist can manufacture inputs A and B at the same cost as buying them, he will set imputed prices for these inputs equal to their former marginal costs when they were obtained from purely competitive outside industries. The combined monopolist of A, B and X will earn the same total profit ($5000) in this situation as a monopolist of X where the industries A and B were purely competitive. Thus, a monopolist of a manufactured final product will have no profit incentive to enter by acquisition or internal growth purely competitive industries which supply its inputs.

MONOPOLIZED INPUT AND COMPETITIVE OUTPUT

A firm that holds a monopoly over an input such as A, where input B and final product X are produced under purely competitive conditions, has no economic incentive to integrate horizontally to industry B or vertically forward to industry X. In this market structure the monopolist of A has the ability to extract all the potential profit from industry X by raising the price of input A. If the monopolist of input A in Fig. 18-1 raises its price to $40, a producer in industry X must accept this increased price for the input as a basic cost. If it is assumed that industry X is only one of many industries requiring input A, and its output is too small to influence the price policies of industry A, the maximum profit available to the monopolist of input A from industry X is $5000. The latter amount is equal to the total revenue from input A (200 $\times$ $40 = $8000) less the total cost to produce this amount of input A (200 $\times$ $15 = $3000).

Under the assumption of pure competition in industry X, there will be no abnormal profits earned in this industry, and the price of X will be equal to the marginal cost of X, MC^*_x. MC^*_x is at a level of $50, since each additional unit of X consists of one unit of input A ($40) plus one unit of input B ($10). The monopolist of input A is able to achieve all of the profit inherent in the production of X by charging $40 for each unit of input A.

The monopolist of input A may also earn profits from sales to final product industries other than X. However, if these profits from sales outside industry X are excluded, and the above assumptions are adhered to, it can be concluded that the same amount of profit is earned by a monopolist in the following market structures: (1) where a monopoly over a final product exists and the related input industries are purely competitive; (2) where a monopoly exists over both the final product industry and the related input industries; and finally, (3) where a monopoly exists over an input industry and the necessary remaining inputs and final product are produced in purely competitive industries.

SUCCESSIVE MONOPOLIES

Successive monopolies are market structures in which a monopolist at one stage of production purchases materials from another monopolist at a higher stage of production. In terms of the preceding model, a monopolist of the final product X purchases one of its basic inputs, A, from another monopolist. Assume that the monopolist of X is one of a large number of purchasers from various industries which require input A, and the output of X is too small to influence pricing decisions of the monopolist of A. If the monopolist of input A raises its price to $40, and input B sells at the purely competitive rate of $10, the marginal cost curve for X will be at the $50 level, or MC^*_x. The latter curve will intersect the marginal revenue curve for X, MR_x at point H. The monopolist will charge a price for X of $62.50 and will have an output of 100 units. The monopoly profit for X at this output is $1250, total revenue is $6250, and total costs are $5000.

The monopolist of input A will receive from industry X a per unit profit of $25 (or $40 less $15), and a total profit of $2500 (100 $\times$ $25). The aggregate profit for both the monopolists of input A and the final product X is $1250 plus $2500 or $3750, which is less than the $5000 profit earned in the previously discussed cases. Therefore, if the monopolist of input A, and the monopolist of final product X would vertically integrate, or at least reach some type of agreement whereby the price of X is lowered from $62.50 to $50, their aggregate profits could be increased to $5000. Thus, on theoretical grounds, the final price to consumers will be higher and output will be smaller in the case of successive monopolies as compared to the single vertically integrated monopolist.

Let us drop the initial assumption that the market for the final product X is too small to affect the pricing decisions of the monopolist of input A. Assume that the demand for input A is derived completely from the demand for the final product X. Marginal costs are no longer assumed to be horizontal, but are assumed to be positively sloped. Under these conditions, it can again be shown that successive monopolists will have a higher price and a lower output than a single vertically integrated monopolist.[2]

Consider the case of successive monopolies in which a manufacturing monopolist sells to a retail monopolist. In Fig. D-2 the demand curve of consumers which faces the retail monopolist is AR_r, and its corresponding marginal revenue curve is MR_r. The latter curve is also the demand curve of the retailer for the product of the manufacturer, provided the retailer has no monopolistic buying power. The manufacturer, with a marginal cost curve MC', will charge the retailer a price RE and offer an output of OR. The retailer, in turn, will charge at this output level a price RA to consumers.

FIG. D-2 Sucessive Monopolies

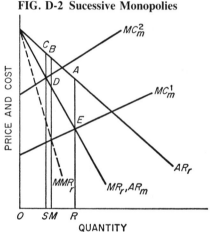

If the manufacturer is stronger than the retailer, so that the latter must comply with the price terms set by the manufacturer, the manufacturer will have a marginal revenue curve such as MMR_r, which is *marginal* to the *marginal* revenue curve of the retailer. The manufacturer with a marginal cost curve MC^1 will produce OM of X, which will ultimately be the retailer's output; the manufacturer's price will be MD, and the retailer's price to consumers will be MB. The above relationship between successive monopolists, a retailer and a manufacturer, results in a higher price and a lower output in contrast to a single vertically integrated monopoly. The explanation lies primarily in the fact that the demand for the manufacturer's product is *derived* from the retailer's demand curve. Consequently, there will occur a "repeated marginalization" of the revenue curves of successive monopolists in determining their profit-maximizing outputs.

In the event the manufacturer attempts to sell its product directly to consumers, the relevant marginal revenue curve will not be MMR_r, but MR_r, which is more elastic for the same quantities than the former curve. The manufacturer would thereby avoid the repeated marginalization of revenue curves. If the marginal costs of the manufacturer remain the same after assuming the retail function, the final price to consumers will fall from MB to RA, and the output to consumers will increase from OM to OR. The forward integration of the manufacturer will benefit the consumers with lower prices and higher output. However, where the manufacturer faces much higher costs, such as MC^2, when undertaking both vertical stages, the consumers may be left worse off than they were before vertical integration. Output will be restricted to OS, and the consumer price will be raised to SC, when the applicable marginal cost curve of the vertically integrated manufacturer is MC^2. Thus, a crucial factor in appraising the economic effects of vertical integration is whether the vertically integrating firm is more efficient in operating the stage that it supplants. If the costs of the manufacturer increase with vertical integration, but the marginal cost curve still intersects MR_r below point D, the consumer will enjoy the benefits of a lower price and higher quantity of the manufacturer's product as a result of vertical integration.

ENDNOTES

1. The following discussion of this model is taken from Burstein, ''A Theory of Full Line Forcing,'' p. 66. His discussion is, in turn, based upon a classroom presentation by Professor Milton Friedman.
2. F. Machlup and M. Taber, ''Bilateral Monopoly, Successive Monopoly, and Vertical Integration,'' *Economica*, Vol. XXVII (May, 1960), p. 102.

APPENDIX E:

SOME THOUGHTS ON THE CALCULATION OF TREBLE DAMAGES

I. SCIENTIFIC METHODOLOGY AND LEGAL DAMAGE THEORIES

Scientific methodology is useful in grouping facts into a unique explanation of a phenomenon. In designing an experiment, the scientist attempts to control all but a few variables in order to predict a given outcome under a fixed set of conditions. Unlike a physical scientist, the antitrust economist need not be confined to searching for a single theory which is a unique explanation of facts. In legal damage cases, there are generally multiple theories of liability and damage.

In one complex damage case, the economic witnesses for the defense were asked by counsel not to converse with each other concerning their proposed testimony. Each advanced at trial his own independent and different theory of calculating damages. The amount of damages which each witness estimated was of a similar magnitude; however, their methods of calculation were totally dissimilar. On cross-examination one of the economic witnesses was asked by trial counsel if the damage computations he had just provided for proving injury, and therefore liability, were "his best calculations of the damages incurred." The witness replied, "no." At this moment the somewhat surprised judge intervened: "Professor, I don't think you heard the counsel's question correctly. He asked if this was your best theory of damages. Is it?" The witness replied, "No, your honor, it is not." A pause which seemed quite long, and the witness continued. "My theory of damages involved a tremendous amount of calculation. I have worked on it for many months. When I began, I did it in a way that seemed reasonably correct, but I have learned a lot from my calculations and if I had to do it all over again, I am not sure that I would do it the same way. So, your Honor, this is not my *best* theory of damages, but I believe it is a reasonably good one." The judge was impressed with the candidness of the witness.

Part of the explanation for the wide flexibility in computing legal damages lies in the metaphysical nature of the problem. We are generally asking a hypothetical question: But for the conduct or action of the defendant, what would have occurred? In terms of time and space, the precise conditions for the experiment cannot be simulated. We are left with *The Fiddler on the Roof* to conjecture: "if I were a rich man." The most we can do is design an experiment close to the conditions that might have occurred "but for" the alleged unlawful conduct of the defendant, and attempt to predict the outcome expected within a reasonable range.

II. GATHERING OF THE BASIC TRANSACTIONAL DATA

Most complex cases involving liability and damage require an enormous amount of analysis of cost data and price data. The mechanics of efficiently compiling these data require the use of computer and microfilm systems. Before copying thousands of documents, it is advisable to conduct a pilot study of a selected number of transactions to ascertain whether the documents are truly responsive to the initial theory of damages. To understand the meaning of transactional data a number of layers of business documents have to be sorted. For example, the price lists might appear to reflect the basic prices being charged in a given period of time. Invoices can be gathered to ascertain the extent to which these price lists were adhered to. However, the invoices only show what was actually shipped. A customer might have ordered five items but the invoices might show only a few items with a delay in shipment noted for the remaining items. A volume discount, if granted, would be based upon the original sales order and, therefore, could not be computed from an invoice covering a partial shipment. Even after the sales orders and invoices have been checked to ascertain which goods have been shipped, the transaction may not be concluded. The customer might have returned some goods, or might have received an adjustment for damages or for defective products. And you still may not have the final price: the order might say, payable in thirty days, and the delay in payment to 120 days without an assessed interest charge might be deemed equivalent to a discount. Also, credit memos are frequently used at the end of a year for the payment of an annual volume discount. This volume discount has to be prorated back to a wide variety of different prices to calculate the final net transactional price.

Who is going to do this kind of work? The law firm will have difficulty having young associates, trained in legal analysis, checking in a somewhat monotonous fashion thousands of numbers. The client company, although an important source of guidance for understanding the meaning of the documents, may not be a particularly willing source of labor. The best personnel in the company cannot be expected to be put on the project since current sales and profits are generally of higher priority. Recognizing that the compilers of the data are working indirectly for the trial attorney, and that they are being interrupted from their everyday jobs as well as from their current flow of progress within the company hierarchy, the ingredients for care, pride and top performance are often missing.

Another alternative would be for the law firm to hire paraprofessionals and attempt to compile the data in the law firm or at a special document center. Personnel would also have to be hired by the law firm to direct the paraprofessionals.

The use of an economic consulting firm, a management consulting firm, or an accounting firm are other alternatives. If a consulting firm has previously performed statistical work for attorneys, the employees in the firm will be impressed with the importance for the numbers to be correct. The employees will know that the trial attorney and his expert witness cannot be embarrassed in the courtroom with faulty computations. Furthermore, mechanical systems for checking and proofreading data have generally been established in an outside consulting firm.

Lawyers are often limited to meeting with a client's General Counsel and a few members high in management. These individuals are generally more attuned to the broad decision-making of the company than the lower level paperwork involving particular transactions and invoices. To be able to "go down the organization ladder" and reach those with the knowledge of the everyday operations is not an easy assignment. Yet this total understanding of business documents is fundamental for a trial attorney's preparation. Somewhere in a relatively obscure spot in a company can exist an individual with the insight and knowledge of critical documents which may be instrumental in a trial attorney's understanding of the evidence. The search for that individual employee may take the fact finder through manufacturing facilities in distant cities, into data processing complexes, into marketing and sales departments, and, in some cases, even to customers and suppliers. All of this knowledge must ultimately be communicated to the trial attorney for his effectiveness in the courtroom.

Certain computing equipment is especially suitable for litigation work. For example, the client company may have an enormous computer which it uses for processing payroll and sales orders. This equipment may not be at all useful for computations involving only a few thousand numbers. A mini-computer and small disc system, which can be easily reprogrammed, is preferable for use in smaller computational problems. The average programming wait in most companies for their large computer system is probably close to a month without a special "high priority" interrupt. Everyday cannot be a "high priority" interrupt day — even for a trial counsel. A separate mini-computer system allows the trial attorney to have continual revisions and recalculations of data. As trial approaches, late answers to interrogatories or amendments and revisions to earlier answers will be received. With the original data base stored on a disc, the task of rerunning computations and summaries with revised data becomes simplified.

The level of knowledge can be expected to rise as one approaches the date of trial. Basic reformulations of damage theories can be expected up to the last minute before trial, as well as during trial, in protracted complex antitrust cases. Manually, it would be close to impossible to recalculate or reformulate large damage theories. If all the relevant names, products and prices are stored on a disc system, the problem is only one of programming. High speed printers, which can output several hundred characters a second, are excellent equipment when a job has to be performed almost concurrently with trial, such as overnight for a cross-examination the following day.

As the speed of retrieving and analyzing information with different sets of assumptions increases, the trial lawyer can have greater flexibility and a wider set of options in terms of affirmatively producing evidence and in defensively meeting evidence.

III. STATISTICAL TOOLS FOR MEASURING LEGAL DAMAGES

In physical science, one can measure with a high degree of precision either heat with a thermometer or length with a ruler. In contrast, it is difficult to measure the qualitative factors that one finds in damage cases: the value of a brand name, what a company would have done in sales had it not been illegally cut-off from its source of raw materials or supplies, or the price customers would have paid if prices were not illegally fixed. The concept of "measurement" of damages presents unusual problems to the antitrust litigator who must quantify various qualitative factors. Furthermore, in the courtroom it may be necessary to prove by statistics even that which may be "intuitively clear."

Rank Correlation

The basic challenge in the measurement of damages is to find one variable to estimate what value another variable would have had "but for" the illegal behavior of the defendant. The *rank correlation coefficient* is a statistical tool to ascertain whether two variables are related and, therefore, whether the value of one of the variables can be used for predicting or estimating the value of a second variable.

Consider an antitrust example. A distributor is unlawfully cut off by a supplier which seeks to boycott him for price cutting. The distributor sues for lost profits. The defense wishes to argue in terms of damage theory that the higher sales would not have necessarily resulted in higher profits. The sales and profits of five companies in the industry are chosen at random. Will the companies with the larger sales be the most profitable? Are sales and profits always correlated? This broader proposition surely cannot be proven from a single sample of five companies, but the methodology of the formula is nevertheless shown in Table E-1. Company A is ranked second in sales and first in profits. Company E, in contrast, is ranked fifth in sales and second in profit. From our limited sample of five companies, it is not obvious that the companies with larger sales will also have higher profits.

TABLE E-1
Correlation of Ranks

Company (1)	X: Rank in Sales (2)	Y: Rank in Profit (3)	D: Difference Col. (2)-(3) (4)	D^2: Squared Difference (5)
A	2	1	1	1
B	1	3	-2	4
C	3	5	-2	4
D	4	4	0	0
E	5	2	3	9
Total			0	18

Spearman's rank correlation coefficient is defined by the following formula:

$$\text{Spearman's Rank Correlation Coefficient} = 1 - \frac{6 \cdot S(D^2)}{N(N^2 - 1)} = 1 - \frac{6(18)}{5(25-1)} = .1$$

Inserting the numbers from Table E-1 into the above formula gives the value .1. The value of Spearman's Rank Correlation Coefficient varies between +1 for a perfect correlation where the array of ranks of sales and profits are identical (the higher a company's sales, the higher its profits) to the value of minus one, where the ranks are inversely related (the higher a company's sales, the lower its profits). In case there are ties, the average of the ranks they jointly occupy is used. Thus, if the second and third ranked companies were tied in sales, the value of $(2 + 3)/2$ or 2.5 would be used as the rank of each. The value of .1 in our example is approximately midway between the extreme values of no relationship (-1) and a perfect relationship ($+1$). The statistical significance of .1 is questionable due to the extremely small size of the sample of companies being analyzed.

The correlation of sales and profits was done in terms of the *ranks* of the data in the sample. We only wanted to know whether the companies with higher sales generally had higher profits. We did not examine the absolute level of profit, say $1 million, but only the rank of the company's profit as compared to the other companies in the sample.

The *correlation coefficient,* in contrast to the previous *rank* correlation coefficient, utilizes the magnitude, and not just the rank, of the data. In Table E-2, the absolute or dollar value of the sales and profits of Companies A, B, C, D, and E are used in computing a correlation coefficient. A value of $+1$ from the formula shows a perfect correlation, and a value of zero shows no correlation. The computations show a correlation coefficient of .98 and an apparent strong relationship between sales and profits. But again the statistical significant of the result is suspect due to the limited amount of data in the example. Other factors affecting sales and profits should also have been studied before even cursory conclusions could be drawn meaningfully from these data.

TABLE E-2
Correlation of Absolute Quantities

Company (1)	X: Sales ($Millions) (2)	Y: Rank in ($Thousands) (3)	XY (4)	X^2 (5)	Y^2
A	6.0	150	900	36.00	22,500
B	4.5	80	360	20.25	6,400
C	5.5	110	605	30.25	12,100
D	5.6	135	756	31.36	18,225
E	4.0	60	240	16.00	3,600
Total	25.6	535	2861	133.86	62,825

Formula: The correlation coefficient, r, is defined by the following formula:

Correlation Coefficient = r =

$$\sqrt[2]{\frac{N \cdot S(XY - S(X) \cdot S(Y)}{[N \cdot S(X^2) - S(X) \cdot S(X)] [N \cdot S(Y^2) - S(Y) \cdot S(Y)]}} =$$

Answer:

$$\sqrt[2]{\frac{5(2861) - (25.6)(535)}{[5(133.86 - (25.6)(25.6)] [5(62,825) - (535)(535)]}} = .98$$

Regression

Another statistical tool for estimating damages is *regression*. A simple model can be constructed to describe how this statistical tool might be used. The model has *output* on a vertical axis and *input* on a horizontal one. Assume that the input is a tenth of a ton of a certain brand of fertilizer per acre, and output is measured by thousands of bushels of onions. Assume there is a hypothetical product liability case in which the farmer sues the fertilizer supplier for providing a defective product which the farmer believes actually decreased his crop yield. As evidence of damages, the plaintiff-farmer wishes to provide evidence of what competitive fertilizers did for other farmers.

Consider the result of various farmers using a tenth of a ton of fertilizer an acre. The example of .1 or .2 tons of fertilizer per acre is for simplicity only. After a certain point additional fertilizer will have adverse or negative effects on yields per acre with the result that the regression line will curve downward. One farmer, who may have been very careful in watering and in eliminating weeds had a high yield, say 200 bushels of onions per acre. (See point *a*). Another farmer who did not irrigate his land as carefully had only 190 bushels per acre. (See point *b*). The third farmer tried hard but lacked the right soil conditions. (See point *c*). He had an even lower yield of 175 bushels of onions per acre. The average output of these farmers that used a tenth of a ton of fertilizer per acre is designated as point X1 on line RR'. A similar analysis follows for all farmers using 3 tenths of a ton of fertilizer and receiving even higher levels of outputs of onions. (See points d, e, and f). The average of these points are at point X2 on line RR'. Line RR' is called a "regression line." The statistical regression line can be used to estimate the damages of the plaintiff farmer. It shows what the plaintiff's output would have been and is based on the average output of those farmers which used the competitive fertilizer without quality problems.

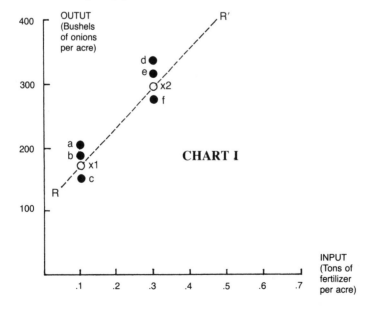

IV. THE ELEGANCE OF SIMPLICITY

The statistical examples selected for discussion were oversimplified in not taking into consideration the multiplicity of other variables that can affect statistical estimates. We seldom find a single variable that can be used uniquely to determine the level of damages. The presence of multiple interrelated variables raise exceedingly complex statistical questions. We are required to translate technical words into a clear explanation for judges and jurors.

The computer can be critical for isolating important variables and in finding a relatively simple theory of damages. In a case in which a plaintiff sued for being unlawfully deprived from technical patents and know-how, the technique of regression was used on a computer to isolate and analyze the time lag between research and development expenditures and the eventual sales of the product several years later. The plaintiff argued that if it had not been unlawfully deprived of the technical knowledge, it could have received the same pay-out with the same time lag from its research and development funds as the defendant. Regression allowed the construction of a sloping line showing the average output in dollar sales for various amounts of research and development expenses. The astute attorneys soon realized that the same proposition could be established without resort to the statistical jargon of regression if they would use only the *average ratio* of a sales to research and development expenditures which occurred two years earlier.

The cross-examination was correctly anticipated. Defense counsel wanted to know what would have occurred if two and one half years, or perhaps only one year, were used as the lag between research and development and sales. The economic witness was sitting with computer print-outs of every imaginable combination of the variables. Defense counsel, as expected, explored whether the witness had considered alternative damage theories, and soon realized that the economic witness had computer print-outs of statistical regression lines and various ratios for every conceivable time lag of research and development expenses. The earlier decision to limit direct examination to simple arithmetic ratios was wise. The small weapon of arithmetic had the tactical advantage of simple exposition over the sophisticated statistical jargon. The computer print-outs of multiple regressions for all configurations of data were not introduced in evidence, although they were made available for discovery by the other side. But their presence was felt in the confidence of the economic witness, and in his ability to anticipate the cross-examination of defense counsel.

The Illinois Brick Controversy

Most treble damage cases are settled rather than fully litigated by parties. The generally wide latitude in the calculation of damages, as well as the questionable ability of jurors to comprehend fully the complex computations of economic witnesses, heighten the risk factor of defending a case even when a client sincerely believes that it did not commit an unlawful act. When the cost and risk of proving innocence in a courtroom is too high for a defendant, the equity of our judicial system is open to serious question. The relationship between treble damage plaintiffs and alleged antitrust violators has been described as a "balance of terror."[1]

In 1968 the Supreme Court decided *Hanover Shoe, Inc.* v. *United Shoe Machinery Corp.*.[2] Hanover Shoe was a manufacturer of shoes and leased show machinery from United Shoe. In 1953, United Shoe was found to have monopolized the shoe machinery market. Hanover Shoe sued its supplier, United Shoe, for treble damages for the overcharges it incurred on its lease payments for the shoe manufacturing machinery. United Shoe attempted to defend itself by arguing that Hanover Shoe was not injured since it was able to "pass on" the higher cost to its customers purchasing the finished shoes.

The Supreme Court rejected this "passing on" defense and required United Shoe to pay damages to Hanover Shoe. The Court explained the economic uncertainties involved in defensively proving how much of an overcharge a purchaser may have passed on to its subsequent customers:

> A wide range of factors influence a company's pricing policies. Normally the impact of a single change in the relevant conditions cannot be measured after the fact; indeed a businessman may be unable to state whether, had one fact been different (a single supply less expensive, general economic conditions more buoyant, or the labor market tighter, for example), he would have chosen a different price. Equally difficult to determine, in the real economic world rather than an economist's hypothetical model, is what effect a change in a company's price will have on its total sales. Finally, costs per unit for a different volume of total sales are hard to estimate. Even if it could be shown that the buyer raised his price in response to, and in the amount of, the overcharge and that his margin of profit and total sales had not thereafter declined, there would remain the nearly insuperable difficulty of demonstrating that the particular plaintiff could not or would not have raised his prices absent the overcharge or maintained the higher price had the overcharge been discontinued. Since establishing the applicability of the passing-on defense would require a convincing showing of each of these virtually unascertainable figures, the task would normally prove insurmountable. On the other hand, it is not unlikely that if the existence of the defense is generally confirmed, antitrust defendants will frequently seek to establish its applicability. Treble-damage actions would often require additional long and complicated proceedings involving massive evidence and complicated theories.

In 1977 the Supreme Court was confronted with an *offensive use* of the "passing on" theory which was considered as a defense in *Hanover Shoe*. In *Illinois Brick Co.* v. *Illinois*,[3] the Supreme Court denied the State of Illinois and 700 local government entities the recovery of overcharges for the concrete blocks used in state and local buildings. Illinois Brick, which was convicted of price fixing, sold concrete block to masonry contractors, which then sold the blocks to general contractors, who in turn made contracts for the building structures using these blocks with the state and local governments. The masonry contractors, who first purchased the concrete blocks from Illinois Brick were allowed to recover treble damages as "direct purchasers." But this case involved the customers of the masonry contractors, namely, the state and local governments which purchased the buildings. These subsequent levels of purchasers are referred to as "indirect purchasers."

The Supreme Court held that the reasoning of *Hanover Shoe* was equally compelling against the Court attempting "to trace the effect of an overcharge through each step in the distribution chain from the direct purchaser to the ulimate consumer.'' The Court summarized some of the critical assumptions which would have to be made as follows:

> Under an array of simplifying assumptions, economic theory provides a precise formula for calculating how the overcharge is distributed between the overcharged party (passer) and its customers (passees). *If* the market for the passer's product is perfectly competitive; *if* the overcharge is imposed equally on all of the passer's competitors; and *if* the passer maximizes its profits, then the ratios of the shares of the overcharge borne by passee and passer will equal the ratio of the elasticities of supply and demand in the market for the passer's product.

Hearings were held by the Senate Subcommittee on *Illinois Brick* after the decision by the Supreme Court. One proposed bill (H.R. 8359) would have overruled the Illinois Brick decision and allowed indirect purchasers to recover treble damages. The bill probably will not be approved primarily because of the complexities involved in the computation and allocation of damages. The problems of economic proof in a courtroom with regard to proving the elasticity or inelasticity of demand at all levels of distribution was described by Professor Richard Posner as follows:

> Normally you would have to have an economist who would have a mathematical model of demand, which he would then try to apply by plugging in data about the industry. These would usually be data concerning prices at different periods in the industry's past and data on quantity. He would try to infer the elasticity from these data, correcting for various other factors. This would be the econometric model. It would be very complicated, and it would be very controversial. So the defendant would have his own expert economist witness who would poke holes in the econometric model and present his own econometric model, and the judge and jury would have a great deal of difficulty understanding what the experts were contending about and where the truth lay.[4]

The existence of a "multiplier effect" or double counting in calculating damages passed on to different levels of distribution was described by Dr. Betty Bock of The Conference Board.[5] If an illegal overcharge of a manufacturer was marked-up 50% by its wholesaler to $1,500,000 and marked up 50% by a distributor to $2,250,000, and finally by an additional 50% by a retailer to the consumer, the final overcharge is $3,375,000, which after being trebled amounts to $10,125,000. The amount of the overcharge to the "direct purchaser" was only $1,000,000, but this amount is duplicated at each stage of distribution which passes on the overcharge. Thus, the original supplier, who overcharged as a result of a price-fixing conspiracy or monopolization, is being held accountable in a repetitive fashion for the same overcharge being passed through each stage of distribution.

If *Illinois Brick* were reversed, the defendant could face damages far in excess of three times the amount he originally over-charged his direct purchaser. The defendant would be subjected to damages far beyond trebling even though the various middlemen below him, to the extent that they passed on rather than absorbed the overcharge, were the ones that profited from the violation once the product left the defendant's hands. The simplicity of the present *Illinois Brick* rule appears as a wiser antitrust policy than subjecting the courts and juries to a wide spectrum of classes or levels of distribution, overwhelming amounts of data with regard to prices, costs, sales and operating margins, and finally, to the highly speculative calculations and estimations of econometricians and (some) economists.

ENDNOTES

1. Statement by the Committee on Trade Regulation of the Association of the Bar of the City of New York before the Subcommittee on Monopolies and Commercial Law, H.R. 8359, (Illinois Brick Hearings) Serial No. 20 (1977), p. 505.
2. 392 U.S. 481 (1968).
3. 431 U.S. 720 (1977).
4. See footnote 1, p. 225.
5. *Ibid.*, p. 503.

INDEX